'For good or ill, mindfulness has grabbed the popular imagination as therapy or self-help. This book is a timely and much needed contribution to the field, which examines assumptions that have shaped our contemporary conceptions of mindfulness, and so in a similar way will change the way we see ourselves.'

Mark Leonard. *Director, Mindfulness Connected, pioneer in 'social mindfulness', writer and author,* Social Mindfulness: A guide to meditations from Mindfulness-Based Organisational Education

'Mindfulness is used in many clinical environments to help people who are mentally unwell get back to normal functioning. This book delivers the next level; mindfulness groups that enhance wellbeing and increase the capacity for joy. The experienced authors generously provide a treasure-trove of practical materials. The appendices alone contain a schedule for an 8 week program, plus the scripts for all the exercises, metaphors and stories. The preceding chapters provide background, instructions and stylistic tips. Well worth buying.'

Dr Christine Dunkley, *Consultant trainer, British Isles DBT Training Team*

This fascinating book introduces an innovative Mindfulness-Based Wellbeing Enhancement program. With deep knowledge of Advaita Vedanta, modern Psychology, and lived experience in a multicultural setting, the authors are uniquely placed in providing insightful guidance for cultural adaptations of mindfulness based programs. Another salient aspect of this work is a scholarly analysis of the history of mindfulness, giving lesser known facts and timelines. This book would be relevant for both students and practitioners, engaged with the field of mindfulness and mental health.

Dr. Jyotsna Agrawal, *Associate Professor of Clinical Psychology, National Institute of Mental Health and Neuro Sciences, Bengaluru, India*

T0386454

Introducing Mindfulness-Based Wellbeing Enhancement

Mindfulness-Based Wellbeing Enhancement (MBWE) integrates the science of mindfulness and wellbeing to bring about human flourishing. This 9-session program, conducted over 8 weeks, enhances wellbeing, happiness, and quality of life through self-understanding and self-awareness.

The first part of the book is devoted to presenting mindfulness, wellbeing, the happiness paradigm and the curriculum of the Mindfulness-Based Wellbeing Enhancement (MBWE) program. It presents the foundations of mindfulness-based programs, and how mindfulness intersects with wellbeing. The authors argue, with the support of evidence, that mindfulness is well placed to promote human flourishing rather than limiting its relevance to stress reduction and preventing depression relapse. Several chapters are devoted to presenting the MBWE program comprehensively with weekly agendas, homework, handouts, facilitation guides, and practice scripts.

The second part of the book presents the evidence base of mindfulness, cultural adaptations for different populations, the therapeutic effectiveness of group learning inherent in mindfulness-based programs and the often-untold history of mindfulness. The authors present the often-neglected Asian roots of mindfulness and justify how secular mindfulness, as taught by Jon Kabat-Zinn, is influenced by multiple wisdom traditions as opposed to it being a solely Buddhist practice.

This book serves as a hands-on resource for trained mindfulness teachers, psychologists, psychiatrists, psychotherapists, counsellors, social workers, practitioners, educators, coaches, and consultants. It is also suitable for anyone who is interested in the appreciation of mindfulness and human flourishing.

Kathirasan K. is the founder and Managing Director of the Centre for Mindfulness (Singapore). He is the author of several books and a renowned scholar-practitioner of Indic contemplative traditions. He is also a leadership and culture consultant; and an executive coach. The Mindfulness-Based Wellbeing Enhancement (MBWE) program was born out of his personal experience with mindfulness and his interest in wellbeing and human flourishing.

Sunita Rai is the founder and Managing Director of the Holistic Psychotherapy Centre. She is a psychologist, psychotherapist, author, consultant, lecturer, and clinical supervisor. She created a unique model of wellbeing called the Integrated Wellbeing Model (IWM) and another brainchild of hers is the Mindfulness-Oriented Counselling and Psychotherapy (MOCP) program.

Introducing Mindfulness-Based Wellbeing Enhancement

Cultural Adaptation and an 8-week Path to Wellbeing and Happiness

Kathirasan K. and Sunita Rai

Routledge
Taylor & Francis Group

LONDON AND NEW YORK

Designed cover image: Shutterstock

First published 2023
by Routledge
4 Park Square, Milton Park, Abingdon, Oxon OX14 4RN

and by Routledge
605 Third Avenue, New York, NY 10158

Routledge is an imprint of the Taylor & Francis Group, an informa business

British Library Cataloguing-in-Publication Data
A catalogue record for this book is available from the British Library

Library of Congress Cataloging-in-Publication Data
A catalog record has been requested for this book

ISBN: 978-1-032-34594-9 (hbk)
ISBN: 978-1-032-34593-2 (pbk)
ISBN: 978-1-003-32295-5 (ebk)

DOI: 10.4324/9781003322955

Typeset in Bembo
by Apex CoVantage, LLC

Contents

Figures

Tables

Preface

We walked into our center's library and randomly picked up three mindfulness books that were known to be bestsellers or popular. Though we have read these books in the past we did not remember what the introduction to the books were like. The first book began by stating that "life is tough" and the second one started by giving an account of how we lay sleepless on our beds unable to quieten our mind or wrestling with our thoughts. The third book presented a story about how a woman was dealing with a divorce. We immediately looked at each other wondering if our lives would have to be so in order for us to discover mindfulness!

It then dawned on us how authors and teachers seemed to present a bleak and hopeless situation in our lives for mindfulness to become relevant. Predictably these books eventually make a point that this broken state can be fixed by mindfulness. This has been the portrayal of mindfulness in the recent decades. These popular books often claim that happiness can be gained by achieving peace and a resolute calm, which would then make us believe that we cannot possibly be happy at a rock concert.

Calmness/Peace = Happiness

Unfortunately, these books do not tell us that life is *not* always tough and that *not* all the time do we lie sleepless wrestling with our thoughts. In fact, we could have had so many things to be grateful for and we are not even looking for peace because peace is not equal to happiness. A fundamentally neutral state of calmness is quite the opposite of being in a state of laughter and glee. Also seeing our thoughts as not facts is not enough to be happy. By examining stress, we become stressful and by delving deep into our unwanted emotions we recreate the very thing we want to overcome. No wonder ancient practitioners of mindfulness were monks who had renounced their worldly desires and left their active life to pursue a life of solitude.

Seeing our lives as being tough and thinking that we live in frantic times are mental interpretations of objective experiences. And as valid as it may be to think so, it is a fact that there was never a time in human civilization that people felt like they were in utopia. In the past, perhaps we were afraid of the floods, catastrophes, predators, and droughts and today we are afraid of rejection, insufficient social media engagements, not being able to secure a first-class ticket amongst others. Have the floods disappeared? No, but our attention has shifted to modern world challenges. In the past, we were happy when the men in the village brought a deer to the dinner table. Today, we celebrate when our loved ones get a promotion or a new car. We have always been oscillating between happiness and sadness all our lives, though we aim to increase the moments of happiness. This is where we found mindfulness to be a great psychological capital that empowers us to be happy.

Our discovery of mindfulness came from an existential need and it took another trajectory. We realized that mindfulness allows us to *be* happy and enhances our wellbeing. And this was what we discovered in our lives. In this book, we present this appreciative orientation to mindfulness, that starts from the same premise and evidence as other mindfulness-based programs (MBPs) but allows you to discover a way of flourishing. Often wellbeing is mistaken to be the absence of stress, anxiety or depression; a belief that has been perpetuated and repeated by the first generation of MBPs that helped people reduce stress and prevent relapses of depression. We, on the other hand, see wellbeing as not the absence of the negative but rather a way of living, with *a paradigm that allows one to be attentive to the positive, accept the negative and interpret experiences purposefully.* We call this the *happiness paradigm,* inspired by the wisdom of mindfulness.

Our unique experience with mindfulness led us to develop the Mindfulness-Based Wellbeing Enhancement (MBWE) program, an eight-week mindfulness program that opens the door to all people, and not only to those who are suffering. One need not be stressed or depressed to walk into the MBWE program. People who are healthy and well can also benefit from mindfulness to prevent mental health challenges and promote human flourishing.

MINDFULNESS-BASED WELLBEING ENHANCEMENT (MBWE)

From our own experience and the global evidence from the MBPs, we had developed a differentiated eight-week MBP, Mindfulness-Based Wellbeing Enhancement (MBWE) program, which not only reduces existing stress, anxiety and a host of other mental challenges but also:

1 supports in the prevention of stress, anxiety, or depression
2 allows one to be happy as a way of being and living
3 promotes human flourishing

The MBWE is steeped in the philosophy of wellbeing, psychology and secular mindfulness; and it can be delivered to a wider population than the population currently targeted by the first generation MBPs which is the Mindfulness-Based Stress Reduction (MBSR) program and Mindfulness-Based Cognitive Therapy (MBCT) program. In this book, we present the theory, practice, and the protocol of the MBWE along with its underpinning philosophy of mindfulness and wellbeing.

HOW TO READ THIS BOOK

This book is written for trained mindfulness teachers and other professionals interested in teaching mindfulness and wanting to appreciate its impact on wellbeing enhancement. The chapters of the book have been divided into two parts.

The first part is essential for teachers and professionals who wish to teach or adapt the MBWE. In chapter 1, we present mindfulness as a secular practice and how it generates insights around its intended outcomes. It presents the fundamental pedagogy adopted by all MBPs. The difference between secular and religious mindfulness is clearly presented in this chapter. In chapter 2, we present what wellbeing is and how mindfulness responds to the limitations of current wellbeing theories. We present the happiness paradigm, inspired by the wisdom of mindfulness. Chapter 3 presents the session plans of the MBWE giving sufficient facilitation methods and recommendations. You will get to see the complete MBWE protocol here. In chapter 4, you will be presented with the fundamentals of facilitating mindfulness practices, didactic content, and exercises of the MBWE. In chapter 5, you will find the adapted approach of facilitating inquiry in the MBWE that brings to life the happiness paradigm through the generation of unique insights. These five chapters form the first part of the book and are essential for the delivery of the MBWE.

The second part of the book is meant for those who would like to gain additional knowledge about mindfulness and teaching MBPs. The study of this part is not essential for the delivery of the MBWE though it may be supportive. In chapter 6, we present how groups learn and how we can enhance learning in MBPs. Chapter 7 focuses on how MBPs can be adapted to different cultures. It discusses how the facilitation process can be enhanced to meet the expectations and attitudes of different homogenous cultures and sub-cultures. Chapter 8 presents the effectiveness of MBPs, its integrity and the evidence of its results. This chapter can be also helpful to those who wish to measure the effects of MBPs. The final chapter focuses on the untold history of mindfulness. Here we debunk the myths around the development and evolution of secular mindfulness, rarely found in books that teach mindfulness.

We have used the initials KK for Kathirasan K and SR for Sunita Rai to indicate each of our personal experiences or views that we have expressed in this book. We have also added quotes and responses from our participants and teachers-in-training in the chapters. Their names have been replaced with pseudonyms.

As you read the book, we invite you to not only consult evidence as we know it today but also listen to your own experience as well as the experience of others that you have encountered in your journey. We also invite you to discover parallels of what is written in this book within your own culture and practice and adapt where necessary to suit your culture, context, group and learning style.

WHO WE ARE

Both of us have a lifelong personal interest in wellbeing and happiness. While we worked and continue to work together in different and shared professional fields, our goal of wellbeing that permeates everything we do has not diminished till today.

I (KK) encountered contemplative practices for the first time in the mid-1990s, when I was serving in the military. My early encounter with mindfulness started with questions about purpose, meaning, and attempting to solve the riddle of life. These questions were entrenched in existential crisis, at a time where I was conscripted in the military to serve my nation. The existential crisis started for me in my twenties and honestly I was perhaps a little stressed or depressed but maybe not in a clinical sense. I was very much functional, performing reasonably well in my career, education, and relationships. But what was not right for me, at least from hindsight, was my worldview and the attitude with which I approached my living. I was an unhappy young adult. Towards the late 1990s I met my spiritual teacher, Swami Satprakashananda Saraswati, and learned from him the insight, philosophy, and mindfulness/meditative practices of the Advaita Vedanta philosophy for several years. We combed through Sanskrit texts and commentaries in the original studying its purport. Those years of practice, interactive dialogue, and self-inquiry transformed my life as I discovered myself becoming and *being* the wholeness that I already am. While I was learning from him, I began to teach meditation/mindfulness, philosophy and Advaita Vedanta and I continue to do that till this day. Years later, I encountered the MBSR and the works of Jon Kabat-Zinn which opened a secular door to what I have practiced and saw as a worldview. Kabat-Zinn's approach took the psychological aspects of mindfulness, universal to all human beings, and made it available to all without any barrier. This is the first time in history when mindfulness got secularized. This approach sat well with me given that I had seen the secularization of yoga, being a certified yoga instructor as well, and witnessed how through that millions of people had benefited. I was mentored and coached by Shamash Alidina on the secular MBCT protocol thereafter.

With my professional interest in positive psychology, appreciative inquiry, and other positive interventions, the inspiration to develop the *radically secular* and universal type of MBP, the MBWE, dawned on me, so that people of all cultures could benefit from the potential of human flourishing through mindfulness, like the way I did.

I (SR) came across mindfulness somewhere in 2005 when I was still studying psychology and I fondly remember one of my lecturers referring to meditation in one of my modules. Meditation is something that has already been part of my spiritual tradition. And that got me interested to want to learn and practice mindfulness. My practice, since 2009, also took me to research and understand the mechanisms of mindfulness. I remember being confused over religious meditation and secular mindfulness and am grateful to the many authors including Jon Kabat-Zinn, Zindel Segal, Mark Williams, and John Teasdale. I attended the MBSR, MBCT, and ACT classes and felt something was amiss but I could not place my finger on it. One of the key questions in my mind, similar to KK's, was if we really needed to be mentally and physically unwell to learn mindfulness as my spiritual mindfulness practices taught me something different. I was also facing a similar challenge in the field of clinical psychology and the first wave of positive psychology which seemed to promote polarity. With these questions in mind, KK and I decided to make a change. Though MBWE is the brainchild of KK, I got more involved in adapting, reviewing, and modifying the elements of psychology into the curriculum. In my professional practice as a psychotherapist and an academic, I advocate an eclectic approach to all solutions whatsoever and thus started incorporating elements of psychology and mindfulness as an integrated practice in my psychotherapy services, lectures, workshops, and facilitation. Inspired by the aforementioned questions, I had also developed a unique model of therapy for wellbeing called, *Integrated Wellbeing Model* (IWM) and incorporated mindfulness into the IWM as part of a holistic approach to wellbeing.

Both of us were born in Singapore and have lived here all our lives. We had inherited the multi-culturalism of this city state that is home to approximately 5.7 million people and being one of the densest places to live. It is impossible to not meet someone upon leaving home within 1–2 minutes. We grew up and continue to live along with people of different cultures and descent. For the last ten years, Singapore continues to be a relatively happy country based on the World Happiness Report, scoring consistently above the global average. It is with this backdrop that we experienced mindfulness and noticing what worked and what did not. These insights led us to not only create the MBWE but also present a different perspective of mindfulness especially since we spent all our lives in Asia while continuing to facilitate, speak, coach, and provide therapy globally. We strongly believe that humanity stands to gain more from diverse perspectives rather than presenting a singular one. We invite you to explore this book with an open mind and heart. And, may you be well.

PART I

CHAPTER 1

Foundations of Mindfulness

I've been practicing yoga meditation for last 20 years but I am curious to know about a structured 8-week approach . . . I am sure I will ace the 8 weeks . . . but I am not sure if I will learn anything new since I already have a deep meditation practice.

–Jake

Jake was a participant in the Mindfulness-Based Wellbeing Enhancement (MBWE) program and he shared the above when I (SR) asked each participant to share their experiences of mindfulness if any. Are mindfulness and meditation the same? Is mindfulness secular or religious? Let us discuss this and more in this chapter.

Mindfulness, as secular practice, has been receiving increasing mainstream attention in the last ten years although it was conceived in the late 1970s. This is due to its science, research, evidence, and the impact it has been creating across a wide variety of settings including clinical settings.

In 2015, the UK Parliament published *The Mindful Nation UK* report which recommended that mindfulness be utilized as a tool to enhance health, education, workplace, and the criminal justice system. Between 2010 and 2020 a total of 6,258 journal articles on mindfulness were published (A. M. R. A., 2021). In 2019, the mindfulness and meditation smartphone apps, Headspace and Calm alone, generated $150 million and $100 million in revenue (McGrath, 2020).

The growth and acceptance of mindfulness in the mainstream is still growing exponentially, especially since the evidence about the results and benefits of mindfulness are largely promising and positive. Since the birth of the first-generation mindfulness-based programs (MBPs) namely the Mindfulness-Based Stress Reduction program (MBSR) and the Mindfulness-Based Cognitive Therapy program (MBCT), acceptance of mindfulness in all spheres of life is steadily growing. The salutary effects of the first-generation MBPs have gotten

DOI: 10.4324/9781003322955-2

researchers intrigued with other potential outcomes beyond stress reduction and depression relapse. From the evidentiary methods of the first-generation MBPs, a second generation of MBPs is emerging as effective treatments for anxiety, autism, schizophrenia, addictive behaviors, work-related stress, anger management and improving relationships, as well as improving human performance.

The second-generation MBPs share the design features of the first-generation MBPs such as incorporating weekly group practice sessions, lecture and psychoeducation components, guided meditation exercises, group discussions, and at-home practice elements. However, they are also different as they are psycho-spiritual or spiritual in nature, teach a greater range of meditative techniques and emphasize ethics (Van Gordon & Shonin, 2019). Moreover, the second-generation MBPs challenge the widely accepted definitions of mindfulness given that the outcomes and aim of these programs are different from the first-generation MBPs.

1 DEFINING MINDFULNESS

Mindfulness can be defined in various ways as well as from different perspectives. Sometimes, we ask participants in our workshops and sessions to give a one- or two-word definition of mindfulness. And the usual responses we receive would be awareness, self-awareness, consciousness, present moment, compassion, acceptance, concentration, and breathing awareness amongst others. We invite our participants to describe their understanding of mindfulness and we have received some very interesting perspectives, such as:

- it is a breathing practice
- a practice that helps raise self-awareness and awareness of surroundings
- bringing self-compassion to ourselves
- not being judgmental of ourselves and our experiences
- a meditation practice that focuses on the body, breath, and mind

Participants also bring a variety of definitions into the room which sometimes bring confusion. We often hear words such as "stillness," "stilling the mind," "annihilating all thoughts" and "brain training" amongst others. Often these definitions come from a casual internet search by the participants or sometimes from other teachers who may have had shared their version of what mindfulness is. Hence there is a need to bring more clarity to the definition of mindfulness.

At one end of the spectrum, we have concise definitions of mindfulness and at the other end we have books with hundreds of pages defining and presenting what mindfulness is. We cannot then conclude that one definition is better than the other as each definition describes mindfulness from different perspectives and deepens one's appreciation of it. People from different stages of life could also define it differently depending on how mindfulness had impacted them. Having worked with people of all ages from different parts of the world, we often see definitions of mindfulness stemming from the benefits it had provided them such as being a tool for stress-relief, managing emotions, grounding, or a technique for enhancing attentional capabilities. Are these definitions wrong? Not in totality.

Sarah Shaw (2020) states that it is indeed our right to define and describe mindfulness in a way that has benefited us. We totally agree that it is indeed possible to describe mindfulness from our experiences and the impact that it has had on us. However, there is also a risk in defining mindfulness as something other than what it is. We believe that there are specific unique characteristics to mindfulness that are not found in other contemplative practices and are therefore dissimilar to them. For example, defining mindfulness as a breathing technique could also mean that it could be the same as *Pranayama*, which is a variety of breath regulation practices that are taught in the yoga systems. Or it can also be confused with other deep breathing techniques that are taught by counsellors and psychologists to help people cope during difficult situations. In mindfulness, breathing is used as an anchor and it is observed with non-judgment as opposed to it being manipulated like in the yoga systems or in other coping techniques. *Therefore defining mindfulness would require an accurateness that helps people to differentiate it from other systems which may otherwise create confusion as well as setting up unrealistic expectations over the practice.*

There have been several operational definitions proposed by practitioners, researchers, and teachers of mindfulness. These definitions often come first from the religious (including spiritual) approach, then the secular approach, or finally, the self-help approach to mindfulness. The diverse definitions, each from one of the three approaches, then beg the question whether they had referred to the *same* practice and produced the *same* outcomes. We agree that mindfulness can be defined from many diverse perspectives with overlapping mechanisms but the question is whether we should, given that mindfulness is truly a distinct practice. While we agree that there could be overlapping outcomes in the religious, secular, and self-help approaches, they are indeed unique in many ways like three different types of fruits which look and taste different.

Therefore, this casual assumption that the definitions are all the same and the acceptance of any mindfulness definition without discrimination becomes bewildering, especially for mindfulness teachers and practitioners. For example, we may equate the "simple act of noticing new things," which is a self-help technique, to reduce mindlessness and the mindfulness approach of "noticing each breath as though we are noticing it for the first time" to be the same. On the contrary, the two approaches are very different in spite of revolving around the same theme of "novelty." Another example would be the practice of mindfulness for the removal of existential suffering which is different from the practice of mindfulness for the relief of physical and mental suffering in the form of pain, depression, and anxiety amongst others. It is also a gross misunderstanding that the latter practices would deliver us from existential suffering which is the goal of the former. The goals are not the same. As you can see, there are differences between mindfulness and other contemplative practices.

Our study reveals that the mindfulness, taught in the first- and second-generation MBPs, is distinctly unique by being secular in its approach and having a well defined method with distinct outcomes. A deeper discussion of these points will be presented later on as these are integral to the appreciation of MBPs and mindfulness.

For us to validate the definitions of mindfulness of the MBPs we need to ensure that they belong to the secular approach of MBPs and not those that may belong to the religious or self-help traditions. Studying the definitions of mindfulness from the MBSR tradition, which has been taught since the late 1970s, is certainly essential as it is the source of all the other MBPs. While we reserve the discussion about the history of mindfulness to the second part of this book, in this section we will confine ourselves to the definitions of mindfulness. In table 1.1, you will find various operational definitions of mindfulness found in literature centered around MBPs. We have systematically excluded religious or spiritual definitions of mindfulness as well as definitions that present the self-help approach to mindfulness, popularized by Ellen Langer, which aims to reduce mindlessness.

Table 1.1 The various definitions of mindfulness

1	Paying attention in a particular way: on purpose, in the present moment, and non-judgmentally (Kabat-Zinn, 1995, p. 4).
2	To simply "drop in" on the actuality of [one's] lived experience and then to sustain it as best [one] can moment by moment, with intentional openhearted presence and suspension of judgment and distraction, to whatever degree possible. (Kabat-Zinn, 2003, p. 148).
3	The awareness that emerges through paying attention on purpose, in the present moment, and non-judgmentally to the unfolding of experience moment by moment (Kabat-Zinn, 2003, p. 145).
4	Mindfulness meditation is a consciousness discipline revolving around a particular way of paying attention in one's life. It can be most simply described as the intentional cultivation of non-judgmental moment-to-moment awareness (Kabat-Zinn, 1996, p. 161).
5	Mindfulness is awareness that arises through paying attention, on purpose, in the present moment, non-judgmentally, And then I sometimes add, in the service of self-understanding and wisdom (Kabat-Zinn, 2017).

6	Psychological and behavioral versions of meditation skills usually taught in Eastern spiritual practices . . . [usually focused on] observing, describing, participating, taking a non-judgmental stance, focusing on one thing in the moment, being effective (Linehan, 1993, p. 114).
7	A state of psychological freedom that occurs when attention remains quiet and limber, without attachment to any particular point of view (Martin, 1997, p. 291).
8	Bringing one's complete attention to the present experience on a moment-to-moment basis (Marlatt & Kristeller, 1999, p. 68).
9	A way of paying attention that originated in Eastern meditation practices (Baer, 2003, p. 125).
10	Mindfulness captures a quality of consciousness that is characterized by clarity and vividness of current experience and functioning and thus stands in contrast to the mindless, less "awake" states of habitual or automatic functioning that may be chronic for many individuals (Brown & Ryan, 2003, p. 823).
11	Broadly conceptualized . . . a kind of non-elaborative, non-judgmental, present-centered awareness in which each thought, feeling, or sensation that arises in the attentional field is acknowledged and accepted as it is (Bishop et al., 2004, p. 232).
12	A process of gaining insight into the nature of one's mind and the de-centered perspective on thoughts and feelings so that they can be experienced in terms of their subjectivity (versus their necessary validity) and transient nature (versus their permanence) (Bishop et al., 2004, p. 234).
13	A process of regulating attention in order to bring a quality of non-elaborative awareness to current experience and a quality of relating to one's experience within an orientation of curiosity, experiential openness, and acceptance (Bishop et al., 2004, p. 234).
14	The first component involves the self-regulation of attention so that it is maintained on immediate experience, thereby allowing for increased recognition of mental events in the present moment. The second component involves adopting a particular orientation toward one's experiences in the present moment, an orientation that is characterized by curiosity, openness, and acceptance (Bishop et al., 2004, p. 232).
15	Maintaining attention on immediate experience and maintaining an attitude of acceptance toward this experience (Houlihan & Brewer, 2016, p .199).

What did you notice about these definitions? There is a common theme among the definitions which either describe the (1) means, as in a practice or the (2) outcomes of mindfulness, or both; though most of them preoccupy themselves with the means rather than the end. It is also worth noticing that among these definitions, the most popular one is from the founder of the modern secular mindfulness movement, Jon Kabat-Zinn:

> Paying attention in a particular way: on purpose,
> in the present moment, and non-judgmentally.

Kabat-Zinn's definition is particularly one that defines the practice (means) and every other definition that came after this was generally built on and developed upon this archetypical or prototypical definition. In fact, Kabat-Zinn had also revised his definitions over the years although not deviating radically from this original definition. In spite of the changes, we believe that this is an effective operational definition for mindfulness practices as it is succinct and it accurately describes the unique features that we are going to discuss in the next section.

2 MECHANISMS OF MINDFULNESS

One of the most challenging questions faced by researchers and practitioners is around the mechanisms of mindfulness. We often receive questions from curious participants as to what aspect of mindfulness actually produces the results. Was it the guiding instruction, the personal practice, the concentrative intensity, the breath or the body? The questions can be endless. Let's use the illustration of a piano to comprehend the mechanisms of mindfulness. When watching a piano recital, all that we see is the pianist's fingers coming into contact with the keyboard. And then the next thing that we experience is the sound. However between the contact of the fingers and the sound that we hear, there is a complex and precise sequential movement within the piano that creates the notes. Between the key and the sound there is a chain reaction involving the jack, hammer, string, and damper. The last movement before you hear the sound of the piano is the hammer coming into contact with the string. In the same fashion, there are many "movements" in a mindfulness practice and we are looking for the *final movement* that produces the outcomes. Hence we are undertaking a study of how mindfulness works and functions to generate the salutary effects and results. This "final movement" before the outcomes are produced is the *mechanisms*. A consistent deployment of these mechanisms is what leads to state and trait mindfulness and will be discussed at the end of the chapter. A good place to start this investigation into the mechanisms would be the study of the various definitions of mindfulness to explore patterns that emerge in them. Our study found four key mechanisms in mindfulness.

The first mechanism, either stated explicitly or implicitly, that stands out in all definitions of mindfulness is the practice of *attention*. Attention is often characterized by other descriptors such as regulated attention, clarity, vividness, observing, describing, focusing, noticing, and being free from distraction. Attention is then the intentional deployment of the mind's capacity to focus on a given thing, sometimes described as *focused attention*. It is like adjusting and directing the lens of a camera to the object that you wish to capture. All contemplative and meditative practices, deploy the attentional mechanism as it is central to these practices. However, in the case of mindfulness, we usually pay attention to the self and its internal experiences such as the breath, sensations, emotions and thoughts. In this regard, mindfulness then is essentially an attentional practice.

The second mechanism is *acceptance*. It is this mechanism that makes mindfulness a unique type of meditation. Acceptance is often characterized by curiosity, openness, de-centering, non-judgment, openhearted presence, and without attachment or being detached. In mindfulness practices, acceptance is explored after attention is deployed. As the participant notices the object in the attentional field, acceptance, sometimes described as *open monitoring,* is brought to the experience of the object, including sensations, thoughts, emotions, and urges. This then promotes a non-reactive experience while sitting with the object of attention. It is like how the ocean accepts the waters from all the rivers that flow into it without rejection.

The deployment of acceptance after attention can be likened to the trajectory of a boomerang. After the throw of the boomerang, it takes an elliptical trajectory to return to you as shown in Figure 1.1. In the same way, after attention is brought to an object, such as the breath, we let that experience just *be* with acceptance.

Object of experience

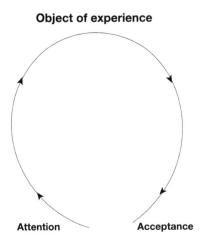

Attention   **Acceptance**

Figure 1.1 A circle showing the deployment of acceptance and attention

The third mechanism is *awareness*, which is perhaps the most abstract one as the quality of awareness is attribute-less in terms of experience. Feldman and Kuyken (2019) call this "simple knowing" without bias or preference. Awareness is often characterized by present-centeredness, immediate experience, being non-elaborative, and moment-to-moment experience. Awareness is unlike attention and acceptance as it is not subject to agency. It is an *intrinsic property of the human mind to reveal things as they are.* Kabat-Zinn (2005, p. 298) states, "Your Awareness is a very big space in which to reside. It is never not an ally, a friend, a sanctuary, a refuge. It is never not here, only sometimes veiled." An apt illustration for awareness would be light and the objects it reveals. The function of light is to "remove" darkness such that the natural perception takes place with regard to objects of experience such as the tables, chairs, floor, trees, mountains, etc. Without the light, we would then not be able to "see" these objects. One key attribute of light is that it does not create the objects it reveals but rather removes the obstacle to perception, which is darkness. In the same way, light does not create perception, as perception is always present, just like awareness. Similarly, awareness reveals thoughts, emotions, behaviors and sensations without creating or altering them.

Awareness being bare and rudimentary, it pervades both attention and acceptance just like how water is inseparably there in the waves. The sustained employment of attention and acceptance only removes the obstruction to "seeing things as they are" which is the nature of awareness. In fact, awareness always functions in the present moment, in the "now." Therefore mindfulness does not *create* awareness, but *restores* or *reveals* it. The result of mindfulness practices is enhanced awareness. Therefore, mindfulness is essentially a consciousness discipline or metacognition.

Some authors consider the attentional mechanism of mindfulness to be awareness, although we do not see awareness as a synonym or mechanism that works in the same fashion as attention. Feldman and Kuyken (2019) describe awareness as possessing intention, insight, understanding, and discernment. Such attributions seem to suggest that awareness operates with a sense of agency that involves evaluation and judgment. The implications of these attributions are that both awareness and attention are the same or function in a similar manner. Awareness as we have described is not subject to will or choice. It is choiceless. It is attention and acceptance that can be subjected to agency. Therefore such descriptions of awareness, from our perspective, are cognitive functions that generate insights and do not belong to the domain of awareness but to the mechanism of attention.

From our brief discussion about the mechanism of awareness, you would now see that *the key role of mindfulness is to enhance awareness through the practice of attention and acceptance* as shown in Figure 1.2.

This leads us to the fourth and final mechanism which is *insight*, often characterized by wisdom, self-understanding, or knowledge of the self. Insight is a cognitive process that is made possible by and depends on enhanced awareness. When we see things clearly for what they are, an intimate understanding of the human self develops. Insight is like a growing clarity that happens as we walk through a dark tunnel toward the light. It is not something concrete and absolute but yet it can lead to positive life outcomes. This is the final outcome

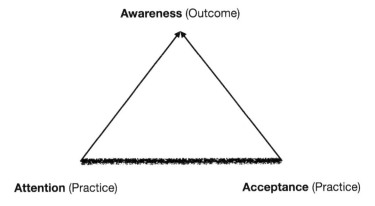

Figure 1.2 A triangle showing how acceptance and attention lead to enhanced awareness

of mindfulness which is facilitated skillfully and experientially by the mindfulness teacher. The purpose of mindfulness then is the progressive generation and development of insight. The insights gained from mindfulness practices could be one or more of the following:

- thoughts are not facts
- common humanity
- identity with awareness
- clarity of purpose and meaning
- knowing the body to be a gauge
- nature of happiness
- self as being whole
- thoughts, emotions, actions, and sensations (TEAS) not affecting awareness

The first-generation MBPs focused on the body, feelings, moods, thoughts, and relating with the world, and using them as a tool to achieve psychological freedom i.e. freedom from pain, stress, depression, anxiety, etc. These are often associated with the Buddhist foundations of mindfulness. However, the positive insights about the self, such as seeing the self as whole and complete, are generally not explicit in the first-generation MBPs, though Kabat-Zinn emphatically and beautifully presents such insights in many of his works. A few excerpts have been reproduced below:

> Although our patients all come with various problems, diagnoses, and ailments, we make every effort to apprehend their *intrinsic wholeness*.
> (Kabat-Zinn, 2011, p. 292)

> We are also what was present before the scarring – our *original wholeness*, what was *born whole*. And we can reconnect with that *intrinsic wholeness* at any time, because its very nature is that it is always present. It is who we truly are.
>
> (Kabat-Zinn, 2013, p. 185)

> When we are in touch with *being whole*, we *feel at one with everything*. When we feel at one with everything, we feel *whole* ourselves.
>
> (Kabat-Zinn, 1995, p. 226)

These positive perspectives of the self are often understated in the first-generation MBPs or totally absent in its curriculum. Perhaps these MBPs were more focused on the removal of suffering of those with clinical needs such that these positive insights about the self had to take a back seat. We were surprised to know that the MBSR, which was created by Kabat-Zinn, did not present these perspectives in its sessions though Kabat-Zinn shares it in his books. We believe that these positive insights about the self are as important as the insights pertaining to stress, chronic pain, depression, and anxiety. We will discuss this aspect of mindfulness and its relationship with wellbeing in Chapter 2.

Our study of the mechanisms, sheds light on the pedagogy of mindfulness and MBPs as shown in Figure 1.3. The image below could be helpful in seeing how mindfulness works.

Figure 1.3 Flowchart on the four mechanisms of mindfulness

To summarize, the pedagogy of mindfulness involves the deployment of attention and acceptance which then leads to the enhancement of awareness. Insights are then generated from enhanced awareness which then create the results such as stress reduction, prevention of relapses of depression, increased levels of happiness, and clarity over purpose among others. Appreciating this process helps us appreciate the pedagogy of any type of MBP, and also empowers teachers to facilitate the MBPs more effectively.

Apart from the four mechanisms stated in our study, various other mechanisms have been proposed in the literature (see table 1.2). We consider these mechanisms to be generally in service of the four mechanisms stated above or similar to them.

Table 1.2 Other mechanisms of mindfulness

Source	Mechanisms
Garland, Froeliger, & Howard, 2014	Focused attention, open monitoring
Jankowski & Holas, 2014	Metacognitive knowledge, metacognitive skills, metacognitive experiences
Shapiro et al., 2006	Intention, attitude
Brown, Ryan, & Creswell, 2007	Insight, non-attachment, exposure, enhanced mind-body functioning, integrated functioning
Baer, 2003	Exposure, self-management, acceptance, cognitive change, relaxation
Baer at al., 2006	Observing, describing, acting with awareness, non-judging of inner experience
Nilsson & Kazemi, 2016	Awareness, attention, present-centeredness, External events, cultivation and ethical-mindedness

3 PEDAGOGY OF MINDFULNESS

The pedagogy of mindfulness consists of four important components. These are

- mindfulness practices
- didactic content and exercises
- seven attitudes of mindfulness
- inquiry and insights

Each of these is crucial to achieving the outcomes of mindfulness. We have come across a few teachers and also therapists, who have good intentions, but mechanically use lesson plans and scripts to conduct mindfulness sessions without a deep appreciation of the pedagogy of mindfulness. We will discuss these four components in greater detail, emphasizing the dependent relationship among the components.

3.1 Mindfulness Practices

Various types of mindfulness practices are available in both secular and religious schools of meditation and mindfulness. In our recent survey of purported mindfulness scripts, we found that there are more than 200 mindfulness scripts available from different mindfulness teachers, and some of them are even on sale for a small fee. This beckons the question as to which of these are authentic. We believe that this question can be answered by examining the practices of the first-generation MBPs which is the MBSR, as well as the MBCT. The practices of the MBSR and MBCT are usually found in all subsequent MBPs, which are:

- body scan
- sitting meditation
- mindful movement or mindful yoga
- awareness of breath
- walking meditation or mindful walking
- lovingkindness meditation
- raisin practice

All MBPs that came after the MBSR and MBCT utilize most of these practices and build upon them. For example, in MBCT, all the above practices are employed and new practices such as the "breathing space" are added for achieving the outcomes of the MBCT. In the Mindful Self-Compassion (MSC) program, there is a centering meditation.

Among these mindfulness practices, a few are considered formal practices which are the body scan, sitting meditation and the mindful movement. Informal mindfulness practices, on the other hand, are usually the ones that are woven into daily routines such as mindful walking, brushing teeth, showering, eating, and dishwashing amongst others. Both formal and informal practices have been found to create positive results, *although the formal ones have been found to create consistent and predictable outcomes.*

One significant point to note is that all of the formal practices would explicitly deploy both attention and acceptance, and allow the recognition of the presence of awareness. These can be clearly seen in the scripts that are used for the practices where various verbs and statements are utilized to deploy attention and acceptance. A couple of excerpts are cited in Table 1.3:

Table 1.3 Verbs and statements for deploying attention and acceptance in scripts

ATTENTION	ACCEPTANCE
• "Noticing your inbreath and outbreath . . ."	• "Not trying to control your breath in any way . . ."
• "Bringing full attention to each breath in each moment . . ."	• ". . . on the inbreath and on each outbreath just letting go"
• "Becoming aware of whatever sensations are there"	• ". . . experiencing and accepting what you feel here"

ATTENTION	ACCEPTANCE
• "Shift your attention to your pelvis. . . . . ." • "Observing the breath deep down in your belly" • "Feeling the abdomen as it expands" • "Bringing it back to the present, back to the moment-to-moment observing" • "Simply seeing each thought as it comes up in your mind"	• ". . . letting go of your lower leg" • "Totally present in each moment. Content to just be, and to just be right here as you are right now" • "Not trying to do anything or change anything" • "Without judging bringing the attention . . ." • "Being here with whatever feelings and sensations that come up in any moment without judging them"

3.2 Didactic Components and Exercises

Along with these mindfulness practices, almost all MBPs incorporate didactic components. The didactic components in MBPs are taught in the service of generating insights. They guide the generation of insights like the way the steering wheel directs the motion of the car. This is where MBPs vary very widely as the didactic components are chosen based on the outcomes of the MBPs. Table 1.4 shows the comparison of the didactic components of MBSR and MBCT.

Table 1.4 Comparison of didactic components of MBSR and MBCT

MBSR	MBCT
• Nine dots puzzle • Optical illusions • Unpleasant events calendar • Pleasant events calendar • Stress theories • Difficult communications calendar • Explorations of assumptions • Changing seats exercise • Letter to self exercise	• Thoughts feelings exercise • Unpleasant events calendar • Pleasant events calendar • Poem reading • Depression/anxiety-automatic thoughts • Nourishing/depleting exercise • Noticing anxiety/depressive relapse signatures • Sustenance plan

One can certainly notice that the didactic components are designed in the MBPs to serve a specific purpose. The purpose is to steer insights in the direction of achieving the outcomes of the MBPs.

3.3 Seven Attitudes of Mindfulness

Kabat-Zinn (2013) in his book, *Full Catastrophe Living*, introduces seven important attitudes that are necessary for practitioners. He added two more attitudes to the seven in later years. These attitudes allow the practitioners to stay open and receptive as they practice mindfulness. He compares them to the function of soil in the way that it supports the cultivation of a crop. These attitudes help in realizing the intention of mindfulness by harnessing the mental energies of the participants in the direction of the outcomes. Here is a brief description of the nine attitudes:

- Non-judging – allowing the experiences to be and allowing oneself to be a witness to them. Noticing the constant judging and reactions that may take place while in the practice.
- Patience – allowing the practice to unfold it its own time without pressurizing for results. It is like the growth of a child where all that is needed is nurturing while the growth takes place in its own time. One cannot rush it.
- Beginner's mind – allowing oneself to meet every practice like it is a new one. Being curious each time without an imposition of a preconceived experience.
- Trust – allowing oneself to trust one's own experiences rather than to validate them through the minds of others. Acknowledging the mistakes that we may make and allowing that to be part of the process.
- Non-striving – without wanting to change what is happening in the present moment and recognizing that we are already where we should be in any given moment.
- Acceptance – bringing acceptance to what is happening *as they are* without reacting to it and wanting to see it differently.
- Letting go – certain thoughts, feelings and sensations might bring resistance during the practice of mindfulness. This resistance could be the result of being unfamiliar, disliking or facing difficulties with the experience. Letting go would mean that we accept the experiences as they are without judging them or expecting a particular result. We let them go like the way a ripe fruit naturally drops from the tree.
- Gratitude – being thankful for being alive, having a functioning body and mind, and being able to practice mindfulness in this present moment. Having a sense of gratefulness to others, including the planet, which has contributed to our practice of mindfulness. Prosocial gratitude includes being thankful in this moment for every being that has helped us in our life journey.
- Generosity – we as human beings have the capacity to bring happiness and wellbeing to ourselves and others. Every small act of kindness brings joy

to people around and also to oneself. By adding value to others around us, we strengthen our interconnectedness.

3.4 Inquiry and Insights

Inquiry is a very important stage in the pedagogy of mindfulness. We will give deeper attention to inquiry in Chapter 4 in the context of facilitation in the MBWE. In this section we will discuss inquiry in the context of pedagogy. Inquiry is where the experience of awareness is processed through an interactive dialogue. Rob Brandsma (2017, p. 103) defines inquiry as:

> A conversation method aimed at exploring a personal practice experience – and reactions to that experience – by inviting participants to transcend their usual way of looking in order to assume a different perspective, one through which participants can acquire insight into unconscious patterns enabling them to be less reactive in dealing with life's challenges.

We agree with Brandsma's definition and intention of inquiry as it packs the fundamentals of the process of inquiry very succinctly. Inquiry takes place in almost every session of an MBP or mindfulness class. This usually happens after a mindfulness practice, regardless of it being a formal or informal practice, a didactic component or an exercise. The teacher skillfully presents question after question in a way that helps in generating personal insights. We emphasize the personal nature of insights as there could never be a wrong insight as each insight is unique to an individual. An illustration of this is like a group of people who are in a dark tunnel and walking in a straight line toward one end of a tunnel where there is light. Each one of them is seeing the light at the end of tunnel to be of different size depending on how far they are from the light. That light is like "awareness" where none of them is wrong in sharing their current experience regardless of the light appearing to be of different size to each one of them. Similarly, the personal insights are not divorced from universal experience of common humanity.

The variance and depth of the insights are largely influenced by the intimacy one has with awareness. Hence, a teacher is not entirely in control of the outcome of the inquiry as it depends on what is emerging in the room and within the selves of the practitioners. This then requires the teacher to possess a certain degree of intimacy with the experience of awareness and diverse insights as well as having the openness to be receptive to newer ones. In addition to the intimacy with awareness, the teacher should be skilled in deepening the inquiry with questions, so as to help contextualize the insights gathered by the participants within the intended outcomes of the MBP. The teacher is not intent on arriving at pre-determined conclusions or world-views, but to allow participants to curiously shift their perspectives to achieve the outcomes of the MBP. As a rule of thumb, all insights would conduce wellbeing, as the outcomes of all MBPs are implicitly aimed at this broad goal. Mindfulness teachers would certainly benefit from the possession of two important assets which are the intimacy with awareness cum insights and the skills to facilitate inquiry.

The continuous engagement with practitioners through inquiry and the generation of insights can be appreciated through the diagram in Figure 1.4. The mindfulness practices comprising of attention and acceptance coupled with the recognition of awareness, didactic components and exercises are a *divergent* process filled with curiosity and openness. It leads to an exploration without pre-defined outcomes. But it is inquiry that harnesses the experiences in a *convergent* manner to arrive at personal insights. The mindfulness teacher facilitates this process in every session of any MBP.

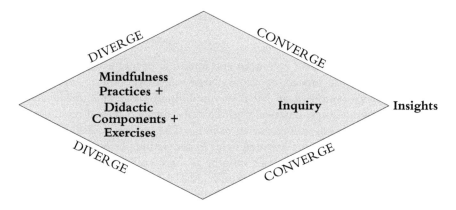

Figure 1.4 Divergent and convergent process of mindfulness components

The complete pedagogical process of mindfulness is presented below in Figure 1.5.

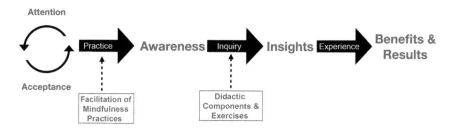

Figure 1.5 The pedagogical process of MBP

4 ARE MINDFULNESS AND MEDITATION THE SAME?

One of the most challenging questions is whether mindfulness and meditation are the same. Many participants continue to ask us this question, sometimes with curiosity and sometimes with prejudice. There are people who "want" to see it as meditation because it is consistent with their beliefs and there are others who do not "want" to hear that mindfulness is a meditation because it sounds like new age, spiritual, and religious jargon.

While there have been discussions around mindfulness and meditation being the same and also of them being different in popular media, not much has been written about this topic. Therefore it definitely deserves deeper exploration. In this section, we will discuss whether mindfulness is indeed meditation and how it is different from other types of meditation.

When studying the literature on mindfulness, one thing that stands out is the usage of the term "mindfulness" as an adjective qualifying the noun "meditation" i.e. mindfulness meditation. Kabat-Zinn too uses the term meditation as a synonym in all his works as he does not make any concerted attempts to use a separate term other then perhaps distinguishing mindfulness meditation to be one that is unique by itself. Before we get into the distinguishing features of mindfulness, let us first explore a few definitions of meditation:

> A self-administered attention-based technique for inner transformation.
>
> (Eifring, 2013, p. 3)

> A family of self-regulation practices that focus on training attention and awareness in order to bring mental processes under greater voluntary control and thereby foster general mental well-being and development and/or specific capacities such as calm, clarity, and concentration.
>
> (Walsh & Shapiro, 2006, p. 228)

> A family of complex emotional and attentional regulatory strategies developed for various ends, including the cultivation of well-being and emotional balance.
>
> (Lutz, Slagter, Dunne, & Davidson, 2008, p. 2)

> Practices that self-regulate the body and the mind, thereby affecting mental events by engaging a specific attentional set.
>
> (Cahn & Polich, 2006, p. 180)

> Deep concentration on any object.
>
> (Adiswarananda, 2007, p. 3)

A cursory study of the definitions above would reveal two important ideas:

- meditation is a term used for a family of contemplative practices, and
- meditation being a mental activity that involves concentration and attention regulation.

Essentially then, meditation is a family of practices that involve mental concentration. The next question would then be about the types of meditation known to us today. Awasthi (2013) presents 11 types of meditation, listed below:

- attentional training
- hatha yoga
- relaxation-based methods
- brain-wave vibration meditation
- automatic self-transcending
- imagery of deities
- mantra meditation
- yoga
- qiqong
- tai chi
- mindfulness

Awasthi has rightly singled out mindfulness as a unique type among the family of meditative practices for the reason that it is worthy of distinction. Do meditative practices then satisfy specific common features? According to Bond et al. (2009), they all do. All the meditative practices share three specific features in common, which are:

- the use of a defined technique,
- logic relaxation, and
- a self-induced state/mode.

The three criteria stated above certainly help us to appreciate meditation as a practice that is well defined, practiced autonomously, and without any need for contemplation. The three criteria apply to the all 11 types of meditation. In addition, Bond et al. (2009) present other auxiliary criteria that may apply to specific meditations, which:

- has a state of psycho-physical relaxation,
- uses a self-focus skill or anchor,
- has the presence of a state of suspension of logical thought processes,
- has a religious/spiritual/philosophical context,
- or has a state of mental silence.

Meditation therefore is a generic term that can denote several permutations of one or more of the criteria presented above. Each type of meditation is essentially unique and differentiated from other types of meditation. In the same manner, mindfulness is then a unique type of meditation. Let us now explore the distinguishing features of mindfulness meditation.

5 DISTINGUISHING FEATURES OF MINDFULNESS MEDITATION

Mindfulness distinguishes itself by satisfying a couple of the unique features stated above. And its two unique features are focused attention and open monitoring. Focused attention is the "voluntary focusing of attention on a chosen object in a sustained fashion" and open monitoring " involves non-reactively monitoring the content of experience from moment to moment, primarily as a means to recognize the nature of emotional and cognitive patterns" (Lutz et al., 2008, p. 2). One would notice that it is the second of the two features, open monitoring, that distinguishes mindfulness from the other types of meditation. All the other types of meditation generally satisfy the first feature, which involves focused attention though the object of attention could be different. We reproduce the summary table from the work of Lutz et al. (2008):

Table 1.5 Summary of features of focused attention and open monitoring

Focused attention meditation	• directing and sustaining attention on a selected object (e.g. breath sensation) • detecting mind wandering and distractors (e.g. thoughts) • disengagement of attention from distractors and shifting of attention back to the selected object • cognitive reappraisal of distractor (e.g. "just a thought," "it is okay to be distracted")
Open monitoring meditation	• no explicit focus on objects • non-reactive metacognitive monitoring (e.g. for novices, labeling of experience) • non-reactive awareness of automatic cognitive and emotional interpretations of sensory, perceptual and endogenous stimuli

The mindfulness approach requires the maintenance of attention in a state of open receptivity, while the exclusive concentrative type of meditation requires the narrowing of attentional focus. The exclusive focused attention style of meditation *without* open monitoring could be limited as it only enhances concentrative abilities without changing one's relationship with thoughts. This style of meditation is popularly attributed to the yoga traditions, especially the patanjali yoga, hatha yoga and some Buddhist yoga schools. At this juncture, it is worth noting that these three schools of yoga, which we will collectively refer to as "yoga traditions" henceforth, are religious and have a clear soteriological goal. Let us now examine the nature of meditation as popularly taught in the yoga traditions.

B. K. S. Iyengar, an early forerunner of the hatha yoga or the postural yoga tradition in the West, defines meditation as "the restraint of mental modifications or as a suppression of the fluctuations of consciousness (mind)" (Iyengar, 1979, p. 20). Vishnudevananda (1999), the founder of the Sivananda Yoga Teachers' Training Course which is one of the first yoga teacher training programs in the West, describes the highest state of meditation where "the awareness of ego gradually vanishes, and reasoning and reflection cease. A higher type of indescribable peace descends" (p. 44). These definitions of meditation are inspired by the often-considered oldest manual for meditation, the Patanjali Yoga Sutra-s (PYS), a Sanskrit text that presents the practice and philosophy of yoga through aphorisms. The PYS is perhaps the most commented text and meditation practice in the yoga traditions in the last 100 years. In the PYS, the goal of yoga is presented as the suppression of all mental activities, a state defined as asamprajnata samadhi. This state is expressed in the PYS's aphorism 1.2 as "yogah citta vrtti nirodha – yoga is the cessation of thoughts." The aforementioned definitions of meditation by Iyengar and Vishnudevananda, as well and many other teachers in the last 100 years revolve around the attenuation or stilling of thoughts. This happens to be the popular view of yoga meditation in the last 100 years where the practitioner enters a state of death-like trance, deep in meditation and motionless like an insentient object where perception ceases. These ideas are also found in the medieval hatha yoga texts (Vivekamartanda (166–9), Hathattvakaumudi (51.15, 18, 54, 73), and Amanaska (1.26–27)). This had become the popular description of the culminating experience of meditation in the last century.

This popular type of meditation is supported in its preliminary stages by breath manipulation (pranayama) and conditioning postures (asanas), which are one of the central limbs of hatha yoga. All of these three practices: breath manipulation, postures, and meditation involve "great effort" which is in fact the direct translation for the word "hatha." There are various types of breath manipulation that involve the regulation of inbreath, outbreath, and retention of breath for fixed intervals. Sometimes the breath is retained within the lungs for as long as 64 counts. The postures are also practiced in a way that there is indeed a *perfect posture* which the practitioners strive to get into. The introduction to the book *B. K. S. Iyengar Yoga: The Path to Holistic Health*, states that "Iyengar used asanas to challenge his students and the Iyengar approach destroys sluggishness in the body" and "Further right alignment and action are required for these postures (Iyengar, 2021, p. 23)." We can certainly see that all of these practices would likely put its practitioners in a striving mode to achieve perfection for all the right reasons according to the philosophy of hatha yoga.

A similar state to asamprajnata samadhi of the PYS appears in the Theravada Buddhist tradition, called nirodha samapatti – the attainment of cessation. In this advanced state of meditation, mental activity gets suspended for as long as seven days (Thera, 2010). This state of mental silence is equally considered to be a state of deliverance, enlightenment, or liberation in the yoga traditions.

Our brief survey of the yoga traditions, which became a huge industry especially in the West in the last five decades, inform us that its practices of meditation coupled with breath manipulation and postural practice are at loggerheads with mindfulness in several key areas. The style of meditation of the yoga tradition appears to be one that requires willful change of state and the attenuation of thoughts. It is practiced in a way that the mind has to be made empty. The mind along with its thoughts are not accepted as they are. While this style is similar to mindfulness in the area of focused attention, it is still very different when compared with the second feature of open monitoring, coupled with acceptance and non-judgment. Further yoga meditation puts the practitioner in the striving mode where the end state of the practice becomes non-negotiable, which is quite the opposite of the mindfulness attitudes of non-judging, non-striving, trust, acceptance, and letting go. Implicitly, yoga meditation teaches the idea that thoughts are unwholesome and freedom from it is a necessity to be free. It encourages mental silence. On the other hand, the attitude of mindfulness comes from the opposite direction where thoughts are not our enemy and mental silence is not a requirement for psychological freedom. Thoughts are noticed for what they are and as they are with an attitude of acceptance and receptivity. The purpose of mindfulness then is not to achieve a state of relaxation or mental suspension but a shift in the cognitive appreciation of the nature of thoughts while in meditation, and the insights gained thereafter. Evidence tells us that this perspective shift results in a variety of wellbeing outcomes.

Another difference is that mindfulness meditation involves using the breath as an anchor without manipulating the way one breathes. Conversely, yoga breathing involves the manipulation of the breath, thus making breath the center of the practice, instead of it being an anchor. The practice of postures in hatha yoga is one that conditions the body with a focus on alignment and a perfect posture. On the other hand, mindful yoga or movement is an attentional practice with acceptance and compassion, that directs one's attention to movement and stillness rather than the culminating posture.

In my (KK) years of practice, I have noticed one key difference between mindfulness and yoga. In mindfulness, we recognize that we are *already* that which we want to be and *already* where we want to be, from the standpoint of *awareness*. There is nothing to be improved in awareness, and it is only available in the present time, so "I am aware" all the time. If I were to then see myself as awareness, "I am" always available regardless of place, circumstances, and time. Kabat-Zinn articulates these subtleties in many of his works and a few excerpts at this stage could be helpful in appreciating these unique features of mindfulness:

> When it comes right down to it, wherever you go, there you are. Whatever you wind up doing, that's what you've wound up doing. Whatever you are thinking about right now, that's what's on your mind.
>
> (Kabat-Zinn, 1995, p. xiii)

> Meditation is the only intentional, systematic human activity which at bottom is about not trying to improve yourself or get anywhere else, but simply to realize where you already are.
>
> (Kabat-Zinn, 1995, p. 14)

> Mindfulness practice means that we commit fully in each moment to being present. There is no "performance." There is just this moment. We are not trying to improve or to get anywhere else.
>
> (Kabat-Zinn, 1995, p. 22)

In our quest to find out if mindfulness is meditation and how it is different from other types of meditation, we have discovered that mindfulness is a unique type of meditation that contains both focused attention and open monitoring, unlike other types meditation that specifically deploys focused attention exclusively. The rise of yoga tradition in the West during the 1960s and 1970s had allowed Kabat-Zinn to integrate its practices into mindfulness and yet distinguish it by its attitudes. We will reserve the discussion of the historical development of mindfulness in Chapter 9. Moreover, the informal mindfulness practices promoted in MBPs are also a unique approach of mindfulness, and are unpopular in the yoga traditions.

Unlike other forms of meditation that have become the means for relaxation and mental silence, mindfulness has taken a cognitive approach to help people with clinical challenges and wanting of purpose and meaning. It is not aiming at mental silence, relaxation, nor suspension of logical thought processes. This could explain why the attempt to disassociate mindfulness from the style of meditation that solely involved concentrative meditation is important.

By making this distinction, we are in no ways deriding or criticizing the yoga traditions. The key thrust of our position is that yoga operates on the premise of a different goal and method which may be productive of its pre-determined outcomes that mindfulness may not be effective in. There could also be an overlap in the outcomes that mindfulness and yoga produce. For example, we discovered some research where the outcomes of MBPs with the absence of yoga were seen to be less effective (Hunt et al., 2018) and the acquaintance with yoga could also enhance mindfulness teacher competence (Salmon et al., 2009). We certainly acknowledge the validity of yoga research and its salutary effects in many spheres of human life. Both yoga and mindfulness are certainly two different vehicles intent on reaching different destinations although they are useful vehicles, nonetheless.

6 SECULAR MINDFULNESS AND ITS APPEAL

I (SR) remember an incident where a participant in the MBWE, who was a practicing Buddhist, kept comparing many of the mindfulness practices to her knowledge and practice of Buddhism. She mentioned during many of the sessions on how she already did breath meditation, walking meditation, etc. and that the Buddhist practice was better. She was resistant in the first few weeks but kept attending and participating in the sessions as we explored together and allowed her to find the space to negotiate her beliefs in a way that worked for her. By sessions 4 or 5, she stopped comparing and started appreciating the differences and similarities with her own practice. She was able to make space for the co-existence of both secular mindfulness and Buddhist meditation.

Many participants in our classes often ask us questions about the secularity of mindfulness. Here is a short list of popular questions that we have encountered:

- Is mindfulness religious?
- Is it Hindu or Buddhist?
- I am a Christian. Should I be even practicing mindfulness?
- Meditation is not permitted in my religion. Are there meditation practices in your classes?
- Are you a trained monk?
- Could I request a mindfulness teacher who has a classical training in meditation?
- Can you provide a teacher who is not religious?

Every time we receive questions along these lines, we take effort to define and explain that mindfulness can also be secular. I (SR) remember guiding the practice of awareness of breath in one of my psychology classes to a group of post-graduate students and I immediately received a pushback from one of the them. He wrote an email to me about how our lectures should not include religious practices and even upon explaining what secular mindfulness is, he insisted that he be allowed to come to class 15 minutes later if we had to practice mindfulness as it was against his religious beliefs. We came to a compromise that he attended class on time and did not participate in anything that made him uncomfortable. The noticing of the breath is not a religious practice. It is just like bending forward to touch your toes in yoga.

In this section, we will discuss what secular mindfulness is and why the secularity of mindfulness is important in specific cultures, especially in Asia where people are familiar with meditation being either Hindu or Buddhist. The first question to ask would be: can mindfulness even be secular? Let us examine this controversial discussion which has become polarized among many teachers and scholars in the last decade.

From the MBSR program conducted in the late 1970s and 1980s, Kabat-Zinn wrote his first book, *Full Catastrophe Living*, about mindfulness and the MBSR. This was possibly the first attempt to disassociate mindfulness from the conventional understanding of meditation influenced by yoga traditions. Since then, he took concerted efforts to secularize mindfulness without denying its religious roots. He states "MBSR is based on rigorous and systematic training in mindfulness. A form of meditation originally developed in the Buddhist traditions of Asia" (Kabat-Zinn, 2013, p. xlix). Kabat-Zinn also makes it very clear in his works that the meditation practices he encountered were from Buddhist traditions, as well as being influenced by the yoga tradition and other philosophical traditions. An elaborate discussion about its influences can be found in Chapter 9. He further states his intention behind secularizing mindfulness:

> Why not develop an American vocabulary that spoke to the heart of the matter, and didn't focus on the cultural aspects of the traditions out of which the dharma emerged, however beautiful they might be, or on centuries-old scholarly debates concerning fine distinctions in the Abhidharma. This was not because they weren't ultimately important, but because they would likely cause unnecessary impediments for people who were basically dealing with suffering and seeking some kind of release from it.
>
> (Kabat-Zinn, 2011, p. 287)

Being a man of medicine interested in healing people, Kabat-Zinn was truly committed to his profession which was to help people find relief from their suffering. It was this primary motive that led to the secularization of mindfulness. However we need to better understand the term "suffering" and not gloss over it. "Suffering" is defined in religious traditions, especially Buddhism, as one that is existential, unlike the suffering that is defined in clinical settings such as depression, anxiety, stress, or chronic pain.

In Buddhism, suffering specifically refers to existential suffering which is defined as dukkha (Pali) or duhkha (Sanskrit). This dukkha is defined as the problem of life in all the schools of yoga traditions. However, in Buddhism *life as a whole* is described to be suffering and this forms the first of the four noble truths of Buddhism. This suffering is further broken down into three types: the physical and mental (dukkha-dukkha), changing phenomena (viparinama-dukkha) and fundamental dissatisfaction (sankhara-dukkha). And Buddhism's eight-fold path puts an end to this suffering. Mindfulness happens to be the seventh limb in the eight-fold path, called Sati or Samma Sati (right mindfulness). Bodhi (1994, p. 74) defines the practice of right mindfulness as the training of the mind to "to remain in the present, open, quiet, and alert, contemplating the present event. All judgments and interpretations have to be suspended, or if they occur, just registered and dropped."

You would have observed that the goal of secular mindfulness and as presented by MBPs, involves the release from suffering, which is similar to the first type of suffering, dukkha-dukkha, i.e. the physical and mental. It does not address the full scope of suffering as defined by Buddhism or the yoga traditions. Neither do we find any evidence within Buddhism that mindfulness *solely* alleviates the first type of suffering, as the entire eight-fold path is driven toward the release from all the three types of suffering. Mindfulness then plays a unique role in the eight-fold path, which Hwang and Kearney (2015) present as:

1. being attentive to the present
2. not forgetting
3. stabilizing the mind
4. formalizing meditation practice
5. guarding the senses
6. wisdom, experience and intelligence
7. discrimination
8. attaining enlightenment via a process

Mindfulness in Buddhism serves as a protective shield from unwholesome thoughts, emotions, and behaviors by staying vigilant. It leads the practitioner to the eighth limb, thereafter, culminating in Nirvana or enlightenment, a unique insight taught by the Buddha, reserved for those who subscribe to the faith.

By now, you would notice that secularized mindfulness retains only the universal aspects of suffering shared by all humans and the universal human capacity to be mindful. And the practices that secular mindfulness shares with the right mindfulness of Buddhism are the bare attentional practices without subscribing to the beliefs of Buddhism. One cannot then argue that the capacity of paying attention with acceptance solely belongs to the Buddhists. These are psychological functions available to all human beings but perhaps first harnessed in patanjali yoga and Buddhist yoga though not confined to these traditions.

Dissociating secular mindfulness from its religious sphere has invited strong criticisms especially from the Buddhist teachers and practitioners. We have summarized their criticisms as follows (Wilks, 2014; Monteiro et al., 2014):

- MBPs diluting the Buddhist dharma, by offering a "one-fold path"
- MBP teachers become qualified within a short time compared to the years of practice by Buddhist practitioners
- MBP teachers neglect the importance of implicit ethics in Buddhism and therefore use mindfulness inappropriately such as in the military or capitalist society
- MBP teachers may not be aware of the profound and uncomfortable experiences that may emerge in people practicing meditation
- MBPs being values-neutral
- MBPs lacking explicit Buddhist ethics in the training

Buddhist critics propose that MBPs should be taught along with Buddhist ethics explicitly. Ajahn Brahm, an influential Buddhist monk, states that secular mindfulness is an oxymoron and that if mindfulness were to be secular, then it should be called "Brainfulness" instead (Buddhist Society of Western Australia, 2017). These arguments are sometimes viewed by non-Buddhist critics as using mindfulness to bring Buddhism through the back door and may we add perhaps even through the front door. Trudy Goodman calls this phenomenon crypto-Buddhism and stealth Buddhism (Brown, 2017). On the other hand, the inclusion of Buddhism in MBPs to make them more effective is an untested proposition and therefore a secular approach is more tenable and has proven to be effective (Baer, 2015). There are other scholars, practitioners, and teachers who welcome the co-existence of both secular and Buddhist mindfulness as different systems. We support this co-existence as long as it is not masked under any other covert agenda.

While some of the criticisms against secular mindfulness are valid, their starting point or the implicit assumption has always been that secular mindfulness is solely a Buddhist practice. We disagree with this assumption. Secular mindfulness is a repurposed practice, like the way a polyethylene terephthalate (PET) bottle can be modified and repurposed into a pot for plants. One cannot insist that the pot is still a PET drinking bottle. These arguments may not be valid anymore. We will gradually dismantle these arguments in Chapter 9 to show that secular mindfulness is quite far removed from its religious roots (especially Buddhism), and has been repurposed from its roots and is profoundly influenced by other schools of thought that do not share the same worldview of Buddhism.

However, Kabat-Zinn's recent responses to these criticisms from the Buddhist circles, and his sympathetic attitude toward it, make the task of clearly setting the boundaries of secular mindfulness more challenging. For example, in an interview with Thrive Global (Baer, 2017), Kabat-Zinn openly repudiates the position that *his* mindfulness was secular. He states "I assiduously avoid the word *secular*. As soon as you say *secular mindfulness*, you're abstracting the sacred out of it." He has made similar responses elsewhere, and to be honest, his responses do not address the concerns over secular mindfulness. In fact, he seems to be circling the issues without resolving it. This could explain why Hyland (2015, p. 178) concluded that Kabat-Zinn's balancing act could be due to his desire to "guard against the possible alienation of religious groups and, in the light of the growth of Mindfulness-Based Interventions (MBI) in schools and colleges in the US and Europe, such an emphasis may well be worth maintaining." However, matters become worse for both the camps, the religious, and the secular, as Kabat-Zinn states at the close of the aforementioned interview:

> The Buddha wasn't a Buddhist. A religion grew around his community. His realizations were universal realizations about suffering, the nature of suffering and the nature of the human mind.

We believe that his position with regards to re-interpreting Buddhism as not being a religion or the Buddha not being a Buddhist had invited very damning criticisms of him and the MBSR (they will be presented in Chapters 8 & 9).

Let us now explore the secular approach to mindfulness. Secular mindfulness is defined as "a solution to many different types of issues, from addiction to pain; from reactivity to stress-management; and as a means to create more productive workers and more efficient soldiers" (Falick, 2020, p. 1). Arat (2017, p. 171) defines it as it being "pure secular stillness" and calming the mind, to relieve stress, and attain an overall state of health and wellbeing.

While Kabat-Zinn takes the ambiguous middle path with his position on whether mindfulness is Buddhist or secular for obvious reasons, the MBCT tradition of mindfulness and its UK base had clearly positioned mindfulness as a secular practice without neglecting its religious roots. For example, the University of Bangor's Centre for Mindfulness and Practice (Bangor University, 2020) states:

> Mindfulness-based approaches are an integration of ancient Buddhist practices and philosophy of mindfulness, with current psychological understanding and knowledge, they are taught in an *entirely secular* way, and *have no religious context at all*.

The Oxford Mindfulness Centre (OMC) (2020) states:

> At the OMC we offer three main mindfulness-based programs. They make the benefits of mindfulness accessible to all. They are based

on a psychological science model of the mind and teach mainstream
cognitive-behavioural and *Secular Mindfulness* practices.

You would have certainly noticed that in spite of these criticisms, secular
mindfulness certainly has its appeal as scholars argue that religious and scientific discourses should maintain a critical distance from each other while
informing each other. And that the sole benefit of secular mindfulness is its
positive impact on mental and physical wellbeing, which are not in the sole
proprietary of religions. Further mindfulness is certainly not inherently religious and the evidence base for reduction in suffering and human flourishing
do not require any belief (Jennings, 2015).

The strong emphasis in the UK for secular mindfulness stems from the
recommendation by the National Institute for Health and Clinical Excel-
lence of MBCT as a National Health Service treatment of choice for people
with recurrent depression. A secular approach would then allow mindfulness to be made available to people who need or want it and would improve
their quality of life without any religious barrier. Is this not what the world
needs? A secular approach provides an opportunity for flourishing without having to worry if mindfulness creates conflicts with one's religious
convictions.

Do we then have a precedence for a successful secularization of a religious practice to alleviate suffering? And the answer is a clear YES. The secular yoga movement in the West is a good example that we can learn from.
Since the 1940s, yoga in the West has been positioned as a type of conditioning calisthenics far removed from its religious roots. The founding fathers of
yoga in the West such as Indra Devi (also known as Eugenie Peterson), BKS
Iyengar, and Pattabhi Jois had their tutelage with the father of modern yoga,
T. Krishnamacharya, who was steeped in the philosophy and practices of
Hinduism. Yet these teachers were able to secularize a sophisticated system
steeped in Hindu philosophy, to non-Hindu audience to alleviate their suffering. Today yoga has crept into secular spaces to help people in physical and
mental fitness, physiotherapy, psychotherapy, and self-help.

Similar to mindfulness in Buddhism's eight-fold path, many yoga postures described in the hatha yoga texts were intended for the purposes of
breath control and meditation in the service of liberation or enlightenment. For example, the "lord of the fishes" posture or seated spinal twist
(matsyendrasana) and the accomplished posture (siddhasana) are specifically
stated in the cardinal hatha yoga text, Hathapradipika (1.27, 1.35) to be
for the purposes of liberation. Evidence from the secular yoga movement
suggests that these postures along with a few others, help in improving
ventilatory function (Rai et al., 1994) and are supportive in the therapy for
diabetes (Kumar, 2012) respectively. If we were to accept the arguments
of mindfulness being Buddhist, then we can argue that the "downward

dog" posture or perhaps the 'tree posture', is Hindu. Postures do not make you Hindu or Buddhist. What makes a posture religious or secular is in its intention.

Contrasting the success of yoga in the West with the secularization of mindfulness, we can certainly see a few parallels. Both yoga and mindfulness have religious roots. Both systems when secularized were criticized by its traditional practitioners for appropriation but yet they were not able to stop its rapid growth. As Kabat-Zinn (Baer, 2017) justified, ". . . that if there were something lost in taking some element of meditative practice at the core of the Buddha's original life and trying to bring it into the mainstream for anybody and everybody, the potential benefits far outweigh the costs." The effects and benefits certainly outweighed everything else for both of these systems. Both yoga and mindfulness succeeded in presenting themselves in a secular way while acknowledging their religious roots.

Given the arguments in favor of secular mindfulness, one can certainly see the value that it brings to society and the world at large. Its appeal is not in its promise but rather in its salutary and evidentiary effects on human flourishing and wellbeing.

7 DIFFERENCE BETWEEN SECULAR AND RELIGIOUS MINDFULNESS

Although mindfulness as taught in the MBPs *resembles* religious mindfulness in some parts, it is distinctly secular. However not much work has been directed to delineating the differences between the two. As cited above in the summary of the criticisms by Buddhist critics, which presumes that mindfulness and MBPs are Buddhist, the superimposition may not be valid. The secular yoga movement in the West could be an example that can be studied to better appreciate the transformation of religious mindfulness into a secular one. In fact, the yoga movement in the West is a good prototype for the study of successful and effective secularization.

Matthew Brensilver's presentation of three key characteristics of secular mindfulness could be an efficacious tool in our quest to distinguish the two systems (Brensilver, 2016):

• Rejection of the notion that some texts or ideas have special, protected status
• Openness to revision based on the evidence emerging from other secular discourses such as science or philosophy
• The primary aim is not a set of beliefs but the engagement with practices that enhance wellbeing.

From our discussion and findings, we propose a simple formula as to how secular mindfulness is derived from religious mindfulness without ignoring the latter:

Religious Mindfulness – Faith/Beliefs + Empirical Evidence for Wellbeing Outcomes = Secular Mindfulness

To make the distinctions clearer, we have compared both secular and Buddhist mindfulness side by side (see Table 1.6) based on its audience, practices, purpose, and the subject.

Table 1.6 Comparison of secular and Buddhist mindfulness

Considerations	Buddhist	Secular
Target audience	People who have taken refuge in the three jewels or triple gems which are: • The Buddha, the fully enlightened one • The dharma, the teachings expounded by the Buddha • The sangha, the monastic order of Buddhism that practice dharmas In early Buddhism the eligible practitioner was a monk or nun, although lay followers were received into the religion and encouraged to live an ethical life.	People who want to enhance their physical and mental wellbeing, as well as desiring to live a wholesome and flourishing life.
Practice or means	Eight-fold path: • Right understanding, • Right thought, • Right speech, • Right action, • Right livelihood, • Right effort, • Right mindfulness and • Right concentration	• Formal and informal mindfulness practices • Inquiry to generate insights • Didactic content to support the generation of insights
Purpose or goal	Enlightenment or Nirvana	Physical, mental, and emotional wellbeing
Subject	Explicit ethics in the form of precepts.	Implicit universal ethics

These comparisons are much needed to demystify the assumed religious superimposition onto secular mindfulness. We liken the secularization of mindfulness to be similar to the modern yoga movement and Kabat-Zinn's role to be somewhat similar to B. K. S. Iyengar, Pattabhi Jois and Indra Devi.

8 STATE AND TRAIT MINDFULNESS

Another important aspect of secular mindfulness is the appreciation of its impact through psychological constructs. Among the many frameworks and models for understanding personality, psychologists have used *state* and *trait* variables to describe the latency of emotions, cognitive states, and behaviors. A stable, enduring, and dispositional quality is described as a *trait* while a temporary and highly transient quality is described as a *state*. It is also known that sustained state experiences lead to trait features.

Similarly, mindfulness can also appreciated through the lenses of *state* and *trait* variables. The cultivation of mindfulness can be organized into three important stages (Black, 2011) (see Figure 1.6):

Figure 1.6 Stages of cultivation of mindfulness

State mindfulness is defined as a momentary condition enhanced by the practice of mindfulness and something that is repeatedly evoked during mindfulness sessions (Baer et al., 2006; Garland et al., 2010). Most measurements of mindfulness do *not* measure state mindfulness.

Trait mindfulness is defined as an effortless tendency to embody mindfulness which is stable over time (Baer et al., 2006; Brown & Ryan, 2003). Trait mindfulness also contributes to the exhibition of mindful attitudes and behaviors in daily living (Kiken et al., 2015). Therefore, trait mindfulness is also called dispositional mindfulness as it impacts the personality of the practitioners. Most measurements of mindfulness actually measure trait mindfulness and not state mindfulness. We cannot also discount the possibility of dispositional mindfulness occurring as a natural trait in the general population without mindfulness training (Burzler et al., 2019).

Mindfulness training facilitates the achievement of state mindfulness. And when it is sustained over a period of time, it then matures into trait mindfulness (see Figure 1.7). The long term effectiveness of mindfulness depends on the sustained practice of mindfulness by the participants. We can then surmise that trait mindfulness is the generator and the predictor of the long term beneficial effects of mindfulness.

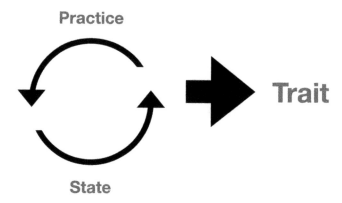

Figure 1.7 Continuous practices leading to trait mindfulness

We also found a growing body of research about the measurement and impact of trait mindfulness. Evidence suggests that higher levels of trait mindfulness are due to sustained state mindfulness over time (Kiken et al., 2015). This eventually contributed to better psychological health. In another research, it was found to decrease psychopathological symptoms such as depressive symptoms (Tomlinson et al., 2017; Martin et al., 2017). It led practitioners to adapt positively to rumination, pain catastrophizing, and emotion regulation. In the areas of life satisfaction, trait mindfulness predicted the benefits through the savoring of positive emotions (Kiken et al., 2017). In fact, higher trait mindfulness decreased gray matter volume in the right amygdala, and in the left caudate of the brain (Taren et al., 2013). The implication of this is that trait mindfulness mitigates the reactive behavior of the amygdala and alters the reward response and stress response associated with the caudate. The military, hospitals and prisons among others found that mindfulness had helped them with being less reactive and thus being more able to be present, focused, and to respond with informed decisions when in stressful situations.

These excerpts from research inform us that the function of mindfulness training is the induction of state mindfulness with the intention of possibly developing it into trait mindfulness. However, one need not wait till the emergence of trait mindfulness to witness the benefits of mindfulness. In another research, it was found that state mindfulness created positive emotions which then reciprocally enhanced one another appreciatively (Du et al., 2019). This could explain the immediate effect participants experience during an eight-week MBP. In our experience, participants often report immediate results while attending a MBP and here are comments from a few of our participants of the MBWE:

> I understood the connection between my inner world and my interactions externally. I see the transformation within me in being more mindful and the automatic need to incorporate mindfulness in my daily activities.
>
> It taught me how mindfulness can improve our lives. I found this course beneficial even without being very consistent with the practices (for myself). My life has been more meaningful with my kids as I don't lose my temper with them as much.
>
> It helped me to be more mindful in my life and put my life into perspective – observing and noticing without judgment has helped me to be more calm and grounded.

With our current understanding of practice, state, and trait, we can now complete the pedagogy of MBPs as presented in Figure 1.8.

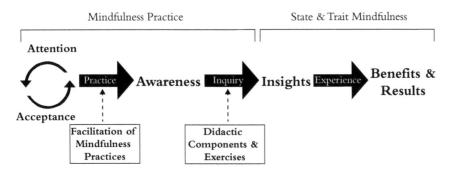

Figure 1.8 Flowchart on the pedagogy of mindfulness-based programs

REFERENCES

Adiswarananda, S. (2007). *Meditation and its practices: A definitive guide to techniques and traditions of meditation in yoga and vedanta* (1st ed.). SkyLight Paths.

A. M. R. A. (2021). *American Mindfulness Research Association – Library*. American Mindfulness Research Association. Retrieved from https://goamra.org/Library

Arat, A. (2017). "What it means to be truly human": The postsecular hack of mindfulness. *Social Compass, 64*(2), 167–179.

Awasthi, B. (2013). Issues and perspectives in meditation research: In search for a definition. *Frontiers in Psychology, 3*, 1–9.

Baer, R. A. (2003). Mindfulness training as a clinical intervention: A conceptual and empirical review. *Clinical Psychology: Science and Practice, 10*(2), 125–143.

Baer, R. (2015). Ethics, values, virtues, and character strengths in mindfulness-based interventions: A psychological science perspective. *Mindfulness, 6*(4), 956–969.

Baer, D. (2017, June 4). *The father of mindfulness on what mindfulness has become.* Medium. Retrieved from https://medium.com/thrive-global/the-father-of-mindfulness-on-what-mindfulness-has-become-ad649c8340cf

Baer, R. A., Smith, G. T., Hopkins, J., Krietemeyer, J., & Toney, L. (2006). Using self-report assessment methods to explore facets of mindfulness. *Assessment, 13*(1), 27–45.

Bangor University. (2020). *What is mindfulness?* Retrieved from www.bangor.ac.uk/mindfulness/what-is-mindfulness.php.en

Bishop, S. R. (2004). Mindfulness: A proposed operational definition. *Clinical Psychology: Science and Practice, 11*(3), 230–241.

Black, D. S. (2011). A brief definition of mindfulness. *Behavioral Neuroscience, 7*(2), 109.

Bodhi, B. (1994). *The noble eightfold path: Way to the end of suffering.* Buddhist Publication Society.

Bond, K., Ospina, M. B., Hooton, N., Bialy, L., Dryden, D. M., Buscemi, N., Shannahoff-Khalsa, D., Dusek, J., & Carlson, L. E. (2009). Defining a complex intervention: The development of demarcation criteria for "meditation." *Psychology of Religion and Spirituality, 1*(2), 129–137.

Brandsma, R. (2017). *The mindfulness teaching guide: Essential skills and competencies for teaching mindfulness-based interventions* (1st ed.). New Harbinger Publications.

Brensilver, M. (2016, September 14). *The secular qualities of mindfulness.* Mindful Schools. Retrieved from www.mindfulschools.org/foundational-concepts/mindfulness-and-secularity/

Brown, C. G. (2017, December 7). *Mindfulness: Stealth Buddhist strategy for mainstreaming meditation?* HuffPost. Retrieved from www.huffpost.com/entry/mindfulness-stealth-buddh_b_6243036

Brown, K. W., & Ryan, R. M. (2003). The benefits of being present: Mindfulness and its role in psychological well-being. *Journal of Personality and Social Psychology, 84*(4), 822–848.

Brown, K. W., Ryan, R. M., & Creswell, J. D. (2007). Mindfulness: Theoretical foundations and evidence for its salutary effects. *Psychological Inquiry, 18*(4), 211–237.

Buddhist Society of Western Australia. (2017, October 27). *Secular mindfulness | Ajahn Brahm* [Video]. YouTube. https://www.youtube.com/watch?v=eGjXEM1HZ54

Burzler, M. A., Voracek, M., Hos, M., & Tran, U. S. (2019). Mechanisms of Mindfulness in the General Population. *Mindfulness, 10*(3), 469–480.

Cahn, B. R., & Polich, J. (2006). Meditation states and traits: EEG, ERP, and neuroimaging studies. *Psychological Bulletin, 132*(2), 180–211.

Du, J., An, Y., Ding, X., Zhang, Q., & Xu, W. (2019). State mindfulness and positive emotions in daily life: An upward spiral process. *Personality and Individual Differences, 141,* 57–61.

Eifring, H. (Ed.). (2013). *Meditation in Judaism, Christianity and Islam: Cultural histories.* A&C Black.

Falick, M. (2020). Mindfulness and the need to minimize the risk of harm: A proposal to implement and enforce standards for secular mindfulness practice. Mindfulness Studies Theses. 33. Retrieved from https://digital commons.lesley.edu/mindfulness_theses/33

Feldman, C., & Kuyken, W. (2019). *Mindfulness: Ancient wisdom meets modern psychology* (Illustrated ed.). Guilford.

Garland, E. L., Fredrickson, B., Kring, A. M., Johnson, D. P., Meyer, P. S., & Penn, D. L. (2010). Upward spirals of positive emotions counter down-ward spirals of negativity: Insights from the broaden-and-build theory and affective neuroscience on the treatment of emotion dysfunctions and deficits in psychopathology. *Clinical Psychology Review, 30*(7), 849–864.

Garland, E. L., Froeliger, B. E., & Howard, M. O. (2014). Mindfulness train-ing targets neurocognitive mechanisms of addiction at the attention-appraisal-emotion interface. *Frontiers in Psychiatry, 4.* 1–16.

Hwang, & Kearney. (2015). *A Mindfulness Intervention for Children with Autism Spectrum Disorders (Mindfulness in Behavioral Health).* Springer.

Houlihan, S. D., & Brewer, J. A. (2016). The emerging science of mindfulness as a treatment for addiction. *Mindfulness and Buddhist-Derived Approaches in Mental Health and Addiction,* 191–210. Springer.

Hunt, M., Al-Braiki, F., Dailey, S., Russell, R., & Simon, K. (2018). Mind-fulness training, yoga, or both? Dismantling the active components of a mindfulness-based stress reduction intervention. *Mindfulness, 9*(2), 512–520.

Hyland, T. (2015). On the contemporary applications of mindfulness: Some implications for education. *Journal of Philosophy of Education, 49*(2), 170–186.

Iyengar, B. K. S. (1979). *Light on yoga: The bible of modern yoga* (rev. ed.). Schocken.

Iyengar, B. K. S. (2021). *B. K. S. Iyengar yoga the path to holistic health: The definitive step-by-step guide* (reissued ed.). DK.

Jankowski, T., & Holas, P. (2014). Metacognitive model of mindfulness. *Consciousness and Cognition, 28,* 64–80.

Jennings, P. A. (2015). Mindfulness-based programs and the American public school system: Recommendations for best practices to ensure secular-ity. *Mindfulness, 7*(1), 176–178.

Kabat-Zinn, J. (1995). *By Jon Kabat-Zinn – wherever you go there you are* (8.2.1995 ed.). Hyperion.

Kabat-Zinn, J. (1996). Mindfulness meditation: What it is, what it isn't, and its role in health care and medicine. *Comparative and Psychological Study on Meditation*, 161–170.

Kabat-Zinn, J. (2003). Mindfulness-based interventions in context: Past, present, and future. *Clinical Psychology: Science and Practice*, *10*(2), 144–156.

Kabat-Zinn, J. (2005). *Coming to your senses: Healing ourselves and the world through mindfulness* (rev. ed.). Hachette Books.

Kabat-Zinn, J. (2011). Some reflections on the origins of MBSR, skillful means, and the trouble with maps. *Contemporary Buddhism*, *12*(1), 281–306.

Kabat-Zinn, J. (2013). *Full catastrophe living: Using the wisdom of your body and mind to face stress, pain, and illness* (rev. ed.). Bantam.

Kabat-Zinn, J. (2017, January 11). *Jon Kabat-Zinn: Defining mindfulness*. Mindful. Retrieved from www.mindful.org/jon-kabat-zinn-defining-mindfulness/

Kiken, L. G., Garland, E. L., Bluth, K., Palsson, O. S., & Gaylord, S. A. (2015). From a state to a trait: Trajectories of state mindfulness in meditation during intervention predict changes in trait mindfulness. *Personality and Individual Differences*, *81*, 41–46.

Kiken, L. G., Lundberg, K. B., & Fredrickson, B. L. (2017). Being present and enjoying it: Dispositional mindfulness and savoring the moment are distinct, interactive predictors of positive emotions and psychological health. *Mindfulness*, *8*(5), 1280–1290.

Kumar, K. (2012). A study on the effect of yogic intervention on serum glucose level on diabetics. *International Journal of Yoga & Allied Sciences*, *1*(1), 68–72.

Linehan, M. (1993). *Cognitive-behavioral treatment of borderline personality disorder* (1st ed.). Guilford.

Lutz, A., Slagter, H. A., Dunne, J. D., & Davidson, R. J. (2008). Attention regulation and monitoring in meditation. *Trends in Cognitive Sciences*, *12*(4), 163–169.

Marlatt, G. A., & Kristeller, J. L. (1999). Mindfulness and meditation. In W. R. Miller (Ed.), *Integrating spirituality into treatment* (pp. 67–84). American Psychological Association.

Martin, J. R. (1997). Mindfulness: A proposed common factor. *Journal of Psychotherapy Integration Discontinued*, 7(4), 291–312.

Martin, K. P. M., Blair, S., Clark, G. I., Rock, A. J., & Hunter, K. R. (2017). Trait mindfulness moderates the relationship between early maladaptive schemas and depressive symptoms. *Mindfulness*, *9*(1), 140–150.

McGrath, M. (2020, October 12). *Meditation giant headspace taps intuit alum CeCe Morken to be its first female CEO*. Forbes. Retrieved from www.forbes.com/sites/maggiemcgrath/2020/10/12/meditation-giant-headspace-taps-intuit-alum-cece-morken-to-be-its-first-female-ceo/?sh=1c0fcb8812c9

Monteiro, L. M., Musten, R., & Compson, J. (2014). Traditional and contemporary mindfulness: Finding the middle path in the tangle of concerns. *Mindfulness, 6*(1), 1–13.

Nilsson, H., & Kazemi, A. (2016). Reconciling and thematizing definitions
of mindfulness: The big five of mindfulness. *Review of General Psychology, 20*(2), 183–193.

Oxford Mindfulness Centre. (2020, October 28). *Learn mindfulness*. Retrieved
from www.oxfordmindfulness.org/learn-mindfulness/

Rai, L., Ram, K., Kant, U., Madan, S. K., & Sharma, S. K. (1994). Energy
expenditure and ventilatory responses during Siddhasana – a yogic seated
posture. *Indian Journal of Physiology and Pharmacology, 38*, 29–29.

Salmon, P., Lush, E., Jablonski, M., & Sephton, S. E. (2009). Yoga and mindfulness: Clinical aspects of an ancient mind/body practice. *Cognitive and
Behavioral Practice, 16*(1), 59–72.

Shapiro, S. L., Carlson, L. E., Astin, J. A., & Freedman, B. (2006). Mechanisms of mindfulness. *Journal of Clinical Psychology, 62*(3), 373–386.

Shaw, S. (2020). *Mindfulness: Where it comes from and what it means (Buddhist
foundations)*. Shambhala.

Taren, A. A., Creswell, J. D., & Gianaros, P. J. (2013). Dispositional mindfulness co-varies with smaller amygdala and caudate volumes in community
adults. *PLOS One, 8*(5), e64574.

Thera, N. (2010). *The Buddha's path to deliverance: A systematic exposition in the
words of the Sutta Pitaka (Vipassana meditation and the Buddha's teachings)*
(5th ed.). BPS Pariyatti Editions.

Tomlinson, E. R., Yousaf, O., Vitterso, A. D., & Jones, L. (2017). Dispositional mindfulness and psychological health: A systematic Review. *Mindfulness, 9*(1), 23–43.

Van Gordon, W., & Shonin, E. (2019). Second-generation mindfulness-based
Interventions: Toward more authentic mindfulness practice and teaching. *Mindfulness, 11*(1), 1–4.

Vishnudevananda, S. (1999). *Meditation and mantras* (Reprint ed.). Motilal
Banarsidass.

Walsh, R., & Shapiro, S. L. (2006). The meeting of meditative disciplines and
western psychology: A mutually enriching dialogue. *American Psychologist, 61*(3), 227–239.

Wilks, J. (2014). *Secular mindfulness: Potential & pitfalls*. Barre Centre for
Buddhist Studies. Retrieved from www.buddhistinquiry.org/article/
secular-mindfulness-potential-pitfalls/

CHAPTER 2

Mindfulness and Wellbeing

I attended courses to manage stress and time. And reduced my expectations of myself . . . yet I feel unfulfilled and unhappy!

–Lilian

The pursuit of happiness to realize wellbeing is an instinct found in all sentient beings, however it may be expressed differently. This pursuit is uniquely complex in human beings. Some animals express their joy and positive experiences but this expression manifests in its fullest form among humans and in human civilizations. We do not have a choice in this matter as we wake up every day hoping that this day will be a happy one. And this instinct has driven people to create wonders that keep us in awe, and atrocities too that question the nature of happiness and what drives it. Fundamentally, our wellbeing and happiness can be broken down into a simple chain of *Desire-Action-Outcomes* (DAO) (see Figure 2.1):

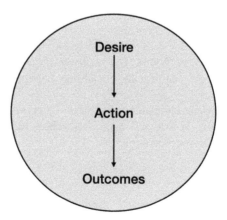

Figure 2.1 Flow of desire and outcome

DOI: 10.4324/9781003322955-3

Our search for happiness starts with a simple desire for an experience or object. To realize that desire, we perform an action. These actions can be either mental, physical, or both and it can also be staged. For example, in a large project, these actions consist of multiple related actions to arrive at the desired outcomes. Each of these actions individually and collectively leads us to specific outcomes. If these outcomes conform to what we desired, we feel happy. And if they do not, we feel unhappy and dissatisfied. The frequency of these happy or positive experiences would determine whether your well-being is high or low. Our life is filled with possibly millions of these chains of DAO. In a given day, you could have possibly fulfilled hundreds of desires, and they are mostly mundane desires such as wanting to brush your teeth in the morning or a few significant ones such as attending a job interview for a much coveted position.

Many terms have been used in both research and popular literature to denote wellbeing. These terms are happiness, positive affect, meaning, purpose, and many more. In fact, we have encountered many different terms used interchangeably thus treating them as synonyms. But we prefer the terms *wellbeing* and *happiness*, for specific reasons. First, wellbeing is generally seen as referring to quality of life, thus inclusive of happiness, positive affect, pleasure, meaning, purpose, and many other known areas. It cannot be limited to wellness, which is a state of being in good health. Second, the term "wellbeing" allows us to include other components that contribute to the attainment of happiness. We also recognize that wellbeing has been popularly associated with human flourishing and that it is certainly valid. The second term, happiness, refers to a private and mental experience of wellbeing. We will henceforth refer to happiness as a private experience and wellbeing as an objective and holistic experience, which includes happiness.

Our endeavor in this chapter is to uncover what wellbeing is and to present the *happiness paradigm*, which is not only the foundation of the MBWE, but also a tool that presents how mindfulness impacts wellbeing, happiness, and human flourishing.

We had discussed in the last chapter that the first-generation mindfulness-based programs (MBPs) thrived on restoring people to mental wellness through reduction of stress and relapses of depression. On the other hand, growing evidence continues to show that mindfulness can positively impact aspects of human flourishing. These have been evidenced through a variety of second-generation MBPs, such as the Mindfulness-Based Wellbeing Enhancement program (MBWE). MBPs have been created for several purposes including (Crane, 2017):

- to discover meaning
- to realize wellbeing
- to develop focus
- to cultivate peace

- to reconnect to the self
- to connect with "bigger than self" concerns

Therefore, we can strongly hypothesize and argue that mindfulness can impact people in ways that transcend the scope of clinical interventions. And the intersection between human flourishing and clinical needs have become more blurred since the advent of positive psychology. Therefore, it is imperative that we understand the intentions and philosophy of positive psychology.

1 POSITIVE PSYCHOLOGY AND WELLBEING

Positive psychology is devoted to the study of wellbeing to improve quality of life and to thrive. The birth of positive psychology in 1998, founded by Martin Seligman, heralded a new school of psychology. Prior to the advent of positive psychology, psychology was preoccupied with the study of mental illness and its cure.

Christian Wolff, a German philosopher, was the first person to popularize the term psychology. However, the birth of modern psychology can probably be traced to Wilhelm Wundt, a German psychologist. He distinguished psychology from philosophy and also established the first experimental psychology lab in Germany in 1879. This was the birth of psychology as a distinct scientific field by itself. Sigmund Freud, an Austrian neurologist, further influenced the field of psychology with his theory of human personality by focusing on the unconscious mind. He is also the founder of psychoanalysis and has influenced many later psychologists such as Carl Jung and Alfred Adler among others. From psychoanalyses, thereafter, many other schools of psychology were born such as the behaviorist, cognitive, biological, evolutionary, and humanistic. All of these perspectives had one thing in common, which was to study pathology. They seem to consider human beings to be passive, vulnerable and subject to unwholesomeness.

The antecedents to modern psychology are often forgotten or have not received much attention for the obvious reasons that they had not been developed into a scientific mold. One ancient antecedent was the Greek philosophers, especially Aristotle. Aristotle's emphasis on "the good life," termed *eudaimonia* cannot be understated as this continues to be the earliest attempt in the Western world to view humans as beings of wisdom and virtues. This perspective re-emerges in positive psychology after a long absence from modern psychology.

In the Eastern world, specifically South Asia, allusions to wellbeing appear as early as the 800 BCE. Archaic meditations in the Indic traditions revolved around the pursuit of both eudaimonia and hedonia. It is also worthy of note that South Asia happens to be the cradle of archaic meditative techniques and later spiritual traditions defined and described these techniques through Sanskrit texts as early as 1000 BCE and further develops through the works of Buddhism and Hinduism. We can certainly see that that the discussion of happiness, wellbeing, and wellness is not something new to the Greek and Indic philosophers.

When we study modern psychology and look for its applications to life, one word that best describes it is *adjustment*. In fact what psychology does is to help people with adjusting to changes or sometimes coping with them. By situating psychology within the domain of wellbeing, we cannot deny or understate its utility. Today psychology has identified many disorders and found ways to support and resolve them successfully. Without it, people would not have found respite from the pain and challenges of debilitating mental health issues. However, we opine that this only solves half the problem, with the other half being in the sphere of realizing the full potential of human existence. We need both approaches. In fact, one without the other is not helpful for human flourishing. Martin Seligman, during his term as president of the American Psychological Association, challenged these traditional paradigms in modern psychology and criticized it for its obsession with mental illness. He wrote in his book, *Authentic Happiness*, "for the last half century psychology has been consumed with a single topic only – mental illness" (Seligman, 2003, p. xi). We consider the work of psychology as generally *restorative* and the work of positive psychology as being *appreciative*, not in the conventionally understood manner, but one that increases in value as opposed to depreciating. Interestingly, mindfulness is one of the unique interventions that is seen to be valuable to the goals of psychology and positive psychology.

The appreciative approach of positive psychology focuses on the goals of wellbeing, happiness, flow, flourish, personal strengths, wisdom, creativity, and imagination. Positive psychology practitioners and researchers have proposed several interventions to realize these goals. We have compiled these interventions in Table 2.1. All of the wellbeing interventions have one single goal which is to *influence* how we desire, act, and measure the outcomes. It provides a structure for us to live life with increased levels of wellbeing.

Table 2.1 Wellbeing interventions and components

Name	Founder(s)	Components
PERMA	Martin Seligman	• Positive affect • Engagement • Relationships • Meaning • Achievement

(Continued)

Table 2.1 Continued

Name	Founder(s)	Components
Psychological wellbeing	Carol Ryff	• Relationships • Autonomy • Environmental mastery • Self-acceptance • Purpose in life • Personal growth
Subjective wellbeing	Ed Diener	Subjective wellbeing = Life satisfaction + frequent positive affect – frequent negative affect
The AIM approach	Ed Diener and Biwas-Diener	• Attention • Interpretation • Memory
Integrated wellbeing	Sunita Rai	• Spatial self • Physical self • Emotional self • Intellectual self • Eudaimonic self
Objective wellbeing		Material conditions such as human rights, environment, safety, security, employment, education, satisfaction of preferences without entertaining positive emotions or meaning in life

Apart from these interventions and components of wellbeing, several other components of wellbeing have been proposed in literature, such as:

1. Wellbeing from neuroscientific approaches
2. Optimism or hope
3. Resilience
4. Values
5. Genetics
6. Personality traits

There are also many other interventions and applications of positive psychology such as the character strengths and virtues, strengths profiling psychometric assessments, positive psychotherapy, positive education, positive organizational scholarship and positive organizational behavior among many others. It is important to be aware that wellbeing interventions directly influence what we desire as shown in Figure 2.2.

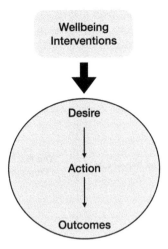

Figure 2.2 Wellbeing interventions influence desires

2 LIMITATIONS OF WELLBEING INTERVENTIONS AND THE MINDFULNESS RESPONSE

Positive psychology and wellbeing interventions have changed the way we looked at human existence. However, they are not immune to limitations. On the bright side, these limitations can be mitigated and resolved through the insights gained from mindfulness and thus mutually strengthening each other's goals and intentions.

The "Flourishing" Confusion

The first and foremost challenge is the lack of clarity in the distinction between eudaimonia and hedonia. Eudaimonia is described as intrinsic wellbeing derived from personal values, virtues, and living life with ethical considerations through our actions and behaviors. Hedonia is described as extrinsic and focused on enjoyment, pleasure, and preferences of the mind and body. A popular assumption by positive psychologists is that there are more overlaps between eudaimonia and hedonia, and that these two should not be treated as separate models in themselves. We, on the other hand, see eudaimonia and hedonia to be distinct approaches to happiness or wellbeing based on a person's *disposition*. We often encounter people generally having either a dominant eudaimonic disposition or a hedonic disposition dependent on their beliefs, life experiences, values, personality, and stage of life among others. Assuming that everyone needs to accomplish all the dimensions of wellbeing betrays the individual dispositions and nature thus putting everyone into a straitjacket. A popular visual presentation of this misconception that appears in several internet sites, is presented in Figure 2.3.

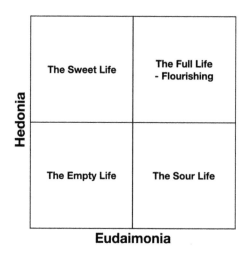

Figure 2.3 The grid of life

In that grid, the casual assumption is that everyone needs to be on the top right quadrant. Being in any of the other three quadrants would then mean that one's life is incomplete or deficient. While there is an ounce of truth that an "empty life" is languishing, but stating that the top left quadrant as being a sweet life and the bottom right as the sour life is highly misleading. Based on this model, a monk or a nun who had renounced his or her worldly attachments would be leading a sour life. If you had interviewed them, you would probably find them claiming to be in the top right quadrant. I (KK) remember meeting a monk in the mid-1990s with a friend of mine. In that conversation, my friend asked him " How do you live a life like this, as a renunciate monk . . . in isolation and without any possessions?" The monk responded by saying "To me, your life is more difficult than mine. That's why I left your lifestyle and adopted the life of a monk." He said this with a benign smile.

Mindfulness on the other hand brings awareness to our happiness disposition. The function of mindfulness is twofold in this regard, one being like a light that reveals one's disposition and the other being like a compass that shows direction as opposed to a destination. We noticed mindfulness practitioners discover that either hedonia or eudaimonia becomes dominant in their lives and becomes a priority at different stages of their lives. The choice is governed largely by their disposition and not entirely by their free will. This discovery allows people to be comfortable in their skin instead of wanting to be fitted into a straitjacket, conforming to a pre-defined mold. People who pursue eudaimonia may feel that hedonia is not their thing and feel a strong disconnection with it, and vice versa for those with a hedonic disposition. We also see a trend with people who are older to possess a eudaimonic disposition although it is not always so. We have also encountered young adults possessing a strong and resonant eudaimonic disposition as well. The other connection we recognize is consistent with Maslow's hierarchy of needs. People who have yet to satisfy their basic needs tend to not notice a eudaimonic disposition within them, although it may not always be so. Mindfulness then allows, through greater self-awareness, to notice one's happiness disposition and be ever curious if it ever changes or perhaps never. This promotes an attitude of self-acceptance with reduced self-judgment.

Mode of Striving

Striving is the excessive effort that we put in to achieve or gain something. This excessive effort leaves us deprived of enjoying what we already have and keeps us preoccupied with the things we want. Viktor Frankl writes the following in his book, *Man's Search for Meaning* (Frankl, 1985, pp.16–17):

> Don't aim at success. The more you aim at it and make it a target, the more you are going to miss it. For success, like happiness, cannot be pursued; it must ensue, and it only does so as the unintended side effect of one's personal dedication to a cause . . . Happiness must happen, and the same holds for success: you have to let it happen by not caring about it.

Being happy is quite different from searching for happiness. Seeking happiness is an agenda for the future but *being happy is an interpretation of experience in the present moment*. When we are in the mode of striving for happiness, we are possibly living in the future without being present. However, any person who is deprived of fundamental needs such as food and safety would naturally be in this state of striving. People who are aspiring for goals beyond food and safety could also get into this mode when they believe that only by the achievement of a particular goal or set of goals would they become happy. I (SR) remember hearing my participants sharing in my MBWE classes that they will be truly happy once they have fully paid up for their homes or for their children's education or succeed in their careers among others. One of my participants excitedly shared that she had five goals to achieve in order to be happy and when I asked her what would happen if she did not achieve some or all of the items in her list, she sounded disappointed but responded that she will "just work harder and harder until it is done." And this then puts them in a striving mode like a hamster running on a wheel, as the goalpost keeps moving. Wellbeing interventions may make people believe that that they need to check every component of the model to live a happy and complete life. This contributes to incessant striving and may lead one to experience the hedonic treadmill. Hedonic treadmill refers to the phenomenon where people continue to find new goals to aim for after achieving their current goals. And this goes on and on without realizing that the happiness gained is momentary and with no incremental effect with every new gain.

Mindfulness mitigates this striving mode by bringing the attitude of non-striving and a more present moment focus. Mindfulness practices do not subject the practitioner to stress through excessive effort. Instead the practices are conducted with a present moment focus without having to think about the future. It shifts the dial from the doing mode to the being mode, where the present experiences are noticed with curiosity and non-judgment. The effort put into mindfulness practices is tampered with compassion and acceptance and therefore the measurement of one's success in practice and its results are not important to a practitioner. It is in hindsight that the practitioner notices the changes without setting up an agenda for change. This attitude of non-striving that is cultivated while practicing mindfulness then pervades into the lifestyle of the practitioner by not subjecting her to excessive striving when trying to realize one's goals. It now becomes a journey, as opposed to it being a race, and a cultivation rather than a catalyst. This then leads to the acceptance of failure with poise, if that happens, rather than it being not an option at all.

Absence of Ethics

The third problem is the absence of explicitly stated ethics. For example, someone could pursue positive affect, engagement, relationships, meaning, and achievement (PERMA) without any ethical consideration to the means and the end. The people in the Nazi regime that persecuted the Jews could have possibly accomplished PERMA through the holocaust. The silence about ethics in Positive Psychology does not help people to overcome ethical dilemmas.

On the other hand, the social dimension of mindfulness helps elicit the universality of ethics through the recognition of common humanity. Common humanity is the recognition that sorrow and happiness are part of the shared human experience rather than being solely individual phenomena. Through the effective leadership and facilitation of insights by the mindfulness teacher, practitioners can recognize that ethics are fundamental to human existence. The gentle inspiration to be kind to oneself and others, as well as through practices like the lovingkindness meditation allow practitioners to recognize that human beings are essentially the same whether we live in the North Pole or in Manhattan. The other person is "just like me" in more ways than we are different. This then leads practitioners to notice the "me, myself and I" syndrome and to see that we are all social creatures who thrive as a community and are not alone. I (KK) remember during my sojourn in the Himalayan ranges where I had stayed and interacted with monks, hermits and nuns. As much as they were solitary, or wandering monks, they still depended on the people and the environment around them for their basic needs such as food. The common people around felt it was their duty and took pleasure in supporting these hermits. Such is the nature of common humanity and mindfulness brings light to this social dimension of human life.

Privatization of Wellbeing

The fourth challenge that positive psychology could pose is the excessive focus on individual happiness as opposed to communal or collective wellbeing. This leads to a "my happiness is more important than your/our happiness" syndrome. Aspersions in favor of narcissism can also be alluded as a result. Individual happiness is placed on the altar and the social dimension of our lives and the fact that we are social creatures could possibly be neglected. Our relationships are therefore seen as a *means* to "my" happiness and not as a *contributor* to it. This "my happiness at all costs" can lead to societal issues and could even widen further the gaps of social inequality and deepen the inequity inherent in many societies today.

Mindfulness has the potential to balance the individual need with the collective need to be happy by directing our attention to the recognition that human beings are connected with everything, sentient and insentient, that surrounds us. We are part of the ecosystem and all relationships are symbiotic. Through acts of kindness, compassion, and empathy, we learn to acknowledge this reality. Every action we take impacts some thing or someone around us or in a distant place. Living in Singapore, we are subjected to the yearly haze, as we call it here. In recent decades, we have been experiencing a thick haze in our atmosphere and it is predictable because it is caused by forest fires that have been started for the sole purposes of clearing land for agricultural uses. This happens during the southwest monsoon season between June and October every year. The fires are in regions 400 kilometers away from Singapore and we feel the brunt of it when the haze attains unhealthy Pollutant Standards Index levels. One single action to clear land in one country affects the lives of millions of people in that country and the neighboring countries.

Rejecting the Negative

Being averse to the negative becomes the fifth challenge that wellbeing interventions could possibly create. Almost all of the wellbeing interventions promote the increase in the frequency of positive affect and the reduction in the frequency of negative affect. This creates and reinforces the belief that negative emotions are bad, useless, and therefore need to be avoided. This is corroborated by neuroscientific theory of negativity bias, inherent in the human brain through its evolution. This bias *directs attention to the negative and in doing so magnifies it and strengthens the negative affect.*

One cannot deny the discomfort one feels when experiencing negative emotions. However, our lives cannot possibly be filled with only positive emotions without any negative ones. A much more pragmatic belief would be that our lives would inevitably be filled with both positive and negative emotions. As much as we want more positive emotions, we could perhaps bring acceptance to our negative emotions such that we can learn to respond to them with poise. Moreover, both negative and positive emotions rise involuntarily because they are mediated by the *mental interpretation* of events and incidents. For example, the proximity to one person X can bring two opposite emotions to two different people. One person could feel an emotion of disgust in X's proximity and the next person could feel admiration toward X. This informs us that *our life experiences are interpreted by our minds* and this does not allow us to see things as they are, a point that we will discuss deeper in the next section of this chapter.

MBPs have a uniform intention to bring across the point that *our thoughts are interpretations* influenced by many factors and hence *they are not facts.* It is on this premise that emotions rise, sometimes even due to an inaccurate evaluation of a situation. For example, mistaking a life-sized bull made of wax to be real can give rise to fear when seen right next to you before realizing it to be what it is and thereby giving rise to amusement and wonder. The information we have and the perspectives that we take can give rise to different emotions with respect to the same object. Mindfulness does not create an aversion to negative emotions, instead it invites you notice it with curiosity and acceptance. This same attitude is applied to positive emotions and neutral situations too. By doing this we arrive at a pragmatic view that our lives would always be filled with positive, neutral, and negative emotions and that this is normal. The comfort and discomfort that arise are results of our interpretations. We need to caution you at this juncture that an interpretation does not make the experience unreal or invalid. Our interpretations are real, as in they are not illusory. With this appreciation, we then create clear intentions about our wellbeing, and what is needed to achieve it, without an aversion to negative emotions. Mindfulness brings light to even these negative emotions thereby revealing our values and wishes. It enhances our self-understanding and awareness.

Interestingly, the second wave of positive psychology, sometimes called Positive Psychology 2.0, has arrived at the same view with regard to the need for a balanced approach to positive and negative emotions. Positive psychology 2.0 is the next generation of positive psychology which promotes a more balanced perspective of the positive and the negative. Both positive and negative emotions can tell us so much about ourselves. In fact, an obsession with positive emotions can sometimes lead us to drastic maladaptive behaviors such as addictive, obsessive, and compulsive behaviors. Another reason is that positive emotions are not the arbiter for ethical dilemmas. A person could experience positive emotions even when committing a crime or something heinous such as rape. And one could experience a negative emotion while doing something wholesome such as feeding a child who constantly refuses to eat. Therefore, *emotions do not report or* validate *wholesome behaviors.*

3 THE HAPPINESS EXPERIENCE

Is happiness a trait or state? If happiness was a trait it would then mean that happier people would have stable experiences of happiness and would be able to "be" happy in most of their daily life experiences. On the other hand if happiness was a state, then people can positively evoke happy moments through will, choice, and effort. This phenomenon is similar to personality traits where conscious and unconscious behaviors are influenced by the former, though a possible exception to this norm may happen when placed in exceptionally demanding situations.

World renowned happiness and wellbeing scientist, Ruut Veenhoven (1993) has suggested that happiness is not a trait, when evaluating happiness with objective measures such as living conditions, good or bad situations, and so forth. We disagree with this position and we are not alone in this camp. It was found that happiness had both state-like and trait-like properties and also that it can endure situational differences (Stones at el., 1995). We acknowledge that viewing happiness as a state can be helpful in formulating social policies and promoting social wellbeing. However, the view that happiness is trait-like, and a private experience can also co-exist with the objective efforts to create social wellbeing. We also found that most of the early contemplative traditions and philosophies, such as yoga and Buddhist mindfulness, tend to view happiness as a state-like phenomenon that grows into being trait-like with sustained practice. This is a phenomenon that is entirely dependent on oneself with less dependence on external situations. A popular quote by the father of secular mindfulness, would convey this position succinctly,

> You can't stop the waves, but you can learn to surf.
>
> (Jon Kabat-Zinn)

Our primary position would be that happiness can become a trait over time through sustained mindfulness practice.

The wellbeing interventions discussed above, present wellbeing as an effect or result dependent on one, more, or a combination of its components. We can then break down each intervention into objects of desires, goals, or wants. While we know that these wellbeing interventions lead us to higher levels of wellbeing, we are yet to investigate into the actual *experience of happiness*. Among the interventions presented above, we wish to single out the AIM approach proposed by Ed Diener and Robert Biswas-Diener. While the rest of the models presented structured interventions, the AIM approach on the other hand had examined the nature of an individual's experience of happiness, as a way of being happy in any moment.

The AIM approach is perhaps one of the most effective models that breaks down the experience of happiness, at any present moment, and guides us to recognize how our happiness can be either trait-like or state-like. In our opinion, it has perhaps not received the attention that it deserves.

Among the triad proposed by the AIM approach, comprising of attention, interpretation and memory, it is attention that holds primacy as the other two depend on it. As we discussed in the last chapter, attention is one of the pivotal mechanisms of mindfulness. The mode of interpretation depends on attention. Therefore, the attentional capability and quality has a significant impact on how we interpret any moment. When we are unable to select what we pay attention to or be able to be flexible, we may experience rumination that could possibly lead to maladaptive behaviors.

Attention – Interpretation – Memory

The interpretation of an experience is a subjective or mental experience. From a mindfulness perspective, it includes the way we relate with our thoughts instead of identifying with it. Thoughts are not facts, and therefore we are able to interpret them differently, when required, as alternative viewpoints or perspectives. With this new insight, you can now willfully appreciate events and experiences differently. We often encounter in mindfulness literature the claim that the awareness of thoughts being more important than the content of thoughts. We do not agree with this as *both the awareness of thoughts and the awareness of the content of thoughts are important*. However, the *development of* being *aware of thoughts should be given primacy as this is what enables one to* relate with *the content of thoughts with acceptance, non-reactivity, and flexibility of attention.*

What we interpret then becomes stored in our memory, which is the third component of AIM. In the AIM approach, memory refers to the type of memories that we recall when we reflect on an experience or respond to a question. For example, in response to the question "How was your childhood?," a happier person is more likely to report the happy and positive events from their childhood. On the other hand, a person who experiences depression would report their unhappy and negative childhood experiences. Sometimes we get attached to specific memories that we cannot let go and they re-emerge and re-appear even in moments where we least expect it. This informs us that we cannot predict our thoughts. This recollection from memory was once something that was paid attention to and interpreted before it was stored in our memories. Research tells us that dispositional happy people interpret neutral objects as if they were positive (Larsen et al., 2003). Therefore, we can see that outcomes of our desire and action can be *re-processed* through AIM in a way that conduces wellbeing.

At this juncture, it is important that we direct our attention to the evidence and knowledge about mindfulness and its impact on memory. Within the school of cognitive psychology, memory is often categorized into long-term and short-term memory (see Figure 2.4).

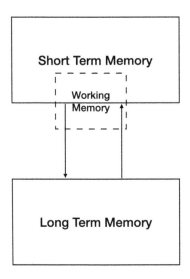

Figure 2.4 Long- and short-term memory

Long-term memory is a mental record of prior events that is often seen as having limitless capacity and endurance. Short-term memory on the other hand has limited capacity and is transient, for the purposes of specific functions. One aspect or part of short-term memory is working memory, an area that mindfulness has shown to impact positively. Working memory is often defined as being responsible for attention, task goals, decision making, and memory retrieval. It is also responsible for the way we pay attention, interpret, manipulate, and evaluate information, and flexibly directing attention. Working memory capacity (WMC) is defined as the "capacity to selectively maintain and manipulate goal-relevant information without getting distracted by irrelevant information over short intervals" (Jha et al., 2014, p. 348). Studying the relationship between working memory and mindfulness is relevant because it is this part of memory that functions at any given present moment. We know from evidence that anxiety and stress decrease WMC and inhibits its function. Also, the working memory experiences reduced mind wandering and functions better with mindfulness training. We also know that competing demands at any present moment create challenges for the working memory. Let us review some evidence about these effects.

People with low WMC suffered from more emotionally intrusive thoughts and not being able to suppress positive and negative affect (Jha, Rogers, & Morrison, 2014, p. 349; van Vugt, 2015). This leads to lowered levels of wellbeing. We can also correlate how WMC has significant impact on intentions, as people with lower WMC might have a harder time staying true to their intentions. In fact, some researchers have hypothesized that the working memory functions are identical to the functions of mindfulness (Gethin, 2015; Davis & Thompson, 2015). Mindfulness has been hypothesized to be strengthening the encoding of information in the working memory which then helps in transferring it to the long-term memory, thus making knowledge available when needed (Davis & Thompson, 2015). These functions could also become a trait when mindfulness becomes dispositional (Zeidan, 2015). We also know that mindfulness reduces the decline in working memory and increases the number of stimuli in it at the same time (van Vugt, 2015).

In summary, AIM reveals the psychological experience at any given moment whether be it positive or negative. It teaches us that the interpretation of events can be influenced by the flexibility of attention, how and what is retrieved from the long-term memory, and that what is put into the long-term memory can be controlled (van Vugt, 2015; van Vugt et al., 2012). This also informs us how memory is formed in our daily interactions. Therefore, flexible attention and the interpretation of events, experiences, and incidents have a significant effect on our happiness experience.

However, AIM is not without limitations. AIM does not account for the negative experiences and subscribes to the widely accepted assumption that positive emotions alone constitute happiness. On a daily basis, people experience more neutral experiences and some negative ones. It is not prag-matic to think that everything is going to go our way. Moreover, AIM does not tell us anything about being able to *cultivate* and be *intentional* about being happy. To overcome this, a person could cultivate a paradigm that allows them to *be* happy by consciously re-interpreting an experience. This is where the wisdom of mindfulness steps in to fill this gap. Mindfulness allows us to train the mind to be intentional and also utilize attention, acceptance, and aware-ness to see things as they are as well as shift perspectives. We call this the *hap-piness paradigm*.

4 THE HAPPINESS PARADIGM

We propose the *happiness paradigm* as an intentional way of cultivating hap-piness as a disposition as well as an on-demand technique. The happiness paradigm is a very helpful equation to *appreciate wellbeing through the lenses of mindfulness*. We propose the following equation that takes into account the insights gained through mindfulness and its evidence:

Happiness paradigm = attention to the positive + acceptance of the negative + purposeful interpretation

Attention to the positive is about using flexible attention to notice the favora-ble and positive experiences including positive emotions in one's life. *Acceptance of the negative* is about bringing acceptance to unfavorable out-comes and negative emotions. It is not about resignation to a situation but having a sense of acceptance toward the emotions and situation rather than fighting it. *Purposeful interpretation* refers to the way we interpret a situa-tion or thought with purpose through what we want and what we know, aided by our insights. Wellbeing interventions then support this happiness paradigm by serving as a guide to what we want to realize in our lives (see Figure 2.5).

In our opinion, the above equation should not be used as a quan-tifiable formula where we derive a final score and match them against a scale to know how happy a person is. Such approaches neglect the eudai-monic and hedonic dispositions that one may have. It would then place people in boxes and thus betraying their personality preferences and innate dispositions. Instead the above equation should be used qualitatively such that we allow people of either disposition (eudaimonic or hedonic) to find their place in it. For example, a person with eudaimonic disposition may find that the low positive affect and high acceptance would be desirable as they would interpret them differently. And a person with a higher hedonic

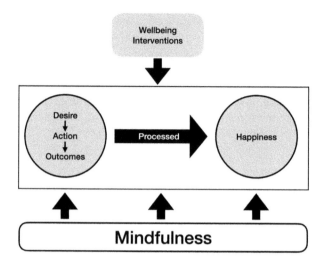

Figure 2.5 Wellbeing interventions support the happiness paradigm

disposition would want to see more frequent experiences of positive affect and acceptance of negative affect, interpreted through their understanding of wellbeing. The equation above is not for the purposes of measurement but rather for appreciation. It should be used like a compass and not as a map.

It is important that we acknowledge that the above equation is about the private experience of happiness. We also need to balance this private experience of happiness with the social dimensions of happiness by connecting it with the objective wellbeing interventions (discussed in section 1 of this chapter) as skillfully argued and presented by Ruut Veenhoven (1993). Balancing this would also make mindfulness a socially engaged practice.

The AIM approach helps us to uncover the psychological mechanisms within the *happiness paradigm* (see Figure 2.6). The conscious directing of attention to the positive and the acceptance of the negative get stored in the memory. With constant practice it could become a trait. The memory of what we know, value, believe, etc., guide us to purposefully interpret or re-interpret an experience. This process of conscious and deliberate interpretation also gets stored in the memory thus possibly becoming a trait as well. We call this positive change within an individual, *wellbeing enhancement.* In the subsequent chapters, we will be presenting how the *happiness paradigm* can be cultivated through mindfulness training via the Mindfulness-Based Wellbeing Enhancement program (MBWE). It is important to acknowledge that the *happiness paradigm* is based on the psychological mechanisms of the AIM approach, though the former has been made more intentional and as something that can be cultivated such that it becomes a trait.

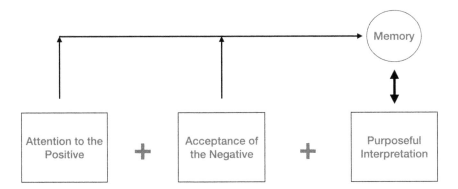

Figure 2.6 The happiness paradigm and memory

Can Happiness Become a Trait?

We have mapped the AIM model with the three-fold criteria for trait as proposed by Ruut Veenhoven (1993) in Table 2.2. The three-fold criteria are stability, cross–situational consistency, and inner causation. Stability refers to the enduring nature of a thing while cross–situational consistency applies to the consistent experience of a thing in different situations. Inner causation ascribes to self-facilitation, meaning that one can influence from within. From Table 2.2 below, you would notice that the AIM approach very much satisfies all the three criteria.

Table 2.2 Mapping of AIM against the three-fold criteria of trait

	Stability	Cross-situational consistency	Inner causation
Attention	X	X	X
Interpretation	X	X	X
Memory	X		X

Understanding the AIM approach from the mindfulness perspectives, insights, and research findings, we hypothesize that happiness can become a trait with sustained mindfulness training, a position that Richard Davidson and Daniel Goleman had also attested to (Goleman & Davidson, 2017).

In summary, through mindfulness training:

- **Attention** can be made flexible and selective.
- **Acceptance** can be brought to an undesirable experience.
- **Interpretation** of situations, events and experiences can be subject to alternative perspectives by acknowledging that thoughts are not facts. This then allows us to re-interpret what we pay attention to and what is retrieved from and stored in memory.
- **Memory** repository and narratives would change as we can now let go of what emerges spontaneously and direct our attention, through inner volition, not to dwell on the past narratives that are not conducive to my wellbeing.

You would have noticed by now as to how attention and interpretation play a pivotal role in the happiness paradigm. The happiness paradigm initially being a state-like experience, gradually develops into a trait.

5 INSIGHTS INTO WELLBEING AND HAPPINESS

Interestingly, the psychological aspects of happiness have been discussed as far back as the 800 BCE in the Indic contemplative traditions of which religious mindfulness found its genesis; as well as by the Greek philosophers (circa 500 BCE). These contemplative and philosophical traditions have given us some rudimentary insights into the nature of happiness and wellbeing. For example, the 6th-century BCE text, Taittiriya Upanishad, states,

> . . . from happiness, indeed, all these beings originate; Having been born, they are sustained by happiness; they move towards and merge in that happiness. . . . of him pleasure is verily the head, delight is the right side, extreme delight is the left side; happiness is the self.

Aristotle (384–322 BCE), in his Nicomachean Ethics, states:

> He is happy who lives in accordance with complete virtue and is sufficiently equipped with external goods, not for some chance period but throughout a complete life.

As we discuss insights into happiness and wellbeing in this section, we will draw on these early philosophical traditions as well as their modern re-appraisals to deepen our insights as well as relate with what we know today from modern authors and researchers. We have organized the topics in this section to answer these questions:

- Are people disposed to different types of happiness?
- What drives the pursuit of happiness?
- Is the locus of happiness within us or is it outside us?
- Are pleasure and happiness the same?
- Do our beliefs impact the way we experience happiness?
- Do positive emotions alone indicate happiness?
- Is happiness entirely in my control?

Hedonia vs Eudaimonia

Ancient philosophical and contemplative traditions have conceptualized happiness as being two distinct types. These concepts were briefly presented as hedonia and eudaimonia in section 2 of this chapter. Hedonia is often described as the affective experience of pleasure, enjoyments, and the absence of discomfort. Eudaimonia is often described as realizing the highest of the human potential through virtues and self-focused behaviors. These two approaches to happiness were presented in the Indic traditions as well as by the early Greek philosophers *as being incompatible*. The ancient roots of mindfulness and its early practice were meant for monks and nuns, of eudaimonic disposition. Modern researchers have also taken a similar view, that both of these approaches are incompatible and having different orientations, behaviors, experiences, and attributes; as Veronika Huta (2018) claims, "there are good reasons to consider eudaimonia as distinct from hedonia . . . eudaimonia is not nearly as necessary as hedonia." Huta's evaluation is astute and is in total agreement with early conceptualizations, though Aristotle considered hedonia to be unwholesome, claiming that "the mass of mankind are evidently quite slavish in their tastes, preferring a life suitable to beasts." Huta has perhaps positioned this tension between eudaimonia and hedonia a little more pragmatically, by stating that,

> Hedonic processes are more *fundamental*, more essential to immediate survival and competition – hedonia is largely about accumulating psychological fuel and getting needed rest. Eudaimonia, on the other hand, is our *higher* function – it literally employs those higher capacities that are so advanced in humans. Sometimes this aids survival. But often it does not.

This tension between hedonia and eudaimonia continues on until today in monastic religious traditions where the world-renouncing religious pontiffs, teachers, and hermits threaten the validity and relevance of the people embroiled in pursuits that are "fundamental, more essential to immediate survival and competition." This dispute can never be settled because it depends not on choice but on disposition. Disposition never lies, as much as choices would. People of eudaimonic disposition would usually polarize the discussion by claiming that eudaimonia is the only conceivable and tenable type of happiness, as evidenced in the quote by Aristotle above. On the other hand people of hedonia claim that enjoyment is of the utmost importance and that alone is happiness. The hedonist Greek philosopher Epicurus (341–270 BCE), states "Pleasure is the first good. It is the beginning of every choice and every aversion. It is the absence of pain in the body and of troubles in the soul."

Many of the wellbeing interventions presented above tend to present a mish-mash version of eudaimonic-hedonia and hedonic-eudaimonia. The eudaimonic dimension in these interventions is usually denoted as purpose and meaning in life. Such conceptualizations can be troublesome, as they do not allow the possibility of being happy with objective pursuits without pursuing meaning and purpose at all. On the other hand, there are people who could be happy with just pursuing meaning and purpose with very minimal dependence on objective wellbeing. We see both types of people in the world today and we will continue to see them. Very rarely do we see people with a balanced disposition of hedonia and eudaimonia, although it is not impossible. It has been our experience that *people would usually have a dominant inner driver that governs behavior, which is a reflection of their happiness disposition.* Therefore, it is immensely important that we are aware of our disposition and bring awareness, acceptance, and attention to it. It also conduces acceptance of one's disposition and helps in not wanting to be someone innately different from who I am.

Desire, the Primary Driver of Happiness

The primary driver for the pursuit of happiness is desire. Desire can be further broken down into *likes* and *dislikes.* The typical human behavior is to direct our efforts to acquire objects and experiences that we *like* and avoid objects and experiences that we *dislike.* These would also include the experience of positive and negative emotions. Both likes and dislikes could also lead to happiness, like a person who gets married to be happy while another gains happiness through a divorce. Dislikes also denote experiences or objects that would hinder or be an obstacle to the acquisition of the objects and experiences that we like. For example, I dislike a policy that might hinder the purchase of an apartment that I desire.

Daniel Kahneman in his book, *Thinking Fast and Slow,* claims that happiness scientists often neglect the dimension of *want* when evaluating happiness. What we want is all about acquiring the likes or the removal of the dislikes, or sometimes both. Kahneman states, "We cannot hold a concept of wellbeing that ignores what people want" (Kahneman, 2011, p. 402). This would then mean that the realization and acquisition of what we "want" has a tremendous influence on how we evaluate our wellbeing. To add a twist to this insight, our wants may not always be right for our wellbeing. If I wanted to rob a bank, or invade another country for its resources, it would mean that upon the realization of these wants, I would be happy. This is because *it is not in the nature of our likes and dislikes to naturally be informed by ethics*. It is not a requirement that wants should be ethically right for me to experience happiness. This calls for the need to ethically engage with our likes and dislikes or wants. The attention to ethics becomes an indispensable condition for happiness.

Happiness is an Internal Experience

One of the implicit beliefs we behold, is that happiness is in the object we desire. For example, I may think that my happiness is in the partner that I want to marry or in the new job role that I am hoping to get promoted into. Almost all happiness scientists take an opposite view on this matter by stating that happiness is an internal experience. Jonathan Haidt in his book, *The Happiness Hypothesis*, states that happiness comes somewhere between within and without. This perspective could be due to defining happiness as consisting of both eudaimonia and hedonia, a view that is hypothesized at the end of his book. Though Haidt acknowledges that happiness is indeed a mental experience or state (or trait) that happens within, his perspective does not account for people's natural disposition toward either one of the happiness approaches. The experience of external objects that consists of attention, interpretations, and memory, are all mental or internal. Our argument is something that many cognitive psychologists would readily agree to i.e. it is within us that the external perceptions are processed. We need to qualify at this juncture that in no certain measure, are we alluding to solipsism by stating this fact.

We can see that happiness is indeed a subjective experience and that the psychological mechanisms of happiness are universal to all. Here comes a question at this juncture. If happiness were an experience within, could we then willfully be happy at any given time without the need for external objects or stimuli? Interestingly research tells us that this is possible with long-term meditators. Richard Davidson's (2005) research with Buddhist monks who were long-time meditators appear to suggest so and so does our experience with expert meditators. However, a word of caution is needed here. We are not suggesting that you replace your objective pursuits with mindfulness meditation or give up your possessions. The point that we are making is that regardless of the objects of happiness existing outside us, the happiness experience takes place within us as a mental experience. This is the normative experience with all human beings.

Emotional Valence

How does the emotional experience of happiness happen? A simple way that we can understand this is through this Figure 2.7:

Figure 2.7 From desire to an experience of an emotion

We can segment the happiness experience into smaller episodes. What is perhaps important here is to see that happiness presupposes a chain of desire (or intention, motivation) and then action. And because the outcomes are not as controllable as the actions are, sometimes we hear of discourses that underrate desire and denounce actions, especially in religious discourses. The ancient roots of mindfulness also find their inspiration from such beliefs that the way to enlightenment is to renounce both desires and action and thereby remove the possibility of disappointments. In fact, the dependency on desire and action itself is seen as a form of suffering. Bhikku Bodhi, an American Buddhist monk, states that the purpose of taking up monastic life is to eschew desire, in his words "break the shackles of desire" (1994, p. 33). He strengthens his position further by claiming that desire:

- and suffering are inseparable concomitants (p. 3 4)
- and its demands are endless and the objects of desire are impermanent (p. 34)
- is attachment and therefore no attachment means no suffering (p. 34)

- ultimately breeds fear and sorrow and that renunciation gives fearlessness and joy (p. 35)
- and sexual desire needs to be reduced and extricated (p. 81)

In ascetic and monastic traditions, desire is seen as the root of suffering. Mindfulness practices in Buddhism too are for the purpose of eschewing sexual and sensual desire as well as to systematically visualize the repulsiveness of the body (Bodhi, 1994, p. 81). It is important to note that this interpretation of desire as being something unwholesome is not confined to Buddhism, but found in many religions and philosophies that espouse and promote austere lifestyles. Modern mindfulness teachers and scholars are confronted with this problem of desire, especially those who wish to situate mindfulness as an authentic and ancient Buddhist practice and yet convince us of its value in this modern capitalistic society. Christina Feldman and Willem Kuyken are classic examples of such interpreters who skillfully re-interpret these doctrines in a more palatable way for secular audiences while acknowledging and justifying their Buddhist roots. In their book, *Mindfulness: Ancient Wisdom Meets Modern Psychology*, they replace the term "desire" with "craving" and in doing so they narrow the scope of desire to confine it to an unhealthy form called "craving."

Our view is that the renunciation of desire and action is unnecessary as they are vital means to our wellbeing and happiness, unless and otherwise one aims to undertake a path of monasticism or lifelong solitude. We acknowledge desire to be the crowning glory of being human and because of desire alone, is action possible. And with action alone can we "change" the status quo to enhance our wellbeing in our environment, innovate products and services, enhance relationships, etc., that include the whole gamut of individual and collective human experiences.

The problem then is not with desire in itself but with the intention behind any given desire. The primary question then is whether my desire, intention, and motivation are conducive to my wellbeing as well as the people in my life and to the larger society. Interestingly, these discussions are usually more popular among spiritual traditions than in modern psychology. The absence of such a discussion, possibly to avert moral issues, happens to be at the root of civilizational challenges as we see invasions of countries, religious extremists destroying and threatening other cultures, and people excluding people who are different from themselves, without any consideration to whether it ultimately leads to individual and societal wellbeing. One of my (SR) therapy clients shared, about ten years back, how she had friendships only with people of the same social status and disliked anyone who did not work hard to be successful. One of her beliefs was that people who are successful make her look good in society so she consciously avoided friends and family members, including her parents, who were deemed to be less successful than her. She also married someone who earned more than her and said that she chose him so that she could "upgrade in life." She only surrounded herself with people who were "successful." Yet, she was unhappy, lonely, and constantly dissatisfied in life. She missed her mother's home-cooked food and gossips; her friends' overseas trips and laughter; her father's wise words and protective nature; her ex-best friend's straight talk and many more. When we exclude those who matter to us and those who connect with us, how can we and they be happy?

Mindfulness softens this challenge by shifting the outside-in orientation to an inside-out phenomenon where the *self* is given the responsibility of desire and action. *We are the locus of desire and we can decide how the realization of our desires impacts others and society.* Shauna Shapiro and Alan Wallace (2006) termed this as "conative balance," the ability to discern if our desires satisfy our own and others' wellbeing. This idea is implicit and explicit in the religious and spiritual traditions of the world, though sometimes ignored in favor of religious zeal and proselytization. This idea is also not new to social psychologists who ask questions about our behaviors and climate change, sustainability, and wealth inequality. This awareness helps in negotiating our desires with wellbeing, something mindfulness enables by providing the strength of intention, action, and insight. Our wants, likes, and dislikes are not the legitimate arbiter for our desires and intentions. With mindfulness, we learn to discern the difference between the pleasurable and that which conduces wellbeing.

Pleasure = Happiness Confusion

Our discussion now leads to the often unconscious association between pleasure vs pain and happiness. The following equations illustrate the mental associations we often make.

Pain = unhappiness
Pleasure = happiness

As an instinct, human beings, like animals, avoid pain. As a result, pain is therefore associated with unhappiness. Because pain makes me unhappy, we form a belief that painful experiences are to be avoided. The same association happens with pleasure as well. We seek pleasure as it produces positive emotions and therefore deem it to be a happy experience. The happy experiences lead us to believe that only pleasurable experiences are to be sought. We come to the conclusion that pleasure equals happiness and pain equals unhappiness. This belief leads us to prioritize "my" pleasurable activities over anything else and as long as something gives me pleasure, it is considered to be ethically okay. We may strive to look for comfort and seek out paths of least resistance when wanting to achieve our goals. As a result, we may fail to see that seeking the wholesome may not always be something comfortable. Many goals that we have set for ourselves may not always be something comfortable to attain, for example giving up smoking or losing weight. As you would have noticed, this creates tension for the conative balance as we could potentially be choosing actions that give us pleasure and comforts rather than that which is conducive to our wellbeing. In the same way, people may discard any practice that requires effort, including mindfulness, as it may not be something pleasurable or comfortable like the way flexing our muscles for the first time in the gym could be for people.

The Power of Perspectives and Beliefs

Research on the efficacy of placebo effect constantly tells us that beliefs have tremendous power. It is important therefore that we are aware of our beliefs, including religious beliefs, because they have the capacity to alter our interpretation of an experience. As quoted above, Daniel Kahneman's observations about wellbeing being dependent on people's wants is a significant point to consider in this discussion. Our beliefs influence what we desire and how we realize and interpret it.

Religion provides purpose and meaning for some people and through its doctrines and tenets create goals and wants. These, however, may not be shared by all. For example, we have met (and continue to meet) sincere and kind human beings who believe that their highest goal in life was to please and serve God. Satisfying this desire is their prime goal of life. Possibly, any of the wellbeing interventions would not work with this group of believers, because they "believe" that pleasing God would be their only truth. This phenomenon does not deserve judgment but rather acceptance, the acceptance that religious epistemologies work quite differently from secular and scientific ones. Religious epistemologies would usually place primacy to revelation, the founder's teachings, and teachings of religious teachers. Believers negotiate their life experiences in light of their beliefs, which is also a phenomenon that is applicable to non-religious beliefs. And we know from evidence that religious people could possibly be happier than those who are not.

With regards to non-religious beliefs, Albert Ellis, the father of Rational Emotive Behavior Therapy (REBT), presents three irrational beliefs, also called the three musts, that are common among people. Michael Bernard (2010, p. xvi), in his book on the legacy of Albert Ellis, states that according to Ellis,

> Humans have an innate tendency to greater or lesser extents to take their desires, preferences, and wishes for love, success, comfort, and for happiness and to formalize them into absolutistic musts, shoulds, oughts, needs, and commands.

These beliefs impact happiness, according to Bernard, by either nurturing or stunting inner causation, vulnerability, acceptance, commitment and scientific thinking. From a mindfulness perspective, we have studied how mindfulness contributes to the transformation of these irrational beliefs, in the Table 2.3 below:

Table 2.3 Irrational beliefs and mindfulness mechanisms leading to alternative perspectives

	Irrational beliefs	Mindfulness mechanisms	Alternative perspectives
1	I must do well and win others' approval or else I am no good.	• Acceptance of oneself • Self-compassion	I am fine as I am and capable of being good.
2	Others must treat me fairly and kindly and in the same way I want them to treat me. If they do not treat me this way, they are not good people and deserve to be punished.	• Non-judgment • Acceptance • Interpretations	I have the capacity to respond to situations with wisdom and interpret them purposefully.
3	I must always get what I want, when I want it. Likewise, I must never get what I don't want. If I don't get what I want, I'm miserable.	• Acceptance of the four types of outcomes	I do not have control over the results or outcomes of my actions. I can bring acceptance to the outcomes.

Diener and Biswas-Diener (2008) bring another perspective to this discussion through their six thinking pitfalls that influence the way we interpret situations:

- **Awfulizing** – people exaggerate how something is unfavorable such that it gets dramatically blown out of proportion, e.g. "My husband did not buy me a gift for my birthday. He does not love me."
- **Distress intolerance** – people underestimate their capabilities to cope and get out of a distressing situation, e.g. "I have lost my job. My family and I are going to perish."
- **Learned helplessness** – people giving up on change or actions that could change a situation, "My staff are not engaged at work. There is nothing I can do about it."
- **Perfectionism** – people strive to be perfect instead of being functionally competent, relevant and successful, e.g. "The work I did won an award, but I think it wasn't good enough as it had cosmetic flaws."
- **Negative self-fulfilling expectancies** – people obtain negative responses or feedback from people by communicating that to them prior, e.g. "Tell me all the ways in which this idea will fail."

- **Rejection goggles** – people view responses that are not in their favor as a rejection, e.g. "You did not like my food? Hmm, oh you must not like me very much then!"

In summary, how we interpret a situation and possibly shift our mind depends on what we know and believe in.

Shifting Paradigms

Read the statement below:

> stcaf ton era sthguoht

You might be thinking that the above is gibberish. Or could it be perhaps a new language? Now try reading the statement from the right to left.

What does this tell us? Our current paradigm is that sentences should be read from the left to the right. The moment when you were told that this sentence would only make sense when you read it from the right to the left, the assumptions have been displaced. A paradigm is commonly defined to be a system of assumptions, concepts, values, and practices that constitutes a way of viewing reality. When we find new ways of viewing reality, our assumptions, values and concepts may shift or gain a new perspective. Mindfulness, with the attitude of curiosity, enables us to look at things with a fresh pair of eyes even things that we already have an intimate relationship with. Through mindfulness practices and inquiry our paradigms about wellbeing and happiness get shifted.

Impermanence and Thoughts

One common thing that we have noted is the widespread discourse about the impermanence of the world in MBPs. Here are several quotes about impermanence from a few books:

> In fact, nothing at all is permanent and eternal. Although some things appear that way since they change so slowly.
>
> (Kabat-Zinn, 2013, p. 299)

> One major realization you might come to is the inevitability of change, the direct perception that, whether we like it or not, impermanence is the very nature of things and relationships.
>
> (Kabat-Zinn, 2013, p. 417)

> Each of us live in a world of conditions that are forever changing, unreliable, and unpredictable. It is not a negative or a positive truth, but simply the inarguable nature of all things.
>
> (Feldman & Kuyken, 2019, p. 72)

> Impermanence, or the reality of constant change, is central to Buddhism . . . it is inevitable that we will come to terms with it. When we resist reality, our suffering increases.
>
> (Shapiro, Wang, & Peltason, 2015, p. 31)

> You will come to learn that everything changes: even the worst-case scenarios imagined in your darkest moments.
>
> (Williams & Penman, 2011, p. 169)

We acknowledge that the above quotes are not exhaustive enough for us analyze the way impermanence has been presented in mindfulness literature. However, these quotes tell us that impermanence can be seen and appreciated from three different perspectives:

- as an indisputable doctrine of Buddhism
- as constant change
- as the world being unreal, an illusion, or empty of reality

It is of utmost importance, especially for mindfulness teachers, to recognize that the doctrine of impermanence and suffering is central to the monastic religious traditions of ancient India, primarily Buddhism, Jainism, and Hinduism. Buddhism also uses impermanence as a corollary to the doctrine of emptiness (shunyata). Apart from seeing the world as impermanent, from an ontological standpoint, the elaborate and radical presentation of the world being unreal is also for the purposes of generating dispassion, which then leads to world renunciation and also turning away from it. As we teach secular mindfulness to people of all faiths, we need to be mindful of views that can come from the opposite end, where the world and its constitutes are seen as beautiful and therefore something to be held in wonder, to be enjoyed or as akin to God itself. There are also equally valid materialist and humanist views that regard the world as being real and not as an illusion.

We have also encountered efforts that direct the insights generated from secular MBPs to rationalizing Buddhist doctrines, such as the work of Christina Feldman and Willem Kuyken (2019). This poses a risk of what we call as passive indoctrination and unconscious subscription to tenets that can be at loggerheads with the one's faith subscription, as discussed in the last chapter. Therefore, when teaching impermanence it is important that we focus on the second perspective which is seeing the world as constantly changing. The world does not have an independent reality as it is made up of many constituents. The purpose of this discussion has to be clear, which is not for the purpose of creating disgust or dispassion, but rather to acknowledge the nature of the world accepted by all, both the religious and the non-religious. Otherwise, stress, the reduction of stress, happiness and wellbeing concepts too could be subject to the same impermanence, thus making it a catch-22 situation.

How can we then position the aspect of "constant change" in a way that people can take away positive insight? As the adage goes "words create worlds," so we can use words to create different worldviews. Study the following statements and compare the left and the right statements:

Thoughts are unreal **vs** Thoughts are not facts
The world is an illusion **vs** The world is constantly changing
The world is false **vs** The world is made up of constituents

The statements on the right could be possibly more pragmatic. The key thrust of these insights is for people to see that thoughts are not facts, but interpretations. They keep changing and every thought depends on a prior thought. These are plain truths and do not require a special type of intuition or subscription to a belief. Mindfulness helps us to bring awareness to these insights, as much as we already know them implicitly, or perhaps unconsciously. Therefore *how we present these perspectives is as important as the perspectives themselves.*

Affect of Attainment

Another important universal experience is the intensity of the arousal of positive emotions. The intensity depends on the level of desirability for an object. The desirable object

1. could be in a mental form, either in anticipation or as a memory of prior enjoyment, or
2. could be within reach, being something attainable in the present moment, or
3. has been acquired, owned or currently being experienced by the five senses.

All of these three situations can give rise to positive affect. Richard Davidson (2002) further helps us to understand these levels of arousal through his conception of *pre-goal attainment positive affect* and *post-goal attainment positive affect.* Davidson found that there were positive emotions in the anticipation of an object of desire which is the *pre-goal attainment positive affect.* Imagine wanting a new dream home and just thinking of it creates positive emotions. This is the first condition in the list above. Interestingly these emotions were found to last longer than the *post-goal attainment positive affect* which is the experience of having attained the object of desire. The contentment that arises at this stage was found to be way shorter than the emotions of anticipation. Perhaps there is some truth in the idiom, "the chase is better than the catch."

Further, Davidson's research also helps us to explain the release of tension that we experience when the anticipation toward an object of desire is dropped. For example, thinking about the dream home and planning to purchase it arouse the *pre-goal attainment positive affect* and when the home is purchased, you jump for joy. That celebratory jump for joy is the *post-goal attainment positive affect* which is a form of a release. Davidson also found that during the stage of contentment, the left prefrontal cortex reduced its activity, thus leading to a release.

Knower-Doer Conflict

The "knower-doer" conflict is one of the many types of cognitive dissonance. We often hear participants in our classes say, "I know that this is what I want but I can't seem get myself to do it." We attribute this challenge to the lack of intrinsic and extrinsic mechanisms to execute an intention. Extrinsic mechanisms are skills such as time management, task management, and supportive aids (e.g. calendaring, productivity applications, etc.). Intrinsic mechanisms refer to the psychological attributes such as prioritization, motivation, attention, and concentrative abilities among others. Mindfulness brings awareness to this reality and further strengthens attention to where we want it to be thus promoting executive action. We had already discussed this as the selective and flexible attention capabilities of the working memory.

Growing Dispassion

Let us bring ourselves back to our childhood days. Can you recollect a toy that you wanted so badly and the joy you experienced when you got it? I (KK) remember my father gifting me a remote controlled car. It was such a joy playing with it but also disappointing each time the battery ran dry in the middle of "driving" the car. Fast forwarding a couple of decades to the present time, I have not touched a remote control car nor desired one since then. Why? Because I have outgrown it. After repeated pre-goal attainment positive affect and post-goal attainment positive affect experiences, our minds develop dispassion toward the very same object. We do not find novelty in it anymore. Similarly, people go through several stages when they form romantic relationships. Our emotions during the dating stage can be quite different from the stage where we are in a committed relationship and with children of our own. Positive affect toward the partner may not be there in the same way it was during the dating stage. The novelty of the experience is again gone. This can lead some people to desire for a new partner so that they can re-create the same pre-goal attainment positive affect and post-goal attainment positive affect, or even introducing new elements into the current relationship to make it more exciting, which is basically re-creating the pre-goal attainment positive affect. We can learn that it is the nature of the mind to outgrow the emotional value we have for an object and look for more novel experiences.

We can illustrate this phenomenon through the balloon effect. When you blow air into a balloon, the pressure within the balloon gets built up. And when you release the air within, the balloon gets propelled into space. How far the balloon travels or how fast the velocity is going to be, depends on the built up pressure within the balloon. The air that is slowly blown into the balloon is the pressure of anticipation, the greater the anticipation, the greater the pressure. And the contentment of release also depends on the pressure of anticipation. An experience of failure in reaching a goal then produces the opposite experience, such as disappointment, anger, and rage. The difference between disappointment and rage depends also on the pressure built by anticipation. To put it simply, we are perhaps just releasing this pressure of anticipation that is burdened in our minds through our search for a release. It is also possible that we are just after this mental experience of release every time we fulfill a desire, although the result is not entirely in our hands.

Is Happiness Controllable?

Why is it that happiness is not entirely in our control? Sonja Lyubomirsky and Kennon M. Sheldon (2021) claim that, *"Happiness can be successfully pursued, but it is not 'easy.'"* Lyubomirsky et al. (2005) proposed that people's happiness was determined by three factors which are genetic set-point, circumstances and intentional activities. Genetic set-point refers to the fact that we inherit our happiness and personality traits from our genetics at birth similar to how depression can be inherited for some. Second, life circumstances also influence our happiness. Where we find ourselves and where we put ourselves can also influence our happiness and wellbeing. Third, intentional and voluntary activities could also impact our happiness as it gives us the autonomy to fulfill desire and do what makes us happy. When we correlate these three influences against our level of control, this is how it would look like in Figure 2.8.

Figure 2.8 Three influences vs level of control

The appreciation of what is within our control, and what is not, helps us in living our life with pragmatism. We do not have any control over our genetics as we do not choose our parentage. Ruminating over the past is equally the same as we do not have any control over it. All that we can do is bring acceptance to this part of our lives. The knowledge of our past and our genetic pre-dispositions can inform our intentions and help us in making informed changes to our lifestyle. While we cannot change the city where we were born in or the circumstances under which we grew up, we can certainly change our current circumstances. If I were born in an urbanized environment and should I wish to move to a quieter and less busy environment, I could possibly relocate to the suburbs or even to a village. Therefore, I do have some level of control over my circumstances. Lastly, intentional activity is something that I have more control and choice over. As much as we know that our genetic set-point and circumstances can either empower or hinder our intentions, we still have a larger sphere of control over what we can do about it or around it. For example, I may not have control over the cards that are dealt to me at the poker table, but I certainly have choice over how I play the game regardless of whether I win, lose, or quit the game. It is important that we recognize the difference between what we can change and what we cannot. We can bring acceptance to what we cannot change and bring attention to what we can. Knowing this difference helps us to be aware of our intentions with more pragmatism and enhance our wellbeing.

6 MINDFULNESS AND HAPPINESS MYTHS

There have been many myths about happiness and wellbeing in both mainstream media and mindfulness literature. Let us examine a couple of them.

Absence of Mental Health Conditions is Happiness

We see no dearth of literature about how the first generation of MBPs, namely Mindfulness-Based Stress Reduction and Mindfulness-Based Cognitive Therapy, have increased levels of happiness. While we do not doubt the veracity of the results, the question remains unanswered if it was the reduction of stress that increased happiness or the mechanisms of mindfulness that did the job, or perhaps both.

In our discussions thus far we had discussed the role of wants in the realization of happiness. These wants were further broken down into likes and dislikes. Certainly stress is something we do not want and we do see that the reduction of stress does restore normal functioning. Perhaps the contentment of having reduced stress makes people feel somewhat happier. To assume that the reduction of stress is happiness, would sound like a wife claiming to be in a happy marriage because her husband does not philander. The absence of negative experiences does not prove the presence of positive experiences, although we know that the former passively facilitates the latter. Using the same rule, we know that the absence of anxiety, depression or any other mental health condition does not constitute happiness. More research is required to delineate how the mechanisms of mindfulness contribute to wellbeing on their own without any mediating factors such as stress reduction, reduction of relapse of depression, or anxiety reduction.

Mindfulness Makes People Happy

Does mindfulness make people happy by the absence of mental health conditions or through the facilitation of the realization of their wants and goals? We believe that the latter is more tenable because all that mindfulness does is that it increases our self-awareness levels via the strengthening of attention and acceptance mechanisms. Through this people generate insights about:

- their disposition for happiness: hedonia or eudaimonia
- their wants, likes, and dislikes
- their values and strengths
- their beliefs and knowledge
- happiness being the prime goal of life; the other goals are its levers

Mindfulness and MBPs play a *facilitative* role in attaining happiness and wellbeing rather than being the *cause* of it. Mindfulness continues to empower the state of *being* rather than coercing people into a state of *doing*. This appreciation of the role of MBPs and mindfulness allows us to set a realistic and pragmatic expectation on mindfulness training.

A Wandering Mind is an Unhappy Mind?

Christina Feldman and Willem Kuyken (2019) came to the conclusion that a wandering mind is an unhappy mind, having cited several research findings.

We take a slightly different view which is that you can be unhappy having a wandering mind, not that a wandering mind is an unhappy mind. These are two different things.

We agree with the cited research findings that a present mind as opposed to a wandering mind is certainly a predictor of happiness. We see a mind that is focused and having concentrative capabilities having a better chance of keeping their attention on the goal and executing it given that the circumstances allow it. We also know for certain that a present mind may not necessarily generate positive affect as it is in a neutral state. The research by John Cacioppo and team (Larsen et al., 2003) shows that happy people can possibly evoke positive feelings with neutral objects, which we can then easily infer that it was not the attention on the object that creates the positive emotions but the lenses (i.e. mental interpretation) through which the information was processed. There is a fine difference between the two. Moreover, we also know that a wandering mind can be beneficial in some situations such as in being creative and problem solving.

Does Mindful Acceptance Make People Happy?

Again, people misconceive that the mechanism of acceptance would by itself directly cause one to be happy. In research by Lindsay and colleagues (2018), it was found that mindful acceptance promoted positive emotions. However, it is to be noted that learning acceptance skills, via mindfulness training, allows people to *notice* the positive experiences in their lives, rather than *creating* them. Therefore, the rise of positive emotions could be due to other factors such as the lowered reactivity that led to enhanced attention. This supports our view of how the repeated practice of acceptance-attention enhances wellbeing through awareness.

The second phenomenon is the strengthening of acceptance toward the four types of outcomes (see Figure 2.7, on page 62). This equanimity helps us to not reject the emotional effect of each of the four types of outcomes but instead allows us to respond to it with non-reactivity.

7 SOCIALLY ENGAGED MINDFULNESS OR SOCIAL MINDFULNESS

One of the dichotomies of mindfulness is the focus on *being* as opposed to *doing*. Mindfulness teachers, like Jon Kabat-Zinn, have repeatedly emphasized the focus on *being* instead of *doing*. This emphasis creates a dissonance within a person when they are brought to spheres where *doing* is very important such as organizations, workplaces, and athletics among others.

The *being* mode is characterized by present centeredness, accepting whatever that rises in the field of our thoughts, being non-judgmental, letting go of interpretations, and having clarity. This mode of *being* is arrived at as a result of sustained mindfulness practices and also facilitated during the mindfulness practices. This mode is presented as being the opposite of *doing* which is characterized by goals, past and future centeredness, evaluations, judgment, non-acceptance of failure, and having a productivity focus.

The prevalent belief that *being* is incompatible with *doing* is perpetuated by polarized discussions about *doing* vs *being*, a pitfall that we need to be conscious of. In contrast, balanced and pragmatic perspectives about *doing* "and" *being* as opposed to *doing* "vs" *being* have also been offered:

> Doing mode is not an enemy to be defeated, but it is often an ally. Doing mode only becomes a "problem" when it volunteers for a task that it cannot do, such as "solving" as troubling emotion.
>
> (Williams & Penman, 2011 p. 36)

> There is nothing inherently wrong with this doing mode . . . We are in no way suggesting that the doing mode necessarily causes problem – it does not.
>
> (Segal, Williams, & Teasdale, 2013, pp. 68–69)

> When you immersed in doing without being centered, it feels like being away from home. And when you connect with being, even for a few moments, you know it immediately. You feel like you are at home no matter where you are and what problems you face.
>
> (Kabat-Zinn, 2013, p. 99)

> No matter what is happening, you can be centered in perceiving and accepting things as they are. Of course, you can also be aware of what still needs to be done in the future, without it causing you undue anxiety or loss of perspective. Then you can move to do it, with your doing coming out of your being, out of groundedness, out of integration, out of a moment of interior balance, of equanimity, of peace.
>
> (Kabat-Zinn, 2013, p. 454)

We particularly find Kabat-Zinn's mindful choice of statements very helpful in removing this dichotomy, for example "with your doing coming out of your being, out of groundedness, out of integration, out of a moment of interior balance, of equanimity, of peace." This positive positioning of *doing* and *being* not as adversaries but being integrated is what we call "Engaged while being." The innate sense of *doing* is natural to being human and is never a problem as stated in the quotations above. If the human organism is not meant for doing, we would not have our limbs, muscles, and a sophisticated nervous system that propels us to move. Neuroscientist Daniel Wolpert (2012) states, "the brain evolved, not to think or feel, but to control movement."

Engaged while being means that we continue to see our *doing* being informed by our *being*, something that continuously happens with mindfulness training. Goals, past and future centeredness, evaluations, or having a productivity focus is no longer seen as a challenge. Why? Because they get negotiated through the appreciation of *being*, without losing focus on its intended outcomes.

We also envision a second corollary to being *engaged while being*, which is the dimension of engaged mindfulness or socially engaged mindfulness.

Social engagement is not new to religious movements such as engaged Buddhism, engaged emancipation of Hinduism and liberation theologies of Christianity and Islam. While these movements used scriptural validation, inspiration and doctrinal re-interpretation for their impetus, engaged mindfulness on the other hand depends on insights into the nature of common humanity to find its impetus. From a mindfulness perspective, social engagement becomes an imperative because we are social beings. We live in a world where we are connected with each other, other beings, and to the environment. As discussed before, kindness, compassion, and empathy are things that arise as a result of the recognition of common humanity. We come to recognize that "the person in the room with me practicing mindfulness is no different from me." We allow this insight to pervade people's lives through their actions or the mode of *doing*. The mode of *doing* now becomes an opportunity for recognizing not only my humanity but the humanity of others. This can be accomplished through simple opportunities that we may have every day to relate with people in our lives and with those who may not be in our immediate environment. This can be done even with nature or in the environment that we are in.

Mark Leonard (2019), in his book *Social Mindfulness*, presents the social dimension of mindfulness training, as something that is "designed to develop insight into the way we create a sense of self and how this creates subconscious biases. It helps people understand their motives, communicate effectively and cooperate in times of change" (p. 15).

Research about gratitude also tells us something interesting. It was found that repeated emotions of gratitude impacted the brain such that people are motivated to support others by relieving them from their stress and the stressors (Fox et al., 2015). Gratitude allows people to re-interpret their experiences and through that, be of service to other people. Higher levels of gratitude were also found to positively correlate with life satisfaction, positive affect, and happiness (Allen, 2018).

By now we could possibly see how mindfulness and MBPs can create a more livable and positive world. What we see outside is not only an internal interpretation but also a product of what we envision and dream within. One of the founding fathers of appreciative inquiry, David Cooperrider states,

> The artful creation of positive imagery on a collective basis may well be the most prolific activity that individuals and organizations can engage in, if their aim is to bring to fruition a positive and humanly significant future.
>
> (1990, p. 93)

This vision, a realistic one, negotiated through experiential insights and enhanced awareness can be advanced through MBPs. Mindfulness is therefore psychological capital that appreciates in value with sustenance and clear intention. What starts within, initially, eventually sprouts to impact the social world that we live in. We can now see from the discussions in this chapter that mindfulness contributes to one's wellbeing and the wellbeing of communities.

In Chapters 3, 4 and 5, we present the MBWE, a unique MBP for enhancing wellbeing and human flourishing through the *happiness paradigm*.

REFERENCES

Allen, S. (2018). *The science of gratitude*. John Templeton Foundation.

Bernard, M. E. (2010). *Rationality and the pursuit of happiness: The legacy of Albert Ellis*. Wiley.

Bodhi, B. (1994). *The noble eightfold path: Way to the end of suffering*. Buddhist Publication Society.

Cooperrider, D. L. (1990). Positive image, positive action: The affirmative basis of organizing. In S. Srivastava & D. L. Cooperrider (Eds.), *Appreciative management and leadership: The power of positive thought in organizations*. Jossey-Bass.

Crane, R. S. (2017). Implementing mindfulness in the mainstream: Making the path by walking it. *Mindfulness, 8*(3), 585–594.

Davidson, R. (2002). Towards a biology of positive affect and compassion. In R. Davidson and A. Harrison (Eds.), Visions of compassion: Western scientists and Tibetan Buddhists examine human nature (pp. 107–130). Oxford University Press.

Davidson, R. J. (2005). Emotion regulation, happiness, and the neuroplasticity of the brain. *Advances in Mind-Body Medicine, 21*, 25–28.

Davis, J. H., & Thompson, E. (2015). Developing attention and decreasing affective bias. *Handbook of mindfulness: Theory, Research, and practice*, 42–61.

Diener, E., & Biswas-Diener, R. (2008). *Happiness: Unlocking the mysteries of psychological wealth*. Blackwell.

Feldman, C., & Kuyken, W. (2019). *Mindfulness: Ancient wisdom meets modern psychology*. Guilford.

Fox, G. R., Kaplan, J., Damasio, H., & Damasio, A. (2015). Neural correlates of gratitude. *Frontiers in Psychology, 1491*, 1–11.

Frankl, V. (1985). *Man's search for meaning*. Pocket Books.

Gethin, R. (2015). Buddhist conceptualizations of mindfulness. In Brown, K. W., Creswell, J. D., & Ryan, R. M. (Eds.), *Handbook of mindfulness: Theory, research, and practice*, 9–41. Guilford.

Goleman, D., & Davidson, R. J. (2017). *Altered traits: Science reveals how meditation changes your mind, brain, and body*. Penguin.

Huta, V. (2018). Eudaimonia versus Hedonia: What is the difference? And is it real? [Special issue]. *International Journal of Existential Positive Psychology: Proceedings of the 2016 Meaning Conference, 8*.

Jha, A. P., Rogers, S. L., & Morrison, A. B. (2014). Mindfulness training in high stress professions: Strengthening attention and resilience. In *Mindfulness-based treatment approaches* (pp. 347–366). Academic Press.

Kabat-Zinn, J. (2013). *Full catastrophe living: Using the wisdom of your body and mind to face stress, pain, and illness* (rev. ed.). Bantam.

Kahneman, D. (2011). *Thinking, fast and slow*. Macmillan.

Larsen, J. T., Hemenover, S. H., Norris, C. J., & Cacioppo, J. T. (2003). Turning adversity to advantage: On the virtues of the coactivation of positive and negative emotions. In L. Aspinwall & U. M. Staudinger (Eds.), *A psychology of human strengths: Fundamental questions and future directions for a positive psychology*. American Psychological Association.

Leonard, M. (2019). Social mindfulness: A guide to meditations from Mindfulness-Based Organisational Education. *Mindfulness Connected*.

Lindsay, E. K., Chin, B., Greco, C. M., Young, S., Brown, K. W., Wright, A. G., . . . & Creswell, J. D. (2018). How mindfulness training promotes positive emotions: Dismantling acceptance skills training in two randomized controlled trials. *Journal of Personality and Social Psychology, 115*(6), 944.

Lyubomirsky, S., Sheldon, K. M., & Schkade, D. (2005). Pursuing happiness: The architecture of sustainable change. *Review of General Psychology, 9*(2), 111–131.

Salagame, K. K. K. (2013). Well-being from the Hindu/Sanatana dharma perspective. In S. A. David, I. Boniwell, & A. C. Ayers (Eds.), *The Oxford handbook of happiness* (pp. 371–383). Oxford University Press.

Segal, Z., Williams, M., & Teasdale, J. (2013). *Mindfulness-based cognitive therapy for depression* (2nd ed.). Guilford.

Seligman, M. (2003). *Authentic happiness*. Nicholas Brealey Publishing.

Shapiro, S. L., Wang, M. C., & Peltason, E. H. (2015). What is mindfulness, and why should organizations care about it. In J. Reb & E. Cho (Eds.), *Mindfulness in organizations: foundations, research and applications*, 17–42. Nova Science Publishers.

Sheldon, K. M., & Lyubomirsky, S. (2021). Revisiting the sustainable happiness model and pie chart: can happiness be successfully pursued? *The Journal of Positive Psychology, 16*(2), 145–154.

Stones, M., Hadjistavropoulos, T., Tuuko, H., & Kozma, A. (1995). Happiness has traitlike and statelike properties: A reply to Veenhoven – Social Indicators Research. Retrieved from https://link.springer.com/article/10.1007/BF01079722

Veenhoven, R. (1993). *Is happiness a trait? Tests of the theory that a better society does not make people happier.* Arbeitsgruppe Sozialberichterstattung.

Van Vugt, M. K. (2015). Cognitive benefits of mindfulness meditation. In K. W. Brown, J. D. Creswell, & R. M. Ryan (Eds.), *Handbook of mindfulness: Theory, research, and practice* (pp. 190–207). Guilford.

Van Vugt, M. K., Hitchcock, P., Shahar, B., & Britton, W. (2012). The effects of mindfulness-based cognitive therapy on affective memory recall dynamics in depression: a mechanistic model of rumination. *Frontiers in Human Neuroscience, 6*, 257.

Wallace, B. A., & Shapiro, S. L. (2006). Mental balance and well-being: building bridges between Buddhism and Western psychology. *American Psychologist, 61*(7), 690.

Williams, M., & Penman, D. (2011). *Mindfulness: A practical guide to finding peace in a frantic world.* Hachette UK.

Wolpert, D. (2012, June 28). The real reason for brains. Retrieved from www.bbc.com/future/article/20120627-the-real-reason-for-brains

Zeidan, F. (2015). The neurobiology of mindfulness meditation. In K. W. Brown, J. D. Creswell, & R. M. Ryan (Eds.), *Handbook of mindfulness: Theory, research, and practice* (pp. 171–189). Guilford.

CHAPTER 3

The Mindfulness-Based Wellbeing Enhancement (MBWE) Curriculum

I have attended meditation sessions to improve myself. I still don't seem to fully understand what gives me happiness. Should I be meditating more?

–Sanjay

In this chapter, we present the Mindfulness-Based Wellbeing Enhancement (MBWE) protocol, a unique mindfulness-based program (MBP) that has its focus on wellbeing and human flourishing. The MBWE empowers participants through mindfulness to enhance wellbeing through insights gained about the *happiness paradigm*. In the following sections we will present the MBWE's intentions, uniqueness, and the session plans as well as the suggested facilitation methods. In Chapters 4 and 5, we present the facilitation of mindfulness practices with exercises and the method of facilitating inquiry to generate insights respectively.

The first generation of MBPs arose in clinical settings for the purposes of clinical needs. Jeff Wilson (2014), in his book *Mindful America*, calls this phase of the secularization of mindfulness as the "medicalization of mindfulness." From these medicalized versions of mindfulness, the world saw promising results that included results beyond stress reduction and depressive episodes, as discussed in Chapter 1.

1 DEFINING A MINDFULNESS-BASED PROGRAM (MBP)

An MBP is certainly unique for the fact that it is *based* on mindfulness and not on any other type of intervention. Some distinct features of MBPs are that it intends to reduce negative emotional experiences and increase positive ones, either actively or passively. They are usually delivered once a week over

DOI: 10.4324/9781003322955-4

a period of 5–8 weeks, or sometimes longer. Each weekly session is usually between 1 to 3 hours, though the average is about 2.5 hours. The outcomes of MBPs are usually measurable.

Rebecca Crane (2017) states that the core aims of MBPs are to serve as a clinical, mental training and/or a self-help tool which explores self-regulation, self-exploration and self-liberation. In addition, the MBP's intention(s) would have to be clear, ethical and free from ideology, dogma, or religious references, thus making it accessible to all, regardless of their faith subscriptions or none. Several scholars (Baer et al., 2019; Crane et al., 2017) state that MBPs:

- integrate theories and practices from contemplative traditions with scientific disciplines
- are rooted in the universal human experience and teach a different way of relating and responding to distress
- provide an intensive training in formal and informal mindfulness practices and exercises
- introduce a new relationship with present-moment experience based on acceptance, compassion, and decentering
- employ a learning process that is highly experiential
- utilize an interactive process known as inquiry that helps participants generate insights about the intentions of the MBP
- aim at intended outcomes such as attentional, emotional, and behavioral self-regulation as well as equanimity, compassion, and wisdom

2 TWO TYPES OF MBPS: RESTORATIVE AND APPRECIATIVE

Our study of the various types of MBPs led us to categorize them into two types; namely *restorative* and *appreciative* (see Figure 3.1). The restorative MBPs primarily aim at rehabilitating people to the baseline level of wellbeing, which is the absence or the alleviation of mental health issues. By using the term baseline, we refer to the quality of life where one is experiencing the usual ups and downs of life, and also has the internal and external resources to cope with them. These include the ability to bounce back from the "downs" and experience a satisfactory frequency of "ups". This is represented by the sine wave in Figure 3.1. On the other hand, the appreciative MBPs aim to bring people from the baseline to achieve the potential of flourishing, aided by the knowledge of oneself and enhancing wellbeing. The usual entry criteria for restorative MBPs would be a debilitated state of wellbeing. The appreciative MBPs, on the other hand, widen the door of entry by admitting healthy individuals who might be interested in exploring mindfulness and its benefit.

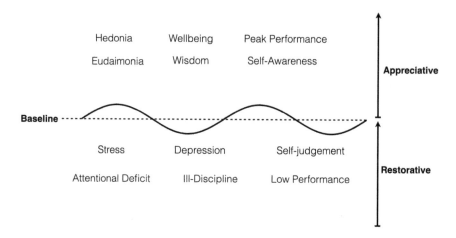

Figure 3.1 Difference between appreciative and restorative MBPs

The power of appreciative MBPs is that they direct our attention to the things that we want more of in our lives. Diana Whitney and Amanda Trosten-Bloom in their book, *The Power of Appreciative Inquiry*, state that:

> The topics we choose to study are fateful. They not only determine what we discover and learn – they actually create it.
>
> (Whitney & Trosten-Bloom, 2010, p. 58).

The more we talk about stress, the more we create stress. One of my (SR) students shared with me on how he was trying very hard to forget his ex-girlfriend. His strategy was to remind himself every morning not to think about her! Was he successful? Definitely not. It is the same with stress. When talking about stress again and again to overcome it, we are empowering the stress narrative rather than reducing it.

The belief that restorative MBPs increase happiness levels is only half the truth. This belief has generated several myths about happiness and wellbeing which we have discussed in Chapter 2. Within modern psychology today, mindfulness continues to support the restorative function by supporting people with mental health conditions. We also see the emergence of mindfulness-informed psychotherapy where mindfulness practices are used as an adjunct therapeutical tool by mental health professionals. An appreciative MBP, on the other hand, dives into human potential and allows the realization of it. It leverages on mindfulness and promotes asset-based mindset focusing on one's strengths, values, purpose, and meaning among others.

3 THE MINDFULNESS-BASED WELLBEING ENHANCEMENT (MBWE)

The MBWE was primarily designed as an appreciative MBP. The MBWE integrates the intentions of both mindfulness and positive psychology 2.0 and thus has a reciprocal influence on each other. Adaptations to the first-generation MBPs are not new as Crane et al. (2017) record that there are three kinds of adaptations already known:

1. adaptations informed by new theoretical frameworks or models that are particular to a new population or setting
2. adaptations to the program that make it more accessible, acceptable and potent for a population
3. adaptations to the program that embed MBPs in a particular context or setting

We developed the MBWE from the evidence base of the first-generation MBPs, wellbeing interventions, and our knowledge and experience to make it available to all healthy populations. We have been teaching the MBWE program since 2015 and over the years, it has undergone minimal modifications except for adaptations needed for different settings. The intentions behind this adapted form of MBP certainly satisfy the three intentions presented by Crane et al. (2017).

The participants' evaluations of the MBWE have been very positive. These evaluations suggest that the MBWE satisfies the conditions of having both *restorative* and *appreciative* qualities. The positive results found from the self-reports were:

- stress reduction
- anxiety reduction
- improved self-awareness
- increased happiness levels
- discovering deeper meaning to life

We had also primarily delivered the MBWE to healthy populations and did not target the program exclusively to people with clinical issues. However, when candidates shared their clinical challenges such as depression, anxiety, and eating disorders among others, we included them in the MBWE program when it was facilitated by a teacher who was also a mental health professional. Interestingly, the feedback from this population had been the same as the healthy populations. This also suggests that the MBWE can be delivered to all populations, even as young as 16. For populations younger than 16 years old, we delivered an adapted form of MBWE to cater to their needs. The ideal group size for the MBWE is around 20 participants. We can hypothesize that appreciative MBPs, while facilitating the realization of one's potential to flourish and thrive, could also have the potential to be restorative as well. We have also delivered adapted forms of the MBWE to audiences composed of these profiles:

- elementary and high school students
- tertiary students
- caregivers
- patients with clinical needs
- staff and employees in corporations
- leaders and management teams in schools and corporations
- the elderly

We encourage and welcome researchers around the globe to rigorously test the MBWE to see how the different populations would respond to the protocol.

4 DISTINCTIVE FEATURES OF MBWE

We compared the MBWE curriculum with the first generation MBPs (refer to Table 3.1). From the table, you will notice that the MBWE curriculum continues in the tradition of the first-generation MBPs, except for a few additional mindfulness practices and some differences and adaptations in didactic components and exercises that focuses on wellbeing.

Table 3.1 Similarities and differences between MBWE and the first-generation MBPs

	Same as first-generation MBPs	Different from first-generation MBPs
Mindfulness practices (formal and informal)	• Body scan • Awareness of breath • Sitting meditation • Mindful movements (mindful hatha, mindful stretching) • Coping breathing space (breathing space) • Mindful walking • Raisin practice • Lovingkindness meditation	• Mindful perception • Gratitude practice • Pro-social gratitude practice • Sitting with a metaphor • Mindful eating

	Same as first-generation MBPs	Different from first-generation MBPs
Didactic components and exercises	• Thoughts and feelings exercise • Poem: *The Guest House* • Nourishing and depleting review *(adapted into meaningful engagement exercise)* • Alternative viewpoints exercise *(adapted into perspective-taking exercise)*	• Wellbeing self-assessment • The brain and mindfulness • Asset-based mindset • Character strengths survey

The primary uniqueness of the MBWE is its implicit intention to generate insights in the participants about wellbeing enhancement and the *happiness paradigm*,

Happiness paradigm = Attention to the positive + Acceptance of the negative + purposeful interpretation

The primary intentions of the MBWE are not to reduce stress nor to resolve a mental health issue. MBWE participants, though they may suffer from stress or a mental health issue, walk into the MBWE as a whole person, not fragmented by their challenges or waiting for the mindfulness teacher to help them piece the fragments together to "become" whole again. This is one of the most significant and distinctive teaching intentions of the MBWE. It is the wholeness of our being that creates the capacity to discover happiness and wellbeing as a phenomenon that is always available and ready to be discovered through mindfulness.

The second uniqueness is that the insights are facilitated in a *balanced* way such that participants get to recognize the positives in their lives along with the negatives. This intention is partly powered by the philosophies of positive psychology and appreciative inquiry. Participants not only get to acknowledge, through the insights facilitated by the teacher, the negatives but also the positives. These insights allow the participants to see that their minds can learn to interpret events and situations differently with flexible attention and greater acceptance, leading to enhanced awareness.

The third uniqueness of the MBWE is that every session begins with a brief meditation on a metaphor related to the theme of the session. These meditations are guided by the teacher, thus intentionally creating an opportunity for the participants to be curious and create their own meaning from each one of them.

The fourth distinction is the conscious expansion of common humanity from within the room to the world outside through various practices, exercises, and home practices. The social dimension of mindfulness often neglected in most MBPs, and often criticized for the neglect by well-intentioned teachers, takes a prominent place in the MBWE.

The fifth distinction is the different set of session themes which are focused on conveying the intentions of the MBWE. They are:

- Session 1 – being curious
- Session 2 – holistic wellbeing
- Session 3 – response-ability
- Session 4 – focusing on what works
- Session 5 – meaningful engagement
- Session 6 – generating perspectives
- All-day retreat – self-retreat
- Session 7 – mindful living
- Session 8 – the future in the present moment

The sixth distinction is that the MBWE does not shy away from the *doing* mode (refer to section 7 of Chapter 2 for a deeper discussion). It presupposes that without doing, which is preceded by desire, one cannot be happy. The MBWE balances *being* and *doing* by allowing *being* to inform *doing*. Therefore, one can find action plans and to-dos in the MBWE, though they are approached with a non-striving attitude.

The above are the six key uniquenesses of the MBWE. As for time investment, the eight-week MBWE follows the same time investment as most MBPs except for the all-day retreat which can be between four to six hours. In total, there are eight sessions of 2.5 hours each and a 4–6-hour all-day retreat.

As you would have already noticed, the MBWE was developed with the prototypical MBPs as its foundations and inspiration, though its structure ascends toward the realization of human flourishing, or wellbeing enhancement in the jargon of the MBWE. While it will be preposterous to claim that everyone would realize their potential in eight weeks, the goal behind any MBP is to prepare the individual for a journey of a lifetime. At the end of the MBWE program, we hope participants begin their journey of a lifetime of wellbeing and not assume that they have reached a destination. Wellbeing or happiness is a paradigm, not a state.

5 MBWE TEACHER COMPETENCIES

If you are a certified mindfulness teacher, trained to teach eight-week MBPs, such as the MBSR or MBCT, the MBWE structure and facilitation methods may not be something very new to you. The key differences are in the didactic components, exercises, and inquiry skills. The most significant differentiated skill is the way the inquiry is facilitated to generate insights. This could be a gigantic shift for some teachers who have been trained in a diagnostic mindset of traditional scientific disciplines. Nevertheless, we invite certified mindfulness teachers trained to teach eight-week MBPs to consult us if in doubt. In our opinion, to teach the MBWE is not rocket science for a certified mindfulness teacher, as along as the teacher has embodied mindfulness through sustained practice and has an experiential and theoretical appreciation of wellbeing and happiness. Therefore, it is our belief that already certified and trained mindfulness teachers of any eight-week MBP could readily use this book as a manual to start delivering the MBWE with no or minimal guidance. Otherwise, it should not take more than a year to complete the training to teach the MBWE.

The increasing concern over the lengthy period of training for MBP teachers is certainly valid. We have also recently noticed that experts are challenging the need for long training periods which can be shortened by changing the program structure with mentorship and supervision (Woods & Rockman, 2021). We support this discourse as it is important to create more mindfulness teachers within a shorter period of time without compromising teaching standards. We have been conducting a mindfulness teacher-training program, based on the MBWE, for several years, while adhering to the program standards of the International Mindfulness Teachers Association (IMTA). The length of our training is a minimum of a year, including mentorship and supervision.

6 PREPARING FOR THE MBWE SESSIONS

Intake Process

The intake process is a very important component of almost all MBPs that help us determine if a candidate is suitable to attend an MBP. With the MBWE, we follow the same guidelines as observed by the first-generation MBPs. The intake process allows the teacher to assess the participant's ability to contain affect; listen and respond in the present; utilize instructional audio tapes and follow classroom instruction; remain in the classroom; practice gentle stretching or similar activities; and organize thoughts, manage logistics, and time commitment (Dobkin, 2011).

The intake process involves of the completion and submission by candidates of the intake form and the informed consent form. Samples of these two forms are in appendix 1. These forms will need to be adapted further to include the teacher's professional background and statutory laws in the candidate's state. We would recommend that you treat the samples as guides rather than something ready for use. In some states, additional personal data privacy use and electronic communication consent may be required. When in doubt, please obtain legal advice.

The intake form allows you to get to know the candidate's personal information such as contact details, occupation, marital status, health, and reasons for attending the MBWE among others. This information helps you to know your participants better and to readily connect with them. The exclusion criteria are necessary too so that you are aware of who might not benefit from the program. The exclusion list includes problems and conditions that would make a candidate potentially unsuitable for the MBWE program such as:

- Psychological safety in a group
- Active substance dependence
- Experienced mindfulness practitioner
- Not proficient in the language of delivery
- Issues that may create challenges when physically in the room
- Inability to attend all the sessions (missing up to two sessions is permissible)
- Brain injury or damage
- Recent loss, bereavement, or crisis★
- Severe anxiety★
- Currently receiving psychological therapy★
- Current or past psychosis★
- Risk of suicide★
- Trauma★
- Depression★

Those conditions listed above with an ★ would require written permission from the candidate's mental health provider if they wish to join the program. In addition, if there is anything else that may require a deeper conversation, the teacher must ask the candidate to clarify whether she can be included into the program without any doubt. For example, one of my (SR) participants stated that she had sustained a spinal injury. We then discussed various ways how she could care for herself while continuing to participate in the sessions. During the mindful movement practices, I would also demonstrate adaptations for her to consider to care for her back. You would have also noticed that it is grounds for exclusion if a candidate is already an experienced mindfulness practitioner. The doubt in this case is whether an experienced mindfulness or meditation practitioner is going to derive benefits from any MBP. If you can ascertain that there is a clear need, then such a candidate could possibly be admitted to the MBWE. So what do we do with candidates who are not suitable for the MBWE? We shall discuss individual coaching and other options for some of these challenges in Chapter 6.

Along with the intake form, the informed consent form would also have to be submitted. This form is for the purpose of indemnifying the teacher and consenting fully to participate in the program. This allows the participant to give their full consent by having all the necessary information such as the period of engagement, expectations of the program, and also the freedom to withdraw from the program at any time.

Once a candidate expresses interest and agrees to participate in the MBWE, these two forms are sent to them for their submission. Once they have completed the forms and sent them to you, you would then review them for possible exclusion and with a clear plan on how to inform and support those who are excluded.

Learning Materials

When it comes to learning materials, there are essential and non-essential ones. Essential materials are absolutely necessary for the program and are non-negotiable.

The first essential material would be a handout that contains two important components: a list of weekly practices and a home practice log sheet for the participants (refer to samples in figures 3.2 and 3.3). In total, there should be enough practice items and log sheets for eight weeks. These could be neatly organized into eight session themes in the handout or journal.

The second essential material would be audio and/or video guides for relevant home practices. It is important that participants are supported with audio and/or video files that are available for downloading before the program commences. These files can be shared via flash drives, file hosting services, online video platforms, smartphone apps, and tablet computer apps among others.

The non-essential components would be books, videos, podcasts, or articles related to mindfulness, happiness, wellbeing among others. We advise that this should be used sparingly and only when necessary. These non-essential components can be a distraction at times, given that the primary commitment and essential engagement, on the part of the participants would be the formal and informal mindfulness practices. The mindfulness practices are the foundational components of any MBP pedagogy.

Home Practices - Week 1

Formal Practices	Informal Practices	Exercises/Explorations/ Readings
Daily - Body Scan with Audio Track*	Daily - Practice Mindful Perception with Audio Track*	Read - 7 attitudes of mindfulness (pg 6-7 of Workbook)
	Daily - To eat One Meal with Mindfulness	Read - Day 1 of Mindfulness in 8 Days
	Daily - One routine activity with Mindfulness	

Figure 3.2 Sample of week 1 home practices

Mindfulness-Based Wellbeing Enhancement (MBWE)

Journal   Week 1

Day	Comments or Observations from your Home Practices
Day: Practice(s):	
Day: Practice(s):	
Day: Practice(s):	
Day: Practice(s):	
Day: Practice(s):	
Day: Practice(s):	
Day: Practice(s):	

Figure 3.3 Sample of week 1 home practice log sheet

Course Information

Sending the course information to the participants is the final preparatory step before the program begins. This could be done via an email or any other preferred method of providing information. Helpful information for the participants would include:

- Dates and times of all the nine sessions
- Venue details and directions including parking
- Recommended dress code
- Mealtime recommendations on the day of the session
- Personal essentials to be brought to the sessions
- Materials given to the participants
- Audio and video guide files
- A short article introducing mindfulness

7 THE MBWE SESSION PLANS

In this section, we present the sessions of the MBWE program, one by one. This will give the teacher a structure and will guide her to deliver the MBWE. We will also share the teaching intentions and facilitation methods for each session component. In total, there are nine sessions delivered within an eight-week period.

Although we present session plans with recommended facilitation methods, it is important for the teacher to be present and change styles and techniques when necessary. The only condition that would have to be adhered to would be the exercise of compassion by the teacher with all participants no matter what they bring into the room. With embodied presence and compassion, we can adapt the session plan and also plan cultural adaptations (the topic of Chapter 7) in advance.

In Figure 3.4, we present the three layers of inquiry to show how we gradually deploy the layers of inquiry over the eight weeks. Chapter 5 will present the methods of facilitating the three-layered inquiry more elaborately. We do not advocate a rigid structure to the facilitation of the layers of inquiry, yet the diagram gives an idea as to how we could prepare ourselves for the session. Though in reality, it requires us to respond to what happens in the present moment in each session.

It is important that you study Chapters 4 and 5 after reading this chapter. We will be referring to concepts by name or very briefly within the session plans. You will learn more in Chapters 4 and 5 how to facilitate the session components and inquiry.

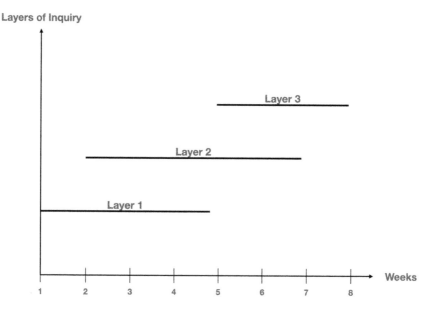

Figure 3.4 Progressive deployment of the three-layered inquiry

Only the session plans are provided in this section. The practice scripts, metaphors, poems and exercises can be found in the appendices. Here is a summary of the appendices which you can refer to along with the session plans:

1. Appendix 1: Intake Process
2. Appendix 2: Scripts for Moving into Specific Postures
3. Appendix 3: Scripts for Formal Mindfulness Practices
4. Appendix 4: Scripts for Informal Mindfulness Practices
5. Appendix 5: Metaphors, Visual Illusions and Stories
6. Appendix 6: Poems
7. Appendix 7: Exercises

Session 1: Being Curious

Theme

- Recognizing that we are on autopilot can be a great way to direct our energies within
- Being curious helps us to let go of judgment and to learn from within

Intention

- To slowly ease the participants into the experience of mindfulness by cultivating curiosity
- To develop new ways of looking at the familiar, the old and the known

Component	Agenda	Time	Facilitation guide
1	Formal welcome • Introductions • Guidelines • Program brief	20m	As the participants walk into the room, the teacher welcomes them informally and settles them on their mats. After the participants take a seat on their mats and at the stipulated commencement time, the teacher welcomes all participants with a 1-min breathing practice. The teacher introduces herself and gets them to introduce themselves. A few questions that can be asked are: • *What brought you to this program?* • *What do you wish to gain from this program?* After the introductions, the teacher shares the guidelines for the program that includes confidentiality, self-care, speaking is optional, not giving advice, silencing devices and attendance recording. Thereafter, the teacher shares how the MBWE is an inside-out approach to learning where we lean on our *own* practice, experience, and insights as opposed to entirely depending on someone else's practice, experience, and insights. It is important to keep this session brief.
2	Siting with a metaphor: the autopilot	5m	The teacher invites participants to close their eyes or to have a soft gaze. She facilitates the metaphor "The autopilot" followed by a 1-min silence.

(Continued)

(Continued)

Component	Agenda	Time	Facilitation guide
3	Centering practice	5m	The teacher invites participants to take a standing posture with eyes closed or with a soft gaze and guides them through a centering practice.
4	Being curious: visual illusion • Young woman or old woman	15m	The teacher shows a visual illusion, "Young woman or old woman" and invites participants to share what they see in the image. It is common for participants to see just one at a time, either the old or the young woman. And then she invites participants to bring curiosity to find a way to see the second woman (i.e. the old woman if they saw the young one first and vice versa).
			The teacher then puts them in groups of three to discuss about what insights they gather from this activity for about 5 minutes. A sample question could be: *What insights did you gather about the mind from this activity?*
			The teacher could then invite participants to share anything that stood out in the discussions as a plenary. The teacher could close the session by teaching briefly on autopilot, curiosity, and how mindfulness helps us be aware of our thoughts, emotions, urges, and sensations.
5	Mindful perception practice • Guided practice and inquiry	20m	The teacher invites participants to sit on the mat and guides them through this practice. After the practice, the teacher could facilitate a layer-1 inquiry with a focus on curiosity.
5	Raisin practice • Guided practice and inquiry • Self-practice	30m	The teacher hands out a raisin to each participant and guides them through the practice. At the end of the practice, the teacher facilitates a layer-1 inquiry as a plenary focusing on autopilot.

Component	Agenda	Time	Facilitation guide
6	Body scan practice • Demonstration of moving into a supine posture • Guided practice and inquiry	50m	The teacher demonstrates how to move into a supine posture and back to a sitting posture and then opens the floor for clarification questions. Once this is done, she guides them into the supine posture before guiding them through the body scan practice. At the end of the practice, the teacher gets them to form groups of three and facilitates a layer-1 inquiry. It is important for the teacher to keep the focus on this layer of inquiry in this session so that participants cultivate curiosity in their present moment experience about sensations, emotions, thoughts, and urges.
7	Home practice 1. *Daily – to practice mindful perception* 2. *Daily – to eat one meal mindfully* 3. *Daily – to practice body scan* 4. *Daily – to perform one routine activity mindfully* 5. *Read – seven attitudes of mindfulness (optional)*	5m	The teacher distributes the journal at this point and guides them to the page where the weekly home practices are stated and briefly explains them. After this, she guides them to the weekly home practice log asking them to write down what they noticed every day after each practice or observations on their life on that day. It is important to state that the journal is private to the participant and at no point during the program would they be asked to show their journals to other participants or the teacher. The teacher bids farewell and wishes them well.

Total Time 2h 30m

Session 2: Holistic Wellbeing

Theme

• Being aware that our intentions are a critical contributor to how attention is directed
• Learning to recognize the habitual patterns of negativity biases

Intention

- To enable participants to see wellbeing as something relational and dependent
- To appreciate that wellbeing is multi-dimensional
- To know how attention can be brought flexibly to aspects of our experiences with mindfulness training

Component	Agenda	Time	Facilitation guide
1	• Welcome • Sitting with a metaphor: a car without a steering wheel	10m	Teacher welcomes everyone briefly and settles them in a sitting posture on their mats. She invites them to look at the "A car without a steering wheel" illustration' and asks a question: *Could I be this car or perhaps not?* This question generates insight into the "sense of direction," which is the purpose of the steering wheel. The teacher then asks, *"Do I know what I want?"* and builds her own insights into the value of being aware of one's own purpose in life and connect it to our desires and goals for wellbeing.
2	Body scan practice • Guided practice and inquiry	50m	The teacher guides the participants into a supine posture and guides the body scan. After the end of the practice, she facilitates the layer 1 and layer 2 inquiry. One specific difference would be to guide the inquiry toward the neglected aspects of what is working well and how gratitude could be brought to the parts of the body that they noticed to be pleasant or no difficult sensations at all. She closes the inquiry by briefly summarizing what was shared in the room and shares that we can also bring attention to what is working well as well as the uncomfortable sensations in the body.
3	Home practice review	15m	The teacher gets the participants to form groups of three and invites them to share how the home practices went for them including what went well. After which, the teacher can invite the participants to share some key highlights from the discussion.

Component	Agenda	Time	Facilitation guide
4	My wellbeing intentions • Assessment using floor activity	25m	The purpose of this exercise is to set wellbeing intentions based on what is working well and what could be better. The teacher facilitates the "My wellbeing intentions" exercise and closes the activity by sharing that we can bring attention to what is working well, and what is not, with our wellbeing. She shares that mindfulness helps in directing our attention with intention to acknowledge what we already have and what we want for our wellbeing. It is important that the teacher stays away from any *doing* mode discussions as the mind has the tendency to react when intentions or desires rise. By keeping to this guideline, we teach participants that a desire can remain as a thought without having to perform an action to realize it.
5	Ways to sit	15m	The teacher demonstrates and shares how to move into a comfortable and firm sitting posture that allows one to be alert. She shows how to use props like a cushion, a rolled yoga mat, or the wall for support. At this point the teacher should not favor one adapted posture over another but emphasize that the participants choose what works for them and is conducive to their wellbeing.
6	Awareness of breath practice • Guided practice and inquiry	20m	The teacher settles the participants in a comfortable and firm seated posture. She then guides a 10-minute awareness of breath practice and facilitates a layer-1 inquiry. The focus of the inquiry could be about curiosity and what they noticed.
7	Didactic teaching: the negativity biased brain	10m	The purpose of this component is to allow participants to see that our brains could respond from an inherent negativity bias. And through mindfulness training, we can learn to direct our attention to the positive.

(Continued)

(Continued)

Component	Agenda	Time	Facilitation guide
			The teacher shares and facilitates how our brain has an inherent negativity bias, developed from the times we were in the forests always looking out for predators. This heightens our flight, fight, and freeze responses in the amygdala. And that we can slowly train the brain to bring flexible attention to the positive, like the way a torch can be used to shine light on the objects that we want to see.
			The teacher explains how the "Pleasant experience journaling exercise," which is one of the home practices for this week, is done and connects this to the brain and torchlight metaphor.
			[Alternative] An alternative approach to open this segment would be to facilitate the "Like a torchlight" metaphor before touching on the brain's negativity bias and bringing flexible attention to the positives.
8	Home practice 1. *Daily – to practice body scan* 2. *Daily – to practice 10-min awareness of breath meditation* 3. *Daily – to journal pleasant experiences* 4. *Daily – to perform one routine activity mindfully*	5m	The teacher briefly explains the rest of the home practices and bids farewell.

Total Time 2h 30m

Session 3: Response-Ability

Theme

- Responding with flexible attention and acceptance allows us to make choices that are aligned with our intentions

Intention

- To recognize that minds possess the ability to respond
- To appreciate the connection of the mechanism of acceptance with response-ability
- To experience how mindfulness can be brought to movements

Component	Agenda	Time	Facilitation guide
1	• Welcome • Sitting with a metaphor: shoot and look or look and shoot	10m	The teacher welcomes everyone briefly and settles them in a sitting posture on their mats. She invites them to close their eyes or have a soft gaze and shares the "Shoot and look, or look and shoot" metaphor and ends it with a question: *Could such a dilemma be in our lives? What are its consequences? Are we responding or reacting?*
2	Sitting meditation practice • Guided practice and inquiry	45m	The teacher settles the participants in a comfortable and firm seated posture. She guides a 30-minute sitting meditation practice and facilitates a layer-1 and 2 inquiry focusing on response-ability.
3	Home practice review • Review pleasant experience journal • Link insights to flexible attention and the brain	20m	The teacher gets the participants to form groups of four and invites them to share about what they noticed in the process of journaling in their pleasant experience journal. The teacher then shares how our brains can be trained to be flexible in bringing attention to what is working in our lives, including the pleasant and positive. The teacher then links to the homework for the week to journal the unpleasant experiences instead of the pleasant ones.

(Continued)

(Continued)

Component	Agenda	Time	Facilitation guide
4	Mindful movement practice • Guided practice and inquiry	45m	The teacher invites the participants to a standing posture on their mats and shares the guidelines for this practice. And then she guides the mindful movement practice for 30 minutes. Thereafter, the teacher arranges them into groups of three before facilitating the layer-1 and 2 inquiry. The focus of the inquiry could be how the mindful movement is different from exercise, yoga, or calisthenics. The teacher briefly shares how mindfulness can be brought to any daily movements and to be aware of the body's ability to respond.
5	Didactic teaching: the brain and mindfulness • 3–6–9 clap *or* Stroop effect activity • Amygdala (3 fs) and the pre-frontal cortex	15m	The purpose of this component is to appreciate the mechanism of acceptance and how it allows us to take a pause and respond, instead of reacting. In this segment, the teacher facilitates the 3–6–9 clap or Stroop effect activity. She shares how our brains have been programmed to react through the 3fs (fight, flight, and freeze) and they can be trained to respond if acceptance could be brought to the stimuli. The teacher briefly presents a simple image of a brain indicating the location of the amygdala and pre-frontal cortex to show how mindfulness reduces the activity in the amygdala and increases the activity in the pre-frontal cortex. This understanding of the mind, its ability to respond with mindfulness is then linked to wellbeing.
6	Coping breathing space • Guided practice	10m	The teacher invites the participants to adopt a standing posture on their mats and guides the A, B, and C of the 3-minute coping breathing space. After the practice, the teacher shares how this practice can be used when we experience unpleasant events or when in unpleasant situations to ground oneself to be able to respond than to react.

Component	Agenda	Time	Facilitation guide
7	Home practice 1. *Daily – to alternate the practice between sitting meditation and mindful movement* 2. *Three times daily – to practice coping breathing space* 3. *Daily – to journal unpleasant experiences*	5m	The teacher briefly explains the home practices and bids farewell.
	Total Time 2h 30m		

Session 4: Focusing on What Works

Theme

- An asset-based mindset allows one to see what is already available within oneself and in our lives
- The social dimension of mindfulness involves being compassionate and kind to oneself and others
- Knowing one's happiness disposition helps us to be intentional

Intention

- To empower participants to bring acceptance to the negative
- To cultivate self-compassion and being kind to others
- To know my happiness disposition

Component	Agenda	Time	Facilitation guide
1	• Welcome • Sitting with a metaphor: camera and lenses	10m	The teacher welcomes everyone briefly and settles them in a sitting posture on their mats. She invites them to close their eyes or have a soft gaze and facilitates the "Camera and lenses" metaphor and ends it with a question: *How might we bring this into our lives? Are we focusing on what's working well in our lives?*

(Continued)

(Continued)

Component	Agenda	Time	Facilitation guide
2	Lovingkindness meditation practice • Guided practice and inquiry	20m	After a short period of silence, the teacher guides the participants in the Lovingkindness meditation and facilitates the layer-1 inquiry and focuses on the self and other-compassion.
3	Home practice review • Review unpleasant experience journal • Link insights to acceptance and the brain	15m	The teacher gets the participants to form groups of three and invites them to share what they noticed in the unpleasant experience journal. She then encourages them to explore together in the plenary on the emotions and thoughts when they recorded the pleasant experiences vs the unpleasant experiences. The teacher then shares how our brains can be trained to bring acceptance to the negatives while bringing attention to the positives. The teacher then links it to the next component.
4	Asset-based mindset • Recognizing "What is working": creating a list of things that are working well • Shifting paradigms I activity • Paper folding activity	20m	In this didactic segment, the teacher shares about how our minds tend to look at what is not there in our lives, a deficit-based mindset, instead of what is there, asset-based mindset. She will invite participants to grab a piece of paper to list things that are already there in their lives such as strengths, opportunities, assets, etc. The teacher shares how we lose sight of what we have and preoccupy ourselves with things we do not have. She invites the possibility of bringing attention to these as well and to perhaps include a sense of gratitude for what we already have. Asset-based mindset is associated with enhanced wellbeing.

Component	Agenda	Time	Facilitation guide
			The teacher facilitates the "Shifting paradigms I" activity and demonstrates how when our paradigm is shifted, we can create meaning out of the meaningless.
			Thereafter, she facilitates the paper folding activity. The purpose of this activity is to demonstrate how neuroplasticity works and we can create new paradigms through mindfulness training.
5	Sitting meditation practice • Guided practice and inquiry	45m	The teacher settles the participants in a comfortable and firm seated posture.
			She guides a 25-minute sitting meditation practice with a focus on acceptance of the negative, unfavorable, and the unexpected. She then facilitates a layer-2 inquiry.
6	Didactic teaching: Integrated Wellbeing Model (IWM) • Eudaimonia and hedonia • The five selves	10m	The teacher shares about how human beings may have a stronger disposition toward Eudaimonia or Hedonia.
			She shares that by knowing our disposition, we can better understand how we can be happy instead of trying to be someone else. She presents the five selves and how people can find fulfillment by setting intentions aligned with one's disposition.
7	Coping breathing space practice	5m	The teacher invites the participants to assume a standing posture on their mats and guides them through the 3-minute coping breathing space.
8	Mindful walking practice • Guided practice and inquiry	20m	The teacher invites the participants to assume a standing posture. She requests everyone to roll up the mats and place them aside to make space for this activity.

(Continued)

(Continued)

Component	Agenda	Time	Facilitation guide
			She then guides a 10-minute mindful walking practice followed by facilitating a layer-1 and 2 inquiry. She could focus the inquiry on attention, acceptance, and compassion.
9	Home practice	5m	The teacher briefly explains the home practices and requests each participant to bring a small snack that can be eaten within 5 minutes to the next session. She may share some options for the snacks to help the participants. She bids them farewell.
	1. *Daily – to practice asset-based mindset*		
	2. *Daily - to alternate the practice between lovingkindness meditation and mindful walking*		
	3. *Daily – to practice kindness to oneself and others*		
	4. *Daily – to practice sitting meditation*		
	5. *Daily – to practice coping breathing space*		
	Total Time 2h 30m		

Session 5: Meaningful Engagement

Theme

- By allowing doing to arise from our being, we can have more meaningful engagements

Intention

- To bring acceptance to what we cannot control
- To discover one's character strengths so that one can increase meaningful engagements

Component	Agenda	Time	Facilitation guide
1	• Welcome • Sitting with a metaphor: are you a passenger?	10m	The teacher welcomes everyone briefly and settles them in a sitting posture on their mats. She invites them to close their eyes or have a soft gaze and shares the "Are you a passenger?" metaphor and allows a few moments of silence.
2	Body scan practice • Guided practice	20m	The teacher invites the participants into a supine posture and guides the body scan. The body scan would be shorter with less guidance and longer gaps of silence.
3	Home practice review • Review asset-based mindset and practicing kindness	15m	The teacher gets the participants to form pairs and invites them to share about what they noticed when cultivating an asset-based mindset and practicing kindness. The teacher then invites a few people into plenary dialogue to share anything that was common in each paired conversation. Their insights are linked to wellbeing.
4	Poem: *The Guest House* by Rumi • Recitation and inquiry • Explore acceptance with four types of outcomes	25m	The teacher refers the participants to the poem, *The Guest House*, in the journal, and then recites the poem line by line giving a 4–5-second silence between each line. If the poem is not in the journal, the teacher can distribute printed copies of it to the participants. After which, she invites participants, in a plenary dialogue, to explore interpreting the poem before she encourages them to study the poem again with the vision of acceptance. She may compare the difference between resignation vs acceptance of a situation that we cannot control. In the last 5–10 minutes of this segment, she shares information about the four types of outcomes in our lives and how acceptance allows us to respond to these outcomes with equanimity.

(Continued)

(Continued)

Component	Agenda	Time	Facilitation guide
5	Character strengths discovery exercise	15m	The teacher shares the 24 character strengths on a projector or distributes them in a printed sheet to all participants. She asks the participants to pick the top 10 character strengths that appear to best define their personality. The teacher gives them 3 minutes to choose them. And then she asks them to select the top 5 from the chosen 10.
			[Alternative] An alternative approach to facilitate this would be to request the participants to obtain a paid report from the VIA Institute on Character's website prior to this session. If a teacher chooses this approach, all required information and instruction would have to be provided to the participants during the previous session's assignment of home practices.
			The teacher then pairs up the participants to share their top strength with each other and one or two examples in their lives when they demonstrated this strength.
			She than summarizes how the discovery of these character strengths help one to deepen meaning in life and be happy. The teacher shares the fact that she will be revisiting this topic toward the end of the session.
6	Mindful movement practice • Guided practice and inquiry	30m	The teacher invites the participants to take a standing posture on their mats and reminds them of the guidelines for mindful movement.
			She guides the mindful movement practice for 20 minutes and asks them to form pairs before facilitating the layer-2 and 3 inquiry.
			After this she invites participants, in a plenary dialogue, to share how being aware of our thoughts, emotions, sensations and actions can help us to be happy.

Component	Agenda	Time	Facilitation guide
7	Mindful eating practice	10m	The teacher requests the participants to take out their snack. She shares the attitudes that we can bring into the eating process, such as curiosity, and deepening attention by engaging all the five senses. She gives them five minutes to consume the snack.
			Sometimes participants may forget to bring a snack or the snack they brought is not edible anymore. Therefore, it is helpful if the teacher could bring a couple of sealed raisins or plain crackers to this session if this happens.
8	Meaningful engagement exercise • Animals within rhino metaphor • Exploring daily activities exercise • Pleasurable and mastery type of activities exercise	20m	The teacher facilitates the "Animals within rhino" metaphor by showing the image for just one second. Participants may notice just one or two animals. And it would usually be the rhino that would catch their attention. After which, she reveals the image again and asks participants to notice the animals within the rhino. The teacher shares about the phenomenon of biased attention, choosing to see things based on its own biases thus limiting perspectives. And when there is constraint in terms of time and other resources, our minds would jump straight into a conclusion. She then asks about how our attention to priorities can be hampered by the limitations of time, biases, etc. The teacher links this biased attention to lower levels of happiness and wellbeing.
			The teacher then invites participants to complete the "Exploring daily activities" exercise followed by "Pleasurable and mastery type of activities exercise." Each of these are facilitated and linked to meaningful engagements and happiness.

(Continued)

(Continued)

Component	Agenda	Time	Facilitation guide
9	Home practice 1. *Daily – to explore engaging with meaningful activities* 2. *Daily – to reflect on a character strength/value that you had embodied on that day* 3. *Daily – to practice kindness to oneself and others* 4. *Daily – to practice mindful eating* 5. *Daily – to alternate the practice between body scan and mindful movement*	5m	The teacher briefly explains the home practices and then bids farewell.

Total Time 2h 30m

Session 6: Generating Perspectives

Theme

- Our living revolves around perspectives of truths more than truth itself. Therefore, thoughts are not absolute nor are they facts. They are interpretations based on many other dependent factors
- Gratitude helps us to acknowledge what we have in our lives, thereby shifting the perspectives of our lives
- People are interconnected like a web. When one part of the web is impacted, another part experiences the effect

Intention

- To recognize that different perspectives can be taken when one sees thoughts as not absolute

- To recognize that one can interpret an experience differently
- To recognize that people are relational beings
- To explore kindness to oneself and others.
- To be grateful for what we already have

Component	Agenda	Time	Facilitation guide
1	• Welcome • Sitting with a metaphor: clouds in the sky	5m	The teacher welcomes everyone briefly and settles them in a sitting posture on their mats. She invites them to close their eyes or have a soft gaze and shares the "Clouds in the sky" metaphor and allows a few moments of silence.
2	Sitting meditation practice • Guided practice and inquiry	45m	The teacher guides a 30-minute sitting meditation practice with a focus on how thoughts are like clouds in the sky of awareness. She facilitates the layer-2 and 3 inquiry and links to how thoughts are not absolute.
3	Home practice review • Review meaningful engagement activity	15m	The teacher gets the participants to form groups of three and invites them to share how the last week went when they engaged in meaningful activities. The teacher invites a few people in plenary dialogue to discuss what was common or uncommon in the group conversations and what are some key insights they got about their wellbeing.
4	Perspective-taking • The blind men and the elephant metaphor activity • Perspective-taking exercise	30m	The teacher shares the *gist* of the *Blind Men and the Elephant* poem and asks the participants as to how might it be relevant to our lives. And then she facilitates the perspective-taking exercise as a plenary activity. The teacher closes this segment by affirming that we have the flexibility to interpret events purposefully with healthier perspectives that are conductive to our wellbeing.

(Continued)

(Continued)

Component	Agenda	Time	Facilitation guide
5	Coping breathing space practice • Guided practice	5m	The teacher invites the participants to assume a standing posture on their mats and guides them through the 3-minute coping breathing space.
6	Social mindfulness: we live in an interconnected world	15m	The teacher gets the participants to form groups of four and shows them the statement "We live in an interconnected world" either written on board or on a projection. She invites them to purposefully interpret what this statement means to them and writes their points concisely on a large sheet of paper. After a few minutes of discussion, she invites each group to hang their paper on the wall and invites all participants to walk and view the gallery of responses.
			The teacher closes this segment by affirming how kindness, compassion, and empathy strengthen human relationships as we are relational beings, and how we contribute to each other's happiness.
7	Lovingkindness meditation • Guided practice	15m	After a short period of silence, the teacher guides the participants through the Lovingkindness meditation and facilitates the layer-1 and 2 inquiry directing the exploration toward compassion and kindness to oneself and others.
8	Five-finger gratitude practice • Guided practice	10m	The teacher guides the five-finger gratitude practice and facilitates the layer-1 and 2 inquiry. The inquiry could be about gratitude for what we have, kindness to people around us, and the environment for providing us with resources or pleasant experiences.

Component	Agenda	Time	Facilitation guide
9	Home practice	10m	The teacher briefly explains the home practices and shares the preparation needed for the upcoming self-retreat. She briefly explains what is going to happen in the retreat including logistics. The teacher specifically shares the information that phones need to be switched off and put away during the session and that for any urgent matters, to request family members to contact the teacher instead. She bids farewell.
	1. *Daily – to practice any one of the three formal practices*		
	2. *Daily – to continue engaging with meaningful activities*		
	3. *Daily – to explore perspective taking in situations*		
	4. *Daily – to alternate the practice between lovingkindness meditation and coping breathing space*		
	5. *Daily – to practice the five-finger gratitude*		
	6. *Daily – to practice kindness*		

Total Time 2h 30m

The Day of Mindfulness: Self-Retreat

Theme

- A half-day silent retreat of 4–6 hours engaging with mindfulness practices

Intention

- To facilitate the mindfulness practices experienced by the participants and being with oneself

Component	Agenda (4 hours)	Time
1	Welcome	10m
2	Setting norms	5m
3	(Strike the chime)Centering	5m
4	Sitting meditation	30m
5	Mindful movement	30m
6	Gratitude for self and others practice	10m

(Continued)

(Continued)

Component	Agenda (4 hours)	Time
7	Body scan	30m
8	Mindful eating + toilet break	30m
9	Mindful walking	20m
10	Mountain, lake, or tree meditation	15m
11	Mindful stretching	10m
12	Lovingkindness meditation	10m
13	Mindful walking with curiosity(Strike the chime)	15m
14	Transitioning out of silence	10m
15	Closing	10m
	Total Time	**4h**

The self-retreat, as we have chosen to call it, is also called the day of mindfulness or the all-day retreat. It is usually held between the sixth and seventh sessions. The self-retreat is a silent retreat where the only source of intentional sounds would be the voice of guidance by the teacher and the chime. The teacher will have to be well-prepared for this session as you would see that there are no extended breaks within. She guides each practice with seamless transitions as one moves to the next practice. There will not be any formal inquiry in this session. It is also acceptable for you, the teacher, to invite past MBWE participants to join these sessions if there are seats available, as an intact group of participants is not a requirement for this self-retreat.

New Practices in the Agenda

There are two components in the agenda that could be new to the participants which are the mountain meditation and mindful stretching. The sample scripts for these practices can found in appendix 4. The mountain meditation could be replaced with either lake or tree meditation if the teacher so prefers. These meditations are visualizations and are technically not mindfulness meditations, though they allow practitioners to see oneself as stable, grounded, and whole.

Facilitation Guidelines

The teacher welcomes everyone briefly and settles them in a sitting posture on their mats. She acknowledges the past MBWE participants in the room so that the current cohort are aware of the reason for having new faces in the room if any. She explains the broad structure of the day, without getting into the specific agenda components and reiterates that self-care is of prime importance during the session. She tells the audience where the restrooms are and that people are free to take a break anytime they need it without having to obtain permission from her. If the experiences during the session become intolerable, participants are empowered to open their eyes, use the breath as an anchor, walk toward the back of the room and stand or sit or drink some water. Participants can also approach the teacher when they feel overwhelmed. All the participants are then invited to place their personal belongings at the back of the room or away from everyone and return to a seated position on their mat. We recommend that the participants place their water bottles beside them to stay hydrated throughout the session.

The teacher presents the norms for the session, which would be to:

- avoid eye contact with each other so that it supports an inward focus
- refrain from using any devices, talking, or reading
- refrain from communicating with each other, verbally or non-verbally
- switch off their personal devices and put them away

After sharing the norms, the session begins with the sound of the chime which would only be struck again right after the mindful walking with curiosity practice. The teacher facilitates each of the items in the agenda one by one seamlessly, while reiterating self-care throughout the session.

The silence is broken after the end of mindful walking with curiosity practice. To transition the participants out of silence, the teacher settles the participants in pairs sitting with their back facing each other, looking in opposite directions. One person would be asked to share with the other person for 5 minutes how the retreat experience was by just whispering over the shoulder. After 5 minutes, the teacher instructs the other person to share his experience for 5 minutes. The teacher shares that she would keep an eye on the time and will let them know when the 5 minutes are up. After this conversation, the teacher invites all of them as a plenary, to share her parting instructions before leaving the retreat venue. In this final segment, the teacher acknowledges the unusual state that they could possibly be in and that this could possibly result also in unusual reactions when going back to everyday life. The teacher suggests being mindful if they are driving, or operating any equipment immediately after the self-retreat. She also proposes that the participants minimize sensorial stimulation for the rest of the day as well as avoid alcohol or partying. The last thing to be mindful about is the way participants share the self-retreat experience with the people in their lives. The teacher advises sharing only when asked and not to sensationalize it unduly.

Session 7: Mindful Living

Theme

* Living mindfully means that we can be happy with bringing attention to the positive, acceptance to the negative and interpreting experiences purposefully and differently

Intention

* To recognize that thoughts are not facts
* To recognize that interpretations have an impact on our wellbeing
* To learn to interpret experiences with flexibility
* To intentionally plan and prioritize one's wellbeing

Component	Agenda	Time	Facilitation guide
1	• Welcome • Sitting with a metaphor: rope and snake	10m	The teacher welcomes everyone briefly and settles them in a sitting posture on their mats. She invites them to close their eyes or have a soft gaze and shares the "Rope and snake" metaphor and allows a few moments of silence.
2	Home practice review	10m	The teacher gets the participants to form groups of three and invites them to share what has been working well for them (including practices and exercises) since the time they started this program.
3	Five-finger pro-social gratitude practice • Guided practice and inquiry	15m	The teacher guides the Five-finger pro-social gratitude practice and facilitates the layer-2 inquiry with specific focus on how it was different from the experience with the Five-finger gratitude practice.
4	Mindful movement practice • Guided practice	20m	The teacher invites the participants to a standing posture on their mats and reminds them of the guidelines. And then she guides a *shorter* mindful movement practice.

Component	Agenda	Time	Facilitation guide
5	Sitting meditation practice • Guided practice and inquiry	40m	The teacher guides a 20-minute sitting meditation practice with guided focus on how thoughts are like clouds in the sky of awareness. She then facilitates a layer-2 and 3 inquiry specifically focusing on how flexibility of attention and acceptance can aid one to be happy.
6	Thoughts are not facts Exercise: John the janitor • Guided activity and inquiry	15m	The teacher facilitates the John the janitor activity and facilitates an inquiry about what they noticed when each of the statement was made. The teacher shares how our minds report an assumption as a fact and link it to how thoughts are not facts and how interpretations impact our wellbeing.
7	My first month of wellbeing	20m	The teacher invites the participants to reflect on what has worked for them among the various practices and exercises and recollects the intentions from the meaningful engagements activity. She invites them to start thinking about what is needed to sustain their wellbeing plan in the future. The teacher then directs their attention to "My first month of wellbeing" sheet to explain the homework.
8	Lovingkindness meditation	10m	After a short period of silence, the teacher guides the participants through the Lovingkindness meditation.
9	Shifting paradigms II activity	5m	Teacher facilitates the Shifting paradigms II activity and reinforces that a new paradigm can be sustained through mindfulness training and at the same time remaining open to new perspectives.

(Continued)

(Continued)

Component	Agenda	Time	Facilitation guide
10	Home practice 1. *Daily – to practice any one of the three formal practices* 2. *Daily – to practice the five-finger pro-social gratitude* 3. *Daily – to practice the lovingkindness meditation* 4. *To plan out the first month of My monthly wellbeing calendar*	5m	The teacher briefly explains the home practices and bids farewell.

Total Time 2h 30m

Session 8: The Future in the Present Moment

Theme

• The consistent practice of mindfulness is more important than the time spent with each practice. This ensures stronger commitment and motivation to practice as one plans to sustain the practice

Intention

• To recognize that mindfulness helps in shifting paradigms about wellbeing and happiness.

Component	Agenda	Time	Facilitation guide
1	• Welcome • Sitting with a metaphor: Rivers and ocean	10m	The teacher welcomes everyone briefly and settles them in a sitting posture on their mats. She invites them to close their eyes or have a soft gaze and shares the "Rivers and ocean" metaphor and allows a few moments of silence.

Component	Agenda	Time	Facilitation guide
2	Body scan practice • Guided practice	15m	The teacher invites the participants into a supine posture and guides the body scan. The body scan would be *shorter* with *less guidance* and *longer gaps of silence*.
3	Home practice review • Review the my monthly wellbeing plan	20m	The teacher gets the participants into pairs and invites them to share their monthly wellbeing plan and what considerations went into the planning. The teacher then invites the participants to the plenary dialogue to share any insights and to clarify any questions.
4	Review of course learning	10m	The teacher summarizes what was learned in the program with a specific focus on the Happiness paradigm.
5	Sitting meditation practice • Guided practice	15m	The teacher invites the participants to take a sitting posture and guides a *shorter* sitting meditation. The sitting meditation will be guided with *less guidance* and *longer gaps of silence*. The guidance could bring the metaphors of the sky and clouds, and waves and ocean into the script.
6	Mindful movement • Guided practice	15m	The teacher invites the participants to take a standing posture on their mats and reminds them of the guidelines. And then she guides a *shorter* mindful movement practice.
7	Assignment of home practices 1. *Experiment with the My monthly wellbeing calendar for a month and then review it in the second month* 2. *Join a monthly silent retreat*	10m	The teacher briefly explains the home practices and encourages the participants to sustain their engagement with mindfulness by attending short monthly sessions or retreats.
9	Mindful letter to self-exercise	20m	The teacher facilitates the mindful letter to Self-exercise and assures the participants that the letter will be mailed to them in 3 months.

(Continued)

(Continued)

Component	Agenda	Time	Facilitation guide
10	Program evaluation	10m	The teacher either distributes a printed evaluation form or invites participants to use their cell phones to complete the course evaluation online, depending on the teacher's preference.
11	Closing	25m	This is an important component of the program where participants share what they are taking away from the program. Depending on the size of the class, this can be done in two ways. If the class size is less than 20, the teacher could form a circle and share what their gratitude statement is in less than a minute per person. If the class size is more than 20, the teacher could form groups of five and invite each participant in their small group to share with their group what they are grateful for.

Finally, the teacher expresses her gratitude to the group, encourages them to continue their mindfulness journey on their own and bids them farewell. |

Total Time 2h 30m

8 PROGRAM ADAPTATIONS FOR ONE-ON-ONE MBWE

We have experimented with one-on-one MBWE coaching sessions and found that it worked well for people with specific needs, such as impairments and social avoidance/adjustment challenges, that justify a one-on-one session instead of a group.

The session plans for the one-on-one MBWE would not have any significant changes except for the omission of small-group discussions and the self-retreat. The absence of small-group discussions would require the teacher to deepen the inquiry to compensate for the limited horizontal inquiry that does not allow for the discovery of common humanity. To make up for the absence of the self-retreat, the teacher could invite their one-on-one participant to attend one of the upcoming self-retreats meant for group programs. This self-retreat could be conducted by the teacher herself or by other teachers who are open to having other participants in their session. As for the time investment for a one-on-one session, each of them could be between 1.5 to 2 hours instead of the 2.5 hour group session.

In addition, when the MBWE is delivered in a one-on-one setting, it borders on being an intervention that lies between a coaching and a therapy session. The ethical standards that guide those in the helping professions such as coaches, psychotherapists, and others would become relevant. It is important that the teacher reviews those ethical standards and abides by them or with reasonable adaptations.

9 TEACHING THE MBWE ONLINE

When facilitating the MBWE online, we need to be aware of several adaptations that are required. It also requires a lot more advanced planning to conduct these sessions online.

Learning materials such as books and journals, would have to be sent at least 2–3 weeks in advance to the participants. An alternative would be to send these materials digitally such as fillable pdf versions.

Usually, for online sessions, it takes the group slightly longer to warm up to each other. So the teacher should plan for more time to be spent bonding by having relevant ice-breaker activities for that purpose. The choice of online platform should be based on the availability of functions such as sharing of screens, chat functions, break-out rooms, use of polls and quizzes, sharing of videos, collaboration tools, and digital white boards. The intention is to be able to keep them engaged especially when facilitating the didactic components or exercises. For the mindfulness practices, we need to give more time for the participants to prepare their mats and space. One recommendation is to inform them of the requirements for the day at least 24 hours in advance. For example, for the mindful movement practice, it might be a good idea to inform the participants in advance to be in a space where there is sufficient room for movement.

There is also the challenge of internet connectivity problems. We recommend that you plan in advance any back-up plan such as using your mobile data should your Wi-Fi fail you. We also suggest that you use another device to log into the session so that you can see what your participants are seeing. That way, you need not disrupt the session by asking for constant feedback if they are able to view your screen.

Safety is another challenge during online sessions. Should a participant suddenly drop out without returning, or is not responsive to questions or has the camera switched off, then there is a risk. The main issue is that the teacher is not able to respond to the participant or her needs should anything have happened to her. One alternative is to agree on a rule that all participants would have to keep their cameras on throughout the session and that the teacher would send a text message or make a phone call to the participant (or the emergency point of contact) if they did not return or were not responsive for more than 15 minutes during the session.

Teaching online means that we need to prepare ourselves and our participants a lot more than onsite teaching. Also, the teacher needs to be well versed with not only facilitating MBPs but also with the technology to create an effective and conducive learning experience.

The MBWE is meant for participants who want to begin their journey of mindfulness and through it desire to improve their levels of wellbeing. Though evidence suggests that participants could benefit from the salutary effects immediately, after or during the MBPs, yet as teachers of MBWE, we want to emphasize that our teaching effectiveness is not measured by the immediacy of the results. Or else we may create the incessant expectation of wanting to taste the fruits as we water a sapling for a couple of weeks. This not only stands in the way of cultivating the attitudes of mindfulness, but also sets up people to be exactly where they were before they started the program.

Instead, we, as teachers could inspire the value of being in a lifelong journey of self-understanding and wisdom that continues to give birth to new experiences, anchored in the happiness paradigm. By doing and being so, we can invite participants who complete the MBWE to recognize that their journey has only just begun, right after the last session. And what they were *doing* throughout the program was like a traveler preparing well for a long journey with all the necessary essentials so that she can face successes, disappointments, excitement, and the mundane with wisdom. At the end of the MBWE program, comes the beginning of a lifelong *journey* of happiness and wellbeing. They walk away with a compass, not a map.

In Chapter 4, we discuss how a teacher could facilitate the mindfulness practices, didactic components, and exercises.

REFERENCES

Baer, R., Crane, C., Miller, E., & Kuyken, W. (2019). Doing no harm in mindfulness-based programs: conceptual issues and empirical findings. *Clinical psychology review, 71,* 101–114.

Crane, R. S., Brewer, J., Feldman, C., Kabat-Zinn, J., Santorelli, S., Williams, J. M. G., & Kuyken, W. (2017). What defines mindfulness-based programs? The warp and the weft. *Psychological Medicine, 47*(6), 990–999.

Dobkin, P. L., Irving, J. A., & Amar, S. (2012). For whom may participation in a mindfulness-based stress reduction program be contraindicated? *Mindfulness, 3*(1), 44–50.

Whitney, D. D., & Trosten-Bloom, A. (2010). *The power of appreciative inquiry: A practical guide to positive change.* Berrett-Koehler Publishers.

Wilson, J. (2014). *Mindful America: Meditation and the mutual transformation of Buddhism and American culture.* Oxford University Press.

Woods, S. L., & Rockman, P. (2021). *Mindfulness-based stress reduction: Protocol, practice, and teaching skills.* New Harbinger Publications.

CHAPTER 4

Facilitating the MBWE Program

I appreciate the short exercises and metaphors in every session. I find it easier to relate with mindfulness and what it can do for me.

–Fauziah

Facilitating a mindfulness-based program (MBP) is more than having a lesson plan and a few scripts. It requires multiple skills apart from adhering to a curriculum. Let us first revisit the MBP pedagogy that was presented in Chapter 1 (see Figure 4.1). In any MBP, including the MBWE, the pedagogy begins by the practice of mindfulness which focuses on strengthening attention and practicing acceptance. The continuous practice of attention and acceptance enhances awareness. The awareness is then funneled through the process of inquiry, aided by didactic components, to arrive at insights about the goals and intentions of the MBP. This then leads to the appreciation of the experience of the results and benefits.

Figure 4.1 The pedagogical process of MBP

In the MBWE, which focuses on wellbeing enhancement, the significant variation, when compared to other MBPs, would be in the stages of didactic

DOI: 10.4324/9781003322955-5

components, inquiry and the insights that lead to experienced results (see Figure 4.2). The content in this chapter would present

- how the mindfulness practices are guided in the MBWE and other MBPs, and
- how didactic components and exercises are facilitated in the MBWE

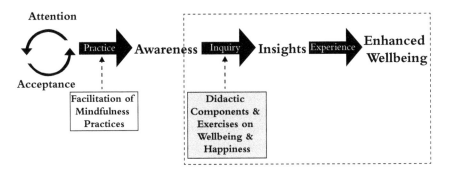

Figure 4.2 The pedagogical process of MBWE

1 FACILITATING MINDFULNESS PRACTICES

You might wonder if mindfulness practices differ in their objectives, methods, and process but the reality is that they are similar in their procedure and goals (Bishop et al., 2004). So, whether one practices the body scan or sitting meditation, the goal is the same which is to increase awareness levels by strengthening attention and practicing acceptance. The process of facilitating MBWE sessions can be seen in Figure 4.2 where the combination of the three elements of practice, inquiry, and experience leads to the outcome of enhanced wellbeing.

1.1 Facilitation, Not Lecturing

Teaching mindfulness is not something that can be easily learned by studying a couple of books or attending one or two seminars. The teaching style is highly collaborative and interactive. The role of a mindfulness teacher is to facilitate, and not just teach, although they are called mindfulness teachers. While teaching is more teacher centered, facilitation is more learner centered. A facilitator's job is to empower others with responsibility and self-direction. So while the mindfulness teacher provides the space, manages the group dynamics, provides guidance on practices and engages in inquiry to lead participants toward enhancing wellbeing, it is the participants who take charge of their lives by using their personal experiences in the session to gather insights about themselves and to continue the practice at home to deepen it. Carl Rogers (1995, p. 44) described this empowerment most aptly: "when I am exposed to a growth-promoting climate, I am able to develop a deep trust in myself, in individuals, and in entire groups." With this trust in oneself, the participants can reduce reliance on the teacher or others and observe their inner experiences and sit with it.

To facilitate mindfulness sessions, one does not require any special or unique dress, tools, or voice. Scripts are provided to support the teacher though we caution against depending too much on the script and missing one's own experience in the process. To facilitate, the teacher needs to be present in the moment and use the processes, lesson plans, scripts, and chime to support herself. In addition, there are facilitation techniques and tools that can make the learning more effective in the sessions. This is a significant area that can help teachers appeal to the different learning styles commonly known as VAK (visual, auditory, and kinesthetics). Today most MBP teachers employ inquiry via asking question and expecting verbal responses to these questions. Using different facilitation tools, other than overly relying on auditory ones, can be very helpful in enhancing the engagement with the didactic components, exercises, and inquiry. This leads to different means through which insights can be generated. We will briefly present a few techniques and tools that can be used in MBPs although it is not an exhaustive list. The images shared herein are from some of our workshops and also used with the permission of the Centre for Mindfulness Pte Ltd except where stated.

- *Post-Its* – the use of Post-It paper notes can be very helpful to organize similar responses in the room. For example, after distributing Post-It notes to all participants, we can invite every participant to write what they noticed during the body scan on Post-It notes, with one response per Post-It note. After which we can request all the participants to stick each of the Post-Its on a wall or whiteboard and get them to organize them under four headings: thoughts, emotions, sensations, and urges. Through these, participants can visually learn not only from the experiences that they noticed with themselves, but also from the collective experience of the room. Here are some samples on the benefits of mindfulness and awareness of internal and external experiences in Figure 4.3:
- *Flip chart papers* – flip chart papers can be used for paired and small group discussions so that participants can write their responses on them and discuss them visually. The written flip chart papers can be mounted on the wall as a reference, or they could be used to teach salient points of the session outcomes. You can combine this with a gallery walk if you wish. Here are some samples from a body scan discussion in Figure 4.4:
- *Gallery walk* – gallery walk is a structured technique that can be used after groups have mounted their written flip chart papers on the wall. You can

Figure 4.3 Sample Post-Its for benefits of mindfulness and awareness of internal and external experiences

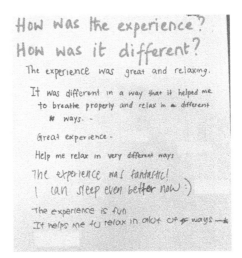

Figure 4.4 Sample flip chart responses from a body scan discussion

ask every group to walk in a particular sequence, as if they are walking in a gallery, to view the written responses on the mounted flip chart papers. This approach saves time and maximizes the engagement of all participants at the same time. Here is a sample of gallery walk in Figure 4.5:

- *Video discussion* – videos can be very helpful for didactic components. Short videos, possibly less than 4–5 minutes, can be shown about mindfulness, the brain, stress, happiness, neuroplasticity, and wellbeing among others. And thereafter participants can discuss in small groups about what stood out for them in the video.

Figure 4.5 Sample of a gallery walk

- *Flash cards* – there are many different types of flash cards that present emotions, values, questions, and test observational skills. These cards can be used at suitable segments of the MBPs with a clear intention to aid inquiry. Here are some samples of question and value cards in Figure 4.6:
- *Images and pictures* – images and pictures can be helpful in bringing curiosity and practicing observational skills. Visual illusions are good options as they are very powerful in revealing the way stimuli, thoughts, and interpretations work.
- *Metaphors and parables* – metaphors and parables can be used for contemplation and for gaining personal insights. Teachers can share a metaphor or a parable so that participants can create their own meaning from them.
- *Poems and lyrics* – reciting poems and lyrics can be another method of creating meaning and gaining personal insights. *The Guest House* by Rumi, is a popular poem used in MBPs.

Question Cards

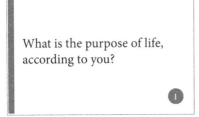

What is the purpose of life, according to you?

What is a high point experience you had in your work/life?

Value Cards

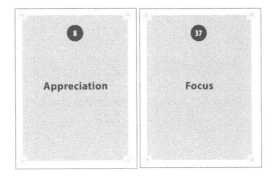

Appreciation

Focus

Figure 4.6 Sample flash cards
(used with permission from Positive Performance Consulting Pte Ltd)

- *Activities and games* – many different types of activities and games can be conducted in the sessions to gain an experiential appreciation of abstract concepts of mindfulness. Stroop effect or model building in total silence as a group are two of such activities that can be used to engage the audience and lead up to an inquiry. Here is a picture of a card tower activity to generate insights about emotions and reactivity (in Figure 4.7):
- *Case studies* – case studies can be helpful in the didactic components of an MBP. While this may not always be relevant in all MBPs, a teacher can use it sparingly if there is a value for participants or for the specific types of MBP.
- *Role plays* – role plays can be helpful in practicing and exercising mental muscles. They can be used in exercises such as the generating perspectives where participants can practice with a partner as to how perspectives can be shifted in a situation.

Figure 4.7 Sample card tower activity to generate insights about emotions and reactivity

- *Worksheets* – worksheets are helpful in exploring concepts, generating, and consolidating ideas, and reflecting on questions without the aid of the teacher. Worksheets are also versatile as they can be used in and out of sessions to deepen learning. An example would be the meaningful engagement exercise worksheets.

The above are just some ideas for facilitation and you can certainly find many more creative ways of engaging the participants. There are of course other competencies that are required of a teacher and this will be further discussed in Chapter 8.

1.2 Instruction and guidance

Mindfulness teachers also use a script as an invitation to experience mindfulness. Every mindfulness practice has a guiding script and principles to adhere to. Each script starts with instructions on posture followed by guidance on how attention is deployed and acceptance is brought to the experience.

Most practices can be between 3–40 minutes. Depending on the population, the teacher can pace the guidance with sufficient silence between instructions. We would suggest that you observe a 15–30 second pause between paragraphs of instructions. Here is an example for the body scan:

> Sitting on the mat with your knees bent, feet on the floor. And then using one hand to support your body as you lean on the forearm of the other arm. And then gently rolling your back such that you are lying on your back with the front of your body facing upwards.
>
> *[15 seconds pause]*
>
> Closing your eyes, and letting your arms lie alongside your body with your palms facing upwards, and your feet falling away from each other. Allowing your body to slowly sink into the mat and being relaxed.
>
> *[15 seconds pause]*
>
> We shall now begin the practice with the sound of the chime.
>
> *[Strike chime/bell]*
> *[10–15 seconds pause and until you can no longer hear the sound of the chime]*
>
> Gently bringing your attention to your breathing. Not trying to control your breath in any way but simply noticing your inbreath and outbreath and noticing your belly. Noticing the sensations there as your belly expands with the inbreath. Then noticing the belly deflate with the outbreath.
>
> *[30 seconds pause]*
>
> And following the rhythmic movement of each breath . . . the expansion of the belly on the inbreath and on each outbreath just letting go, letting your body become heavy as it sinks a little bit deeper into relaxation. Just bringing full attention to each breath in each moment.
>
> *[30 seconds pause]*
>
> Now bring your attention to the right leg, and then to the right foot, becoming aware of whatever sensations are there . . .

Teachers can adapt the existing sample scripts in appendices 2 to 4 by replacing some of the words with familiar ones that may suit your language, style, and culture, as long as the intention is not compromised. For example, let us look at the last sentence above from the body scan "*Now bring your attention to the right leg, and then to your right foot, becoming aware of whatever sensations are there.*" This could be made more descriptive if that works for your participants. For example, it could sound like:

> Now bring your attention to the right leg, and then to the right foot, all the way down to the toes. Becoming aware of whatever sensations that are there in your toes and between the toes. Noticing perhaps the sensations on the sole of your foot . . .

Again, the intention should be to support the participants to notice the sensations and yet allowing for appropriate amounts of silence to focus on the sensations. For example, if we take the above example, it might sound something like this:

> Now bring your attention to the right leg, and then to the right foot, all the way down to the toes.
>
> *[3–5 seconds pause]*
>
> Becoming aware of whatever sensations are there in your toes and between the toes.
>
> *[3–5 seconds pause]*
>
> Noticing perhaps the sensations on the sole of the foot . . .

As you advance through the eight-week program, you could allow for more silences and less guidance. This would mean that a 30 second pause might become 45 seconds and instead of describing the foot and toes, you might just mention to bring attention to the foot without going into the details.

Now when you decide to adapt a script, remember to strike a balance between the present participle and imperatives. Here is an example:

> And then gently rolling [present participle] your back such that you are lying [present participle] on your back with the front of your body facing upwards.

Besides using the script, you also need to consider your own posture and experience in the room. You could sit on the mat with your legs crossed and could also use a meditation cushion to support your posture. Do teachers have to keep their eyes closed while guiding a sitting meditation practice? We do not recommend closing your eyes throughout the practice. Instead, we suggest that you guide your participants with your eyes closed and opening your eyes occasionally when needed to observe your participants and the environment for safety and to also be able to adapt the script based on both your internal and external experience. Rob Brandsma (2017) states that our attention should be divided between the group, the script, and the teacher's meditative consciousness. Adding on to that, we would like to suggest that the teacher adhere to the 50/50 principle in the room when guiding participants. Fifty percent of the guidance comes from the script while the other 50 percent comes from the teacher's meditative consciousness, which includes the relational experience with the participants and the external environment. You can see a diagram of this in Figure 4.8 below.

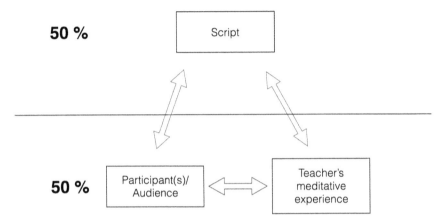

Figure 4.8 50/50 principle of guiding mindfulness practices

I (SR) was conducting the MBWE session in a uptown yoga studio in 2018, and while we were practicing the body scan, suddenly there was an unexpected loud drilling noise. I suspected that the participants might be feeling disturbed by the sound and so I acknowledged the sound in my guidance and directed their attention to notice the sound and the vibrations on the ground before coming back to the body and noticing the impact on the body, emotions, and thoughts. This allowed them to accept the "distraction" and return to their practice rather than fighting between two conflicting stimuli. Now imagine the consequence if I insisted on staying with the script, while their minds were struggling to stay focused on my instructions. This is why the 50/50 principle is important in guiding participants while being aware of one's own meditative consciousness and that of the participants.

Wolf and Serpa (2015) state that if we blindly follow a curriculum, read scripts, and intellectualize the experiences, we could be doing more harm than good to our participants. I (KK) have noticed numerous times in supervisions where trainee teachers come prepared with a list of questions to ask the group instead of responding to what is happening in the room in the present moment. It is imperative that teachers facilitate groups with authenticity and sincerity which includes our personal practice, and our practice and experience in the room.

1.3 Tone of Voice

Often we see teachers who suddenly change their tone of voice from their usual one when guiding mindfulness practices. The voice becomes extremely calm, softer and tranquil. Is that necessary? We do not think so. It is necessary that you be yourself and be genuine in your guidance. Slowing down the pace and being mindful of what you say is important but it is not necessary to change your voice into something that is not you. Of course as you instruct from your meditative consciousness, you might become calmer and with that, your voice might change and that is acceptable as long as you are being authentic. It does help to sound confident when instructing and it is helpful to practice the scripts again and again so that they flow well for you. Other than that, there is no special voice or tone for guiding mindfulness practices.

2 INQUIRY

Practices, exercises, poems, and metaphors are some of the things that need to be supported with inquiry for participants to generate insights into their experiences. These experiences include inquiring into the bodily sensations, thoughts, emotions, and urges in each moment. Without inquiry, the participants are left hanging with an experience *without understanding nor learning from the experience*. Mindfulness apps are helpful with guidance and practices, but cannot conduct an interactive dialogue about the experience in the moment. You can read more about inquiry in Chapter 5 where we have an in-depth discussion on inquiry and how to facilitate it.

3 DIDACTIC COMPONENTS

Didactic teachings support the inquiry and deepen the insights gathered. Didactic components focus not only on the personal experience of the participants but also take into account the universal human experience. For example, when we teach about happiness and wellbeing, it is about universal human desire and not limited to one or a select group of individuals. We might, however, differ on how we go about seeking it. According to Rob Brandsma (2017), the intention of didactic teaching is to further develop and boost insight while increasing the trust in the process. He further states that didactic presentations function as an explanation of how something works; help in recognition that one is not alone; create support in a group that everyone is in the same boat; help people connect the dots of patterns in their life, and register their patterns so they can recognize them next time they occur.

In MBPs, some parts of the content is related to the program outcome while others are related to the mechanisms of mindfulness. It is of the utmost importance that the reading materials chosen for teaching are directly relevant and related to the outcomes and results of the program. In the MBWE, you will have noticed that the focus is on mindfulness, happiness, and wellbeing and as such, the teachings are centered around that.

During didactic segments, the mindfulness teacher moves from being a facilitator to a teacher. A teacher must possess a level of subject knowledge. Unlike a facilitator who needs to know only processes, tools, and strategies, a mindfulness teacher also needs to be strongly grounded in the foundations of mindfulness and the contents relevant to the program outcome. As such, a mindfulness teacher needs to be highly versatile to smoothly switch between the two roles when necessary.

Some didactic teachings may happen spontaneously and are not pre-planned before the session. I (SR) remember being in the middle of a discussion on wellbeing and a participant asked if seeking happiness is all there is in life. This was an opportunity to discuss purpose and meaning in life and also to differentiate between happiness and wellbeing. The intention is to lean onto the participants' own experiences and insights to weave in the didactic concepts of mindfulness where possible instead of lecturing or adhering strictly to the curriculum.

A teacher therefore needs to be able to balance between didactic teaching and dialectic facilitation throughout the eight-week program. Here is a sample of the difference between didactic teaching and dialectic facilitation:

Table 4.1 Difference between didactic teaching and dialectic facilitation

	Didactic: direct instruction	Dialectic: constructivist/facilitative
Goals	• Acquire knowledge • Facts; concrete	• Explore ideas, experiences and values • Concepts and principles; abstract
Means	Lectures, textbooks, worksheets, scripts, videos, etc.	Inquiry, active participation
Focus	Teacher centered	Learner centered

4 COMPETENCIES AND ATTITUDE OF A MINDFULNESS TEACHER

The role of the teacher is of the utmost importance in experiencing the outcomes of any MBP. It is not about how she looks but is very much related to her embodiment, personal practice, and competence in guidance and teaching of mindfulness. Several UK universities came together to create a competency checklist and assessment criteria for mindfulness teachers called the *Mindfulness-Based Interventions: Teaching Assessment Criteria* (MBI:TAC). There are six competencies on which a teacher is assessed over a period of time and this is discussed in Chapter 8.

Teaching mindfulness requires the teacher to be grounded in a wide variety of approaches, tools, and methodology as well as other qualities. While in many other professions, the trainers and facilitators may not be required to have embodied what they are teaching, in mindfulness it is an essential pre-requisite. To be able to facilitate mindfulness practices, it is essential that the teacher must have first practiced mindfulness for a length of time. Our recommendation is to have practiced it for at least a year or longer. The second important requirement is having been guided, trained, and mentored by another experienced mindfulness teacher. Constructive feedback helps a lot with the facilitation of MBPs.

I (SR) remember once being asked by a trainee teacher if it was acceptable for a teacher to be dressed in jeans and T-shirt during sessions rather than being dressed for yoga. We discussed her thoughts on "yoga type" clothing. While I acknowledged her question, I asked her to wait for a week before I answer that question. For the time being, I suggested that she search for images of mindfulness from the Internet and share with me about her perception of how mindfulness teachers generally dressed. A week later, she told me that she had found her answer. And she then asked me why I was not adhering to the "norm" discovered through internet search results. I asked her to reflect if my teaching was impacted by my dressing in any manner. We discussed for some time on what was appropriate and what was not. For example, wearing clothes with provocative messages or images is not acceptable as it may cause harm. In the same way, when I conduct mindfulness sessions in the park, I would naturally wear something suitable for hot weather since Singapore is usually hot and humid all the year round. A mindfulness teacher needs to dress professionally, respectfully, and in accordance with the time, place, and circumstance. There is no special dress code. So what matters then?

Your life of personal mindfulness practice, continuous learning from your own experience and that of others, attending mindfulness retreats, and continuously teaching mindfulness to others is what matters. Allowing all of these to inform your wisdom is what helps you to be effective as a teacher.

5 TOOLS FOR A MINDFULNESS TEACHER

5.1 Core Tools

A question that might pop up in our minds is whether we need any specific tools and gadgets to be effective as a mindfulness teacher. While there are tools to aid you, the most important "tool" in the room is your "being." *The self is the primary instrument for a teacher when she is teaching mindfulness.* You can use other tools to support your sessions as long as they are not a distraction to the participants and contribute to the generation of insights.

There are some secondary tools and accessories that are necessary for a mindfulness teacher such as a yoga or exercise mat, a mindfulness chime, scripts, and a stopwatch. The yoga or exercise mat is useful for sitting throughout the sessions as well as for all the formal practices such as the body scan, mindful movement, or sitting meditation. An alternative to the yoga mat is a non-slip towel or rug.

A mindfulness chime is usually used to begin and end a practice. You can choose to use any chime or bell that produces a single note upon striking it. An effective chime should emit a strong and deep single note that is neither too high nor too low in pitch. It should also be able to sustain the note for a few seconds. We encourage teachers to not speak after they have struck the chime and allow everyone to sit in silence and just notice the sound of the note until it fades into silence. Only in silence do we instruct so that participants need not focus on two things at the same time. Also the chime is only to be used during the beginning and end of a practice session and not for any other purposes so that participants associate the sound of the chime to the practice of mindfulness.

The mindfulness script is used as a guide for practices mentioned earlier. A stopwatch or a small clock is helpful in managing the time needed for guiding each practice. We do not recommend using a smartphone or a tablet app for this as we encourage teachers to put away all devices during the sessions as we can possibly be distracted by notifications or calls, even if they are placed on a silent mode. As you get more familiar with the guidance and session deliveries, you may no longer need the stopwatch or the script.

5.2 Optional Tools

While the core tools are more than enough to teach, there are some optional nice-to-have tools. These include, but are not limited to, a meditation cushion, yoga block, and a singing bowl. Each of these can be used depending on the context and need as additional aids.

6 POSTURES FOR MINDFULNESS PRACTICES

A question might arise in your mind if there is a special way to sit or stand when practicing mindfulness. Well the answer is both yes and no. There is nothing special about the way we sit or stand but there are some recommendations taking into consideration comfort, the ability to stay alert, and safety. For example, we do not perform sitting meditation while standing (obvious from the term "sitting") as a participant may risk a fall while meditating standing for 30 minutes, completely unaware of their environment at that moment or may fall asleep or into deep absorption.

We have added scripts for moving into starting postures in appendix 2 for mindfulness practices which include standing, sitting, and supine as these are the standard postures for most mindfulness practices. This will allow teachers to pick any script and add it to the relevant practice script.

Most of the practices are done with the eyes closed. However, people who may experience anxiety or have experienced trauma may not be comfortable closing their eyes. They can opt to lower their gaze toward the ground by about 45 degrees, 2 meters ahead of them. We call this "soft gaze" which is a gentle way of looking at an area or object without much tension.

7 MINDFULNESS PRACTICES

There are numerous mindfulness practices and the list is growing as we write. However, we can categorize most of the mindfulness practices into either formal or informal practices.

All mindfulness practices help us to direct our attention inwards instead of engaging with the external sensory world. In a way, it is an appointment with oneself. When practicing mindfulness, we are fully observing ourselves and inviting ourselves through a process of self-discovery and inquiry by engaging with our body, senses, thoughts, feelings, actions and through these we relate to the external world.

One important feature of guiding mindfulness practices is that the instructions can be more spaced out with lesser guidance and more silence as the MBP progresses. For example, we give more guidance instructions in the body scan in week 1 with shorter gaps of silence as this is the first time the participants are probably exploring mindfulness and we want to ease them into the practice. However, by the last session, there is more silence between the instructions and less guidance.

7.1 Formal Mindfulness Practices

The body scan, sitting meditation, and mindful movement (or mindful hatha) are considered the core or formal mindfulness practices (Crane, 2017). Formal mindfulness practices would be longer practices that require a minimum of 30 minutes and time will need to be set aside for practice. We have provided sample scripts for the formal practices in appendix 3.

Body Scan

The body scan is practiced lying down on a mat in a supine posture. Participants are guided on how to lie down on their back and how to sit up before they start the practice. The intention is to ensure that they do not injure themselves, especially their back, as they lie down and come up. Participants who find it difficult to lie down can consider sitting against a wall to support themselves and with their feet away from their body. If this is not suitable, they can consider sitting on a chair in a comfortable posture that does not risk falls.

In the body scan practice, the teacher guides the participants to lie down on the mat and then allowing their body to relax into the mat. This is followed by bringing their attention to the breath followed by gently shifting their attention from their toes all the way to the top of their head. The teacher directs the attention of the participants to sensations on the surface of the skin, the bones, the muscles, pulses, organs, and the flow of blood. The teacher provides guidance to be intentional, curious, and to explore all of the sensations in each part of the body with a sense of exploration and acceptance rather than rejection or the urge to change. It is a way of allowing the body to be as it is rather than trying to change it or to achieve a specific state. The teacher also acknowledges that the mind might wander and to bring it back to the body each time it happens with compassion and kindness.

Sitting Meditation

Sitting meditation is done sitting on the floor on a mat or on a chair. The teacher demonstrates the various ways to sit with proper support before beginning the practice. This gives the participants an opportunity to explore sitting in a way that supports their practice without too much discomfort and allows them to be alert.

In sitting meditation, the practice starts with sitting comfortably followed by bringing attention to the sensations of the breath before moving into the bodily sensations and finally focusing on emotions and thoughts. The breath and body form an anchor in sitting meditation while the participant is encouraged to be curious about the thoughts that are rising and disappearing in the mind, the patterns, insights gathered, and also about the mind itself wandering.

The intention here is really to become more intimate with the mental patterns without having to prevent the mind from wandering and to allow noticing instead of thinking (Segal et al., 2013). Sitting meditation helps participants to understand *how* the mind functions instead of having to reject thoughts or constantly fighting them. There is a sense of acceptance of the mind and the body and letting go of wanting the mind to be still or the body to be different.

Mindful Movement

While the body scan and the sitting meditation practices are done in stillness, mindful movement explores a whole range of motions. Mindful movement in fact builds on the body scan as it is about being aware of the bodily sensations while in motion rather than stillness.

Mindful movement has four key postures: standing, sitting, supine, and prone. The teacher can start from standing to prone or supine. Alternatively, the teacher can also start with supine and move up to a standing posture.

I (KK) saw one of our trainee teachers doing an entire mix of movements from sitting to standing and then supine, followed by prone, and back to standing followed by seated. This led to some participants feeling a bit uneasy and one participant said that she felt dizzy. It is important that we have a smooth flow of motion such as not expecting participants to move from prone or supine to standing. Only from a seated position should they be asked to stand up or move into supine or prone position.

In mindful movement, the focus is not on a perfect posture. The teacher instead instructs participants to notice and pay attention to the actual process of movement: the stretches and contractions on the various parts of the body; the tightness, tensions, or pain if any; the weight or heaviness of the different body parts; the flow of blood upwards or downwards depending on the movement; how the body feels in movement vs stillness; and the limitations and appreciation of the body. The intention is to also notice as we move and while in posture and to adhere to the natural breathing patterns while we are moving into or out of a posture where possible. It is a state of being fully awake to the moment-to-moment movement including the appreciation of the body and its abilities including its limitations.

Mindful movement invites participants to relate to the body with friendliness and to see movements and postures as offering an embodiment of life experiences and processes (Crane, 2017). Further working with physical boundaries/intensity offers a parallel to working in similar ways with emotional experience and experiencing that physical movement can change emotional experience. I (SR) remember exploring mindful movement with a client who was diagnosed with clinical depression and had childhood trauma. He candidly admitted after 4–5 sessions, during the mindfulness-oriented therapy, that he was "super bored and frustrated" when he tried sitting meditation whereas his mind could easily follow his body in mindful movement. He was appreciative of "another way to be mindful and to be present." He found new ways to relate to his emotional and physical pains through mindful movement.

In mindful movement, we do need to be mindful about safety. One of the key consideration is the limits of the practice. Some participants are encouraged to consult a medical professional before starting the practice. I (SR) once had a candidate who had spinal injuries and recommended that she consult her doctor before starting the eight-week program. Her doctor cleared her and the participant and I spoke about what postures might be challenging for her and gave her permission to skip those movements and to practice the alternatives that I recommended for her.

After every posture, it is of utmost importance to allow for rest and stillness. Moving too fast and too often can cause dizziness, nausea, and other discomforts. Resting between postures also allows the participants to tune in to the body in motion vs stillness. Other considerations for adaptations include age, flexibility of movement, and the health of the participants. For example, for participants who are in their seventies and with chronic pain, we recommend movements that do not require too much flexibility.

The venue and space should be considered too. For example, when we conduct mindful movement in classrooms with 30–40 school students, we tend to choose movements that require less space compared to a yoga studio with just ten participants. The available space for movement can limit the choices of postures.

The types of clothes that participants wear also impacts our choices of postures. For example, when we were conducting a session at a local college, we omitted all the postures that required legs to be raised as there were students in skirts. We might also want to consider any cultural dimensions when exploring movement. For example, when we were working in a setting where men and women are not allowed to be in close proximity, we separated them before we started the practices and we also asked them to face away from one another during the supine postures.

7.2 Informal Mindfulness Practices

Any practice that is not a formal practice can be placed under the category of informal practice. Informal practices generally are for durations of 3–20 minutes depending on the practice. While some practices require you to set time aside to do them, others can be combined or done as part of a routine daily activity such as washing our faces or brushing our teeth mindfully.

We have provided sample scripts for informal practices in appendix 4.

Centering

Centering is a practice that is helpful at the beginning of a session. It helps an individual to know where they are in space and time. It grounds you in the present moment so that you are poised to begin the session. In this practice, the participant brings their attention to the feet as they stand and tilt their body in different directions. They are also encouraged to notice the sensations when the body moves as compared to when it is still. The practice usually takes 2–5 minutes.

Mindful Perception

Mindful perception introduces curiosity in a simple way by directing attention to the five senses. It is a short practice where participants are easily able to stay engaged and focused while practicing.

This practice can be done sitting or while standing, if it is shorter than 5 minutes. In terms of time, it is usually practiced for 2–10 minutes. We have provided a ten-minute script which you can adapt to shorten the practice if needed.

Raisin Practice

Raisin practice helps us to appreciate that mindfulness is about noticing the ordinary, not something unusual or mystical. During raisin practice, participants are invited to see a raisin with a fresh pair of eyes and with curiosity. Raisin practice helps one to notice how the mind functions in an autopilot mode and how, by just paying attention, we are able to notice things that we had missed or taken for granted.

The teacher would need to first sanitize her hands and those of the participants. Then the teacher pours raisins into a bowl and uses a spoon to serve one raisin to each participant. She is encouraged to serve each participant individually rather than pass the raisins around. She then sits and guides the participants through the raisin practice by engaging the five senses. Once the practice has ended, she inquires into the experience followed by another round of raisin practice. In the second round, the teacher does not guide and opens the space for self-exploration with the raisins. After about 5 minutes, the teacher gives each participant a sanitary wipe to clean their hands and clears all the used materials before proceeding on with the rest of the session plan.

It is important that we consider alternatives to the raisin if adaptations are required. Some alternatives might be grapes, berries, dates, or prunes among others. The teacher must be aware of possible food allergies when considering what to use for the raisin practice.

Sometimes, it is not an allergy about which we are concerned. At times it is about dietary preferences or restrictions, which a teacher needs to respect. Here are some examples to consider:

- Lactose intolerance
- Gluten intolerance
- Diabetes
- Dairy free
- Keto/Paleo/Low carb

- Raw food
- Veganism
- Fruitarian
- Vegetarianism (Hindus/Buddhist/Others)
- Lacto-vegetarian (Sikhism)
- Halal (Islam)
- Kosher (Judaism), etc.

You might be wondering how a teacher would know all of this information. Well, our recommendation is to include it in the intake form. Alternatively, you could ask the participants in your optional pre-session conversation with them.

It is also important to note that participants might find the throat drying after eating a raisin. It is therefore important that the teacher has water available for participants if needed.

Awareness of Breath Meditation

Awareness of breath is a quasi-formal practice among all the informal mindfulness practices given that it prepares a participant for the longer sitting meditation practice. This seated practice can be explored for 5–20 minutes. We have provided a script for 20 minutes so you can adapt it if you wish to guide a shorter version.

The practice focuses on building awareness of the breath. The practice starts with a focus on the breath and the breath is used as an anchor because breathing is always available. Whenever the mind wanders, there is an acknowledgment of the mind being distracted and a gentle shift back to the breath.

Coping Breathing Space

The coping breath space practice is one of the shortest informal practices. This is a standing or seated practice which can be practiced for 3–10 minutes. The script provided is for a three-minute practice and the teacher can adapt it to deepen it. This brief practice can be used when we find our thoughts or mood spiraling downward in a negative direction.

The teacher guides the participants out of autopilot and gently brings their attention to the body to become aware of the body from the toes to the head, like a micro-body scan. This is followed by shifting the attention to the breath at the nostrils, chest, or belly. Finally, the teacher guides the participants to expand their awareness to the body as a whole and to allow any experience to be present. The coping breathing space is like a mini-mindfulness practice that we can easily practice in daily living especially when our thoughts are spiraling or when we feel stressed, anxious, or depressed.

Lovingkindness Meditation

The lovingkindness meditation is one of the most interesting meditations as it nearly always evokes many emotional responses from feelings of love, grief, empathy, regrets, kindness, generosity, goodwill, forgiveness and compassion. We have seen participants crying after this practice as it has the capacity to evoke strong emotions.

This is a seated practice of about 15–20 minutes. The teacher guides the participant to first focus on their breath followed by bringing to mind some-one that they love and offer lovingkindness to that person. This is followed by offering lovingkindness to someone for whom we have deep feelings of love, to oneself, someone who supports us, someone with whom we have difficulty with, and finally to the broader community. We have often received feedback that giving lovingkindness to oneself, and to someone to whom we have strong negative feelings, is difficult. In fact, this practice is a great opportunity to practice letting go of resentment. Many of our participants have also shared how over weeks of practice, they noticed that the intensity of unhappiness, with the person that they were unhappy about, had reduced and some were even able to forgive that "difficult" person. This practice can be extended beyond humans so that we can give lovingkindness to our pets, flora and fauna, and to the entire planet.

Mindful Walking (or Walking Meditation)

Mindfulness is definitely not about staying still as you can see from the practice of mindful movement. Mindful walking integrates mindfulness into daily life as we walk all the time and perhaps it is one of those activities that we do the most. We have also noticed over the years that mindful walking (and mindful movement) is welcomed by those who find sitting meditation and body scan anxiety-provoking and, like the awareness of breath, it forms a bridge between formal and informal practice. It is especially useful for people who feel restless in stillness and are unable to settle.

The practice is usually explored for 10–20 minutes. The teacher guides the participants to focus on the bodily sensations while in movement starting from the feet. Attention is given to the heel, ball of the foot, and the toes, as the body moves, and also to observe the balance and weight of the body in motion (see Figure 4.9). Each time the mind wanders, the teacher guides the attention back to the body and the walk. The teacher can experiment with walking slow vs fast, walking forward vs backward, walking vs stillness, and walking alone vs following someone. The intention is to notice with curios-ity the sensations in the feet and legs, emotions, and thoughts while one is walking.

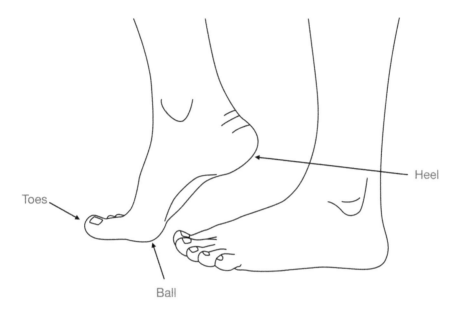

Figure 4.9 Parts of the foot

Five-Finger Gratitude Practice

The five-finger gratitude practice is a way of reminding ourselves to be appre-ciative and to be intentionally grateful in daily living. It can be practiced within 3–5 minutes. Participants are encouraged to recall five experiences that they are grateful for and count them using their fingers. As they do this, they are also invited to be curious and notice any bodily sensations as they recount all the experiences and things for which they are thankful. Attending to what we appreciate in daily life can lighten our mood, train our mind to be more positive, and enhance our wellbeing. It is primarily an exercise of directing attention to the positive.

Five-Finger Pro-Social Gratitude Practice

This practice is similar to the five-finger gratitude practice. The difference here is that we focus on the other people who are not part of our immediate family, environment, or the things that do not belong to us. Here we take about 3–5 minutes to be grateful for all the people we have met in the day (or week) and notice the sensations in the body. This can include friends, colleagues, neighbors, the community, or anyone else. This practice can enhance relationships with people that we consider as the "others." It also helps us to see the symbiotic relationship we have with everything around us.

Mindful Eating

Mindful eating is similar to the raisin practice. Eating mindfully is all about the awareness we bring to the entire process of eating from food selection to digestion. We slow down the pace of eating to be able to savor every bite of the food and this also aids in digestion.

The difference between mindful eating and mindless eating is mainly in the process rather than the actual outcome of eating. For example, in mindless eating, we may pick any nearby restaurant to eat without considering our dietary needs or even forgetting our dietary plan if any. In mindful eating, we are able to take a break and select a place that meets the nutritional needs of the body.

In the mindful eating practice during the MBWE, participants are encouraged to bring their own snack which they can consume within 5 minutes. The teacher could provide examples. The teacher brings along the hand sanitizers, sanitary wipes, and a garbage bag if necessary.

Mountain Meditation

The metaphor of the mountain helps us to connect with our inner strength and stability in the face of internal and external challenges. By visualizing oneself as a mountain, it helps us to cultivate resilience and calmness. This is a seated visualization practice of about 10–15 minutes.

The teacher can consider replacing the mountain with the tree or the lake as metaphors. The visualization behind each is slightly different, so depending on what may support the audience, the teacher can pick the right metaphor for meditation. The intake process would also reveal any possible phobia or trauma relating to water or mountains and thus one can adapt accordingly. In one of the teacher-training cohorts, a trainee shared her anxiety about mountains, and I (SR) asked her if she would like me to change the metaphor but she decided to give it a go. It took a lot of courage and effort from her and now she is able to guide others in the mountain meditation. However, you can consider replacing the metaphor completely if required.

Mindful Stretching

Mindful stretching is similar to mindful movement but is a less intensive practice which can be done in 10–15 minutes. This is a standing practice though it can be done seated. The teacher guides the participants through gentle stretching exercise with a focus on moving and stretching the joints. Generally, the stretches can be done at the neck, shoulders, chest, trunk, lower back, upper back, hips, knees, and ankles. The participants are directed to focus their attention when moving, the areas of stretch and contraction, and when the stretch is released. Many of our participants shared that they found practicing mindful stretching helpful during the start of the day.

Bringing Mindfulness to Routine Activities

Mindfulness can be practiced anywhere and anytime. One of the easiest ways to do this is to bring a sense of awareness to our daily activities. One can bring attention to any daily and ordinary activity right down to every single detail of that experience from the start till the end. This includes engaging all of our five senses, if possible, just like mindful perception and notice all of our movements moment to moment. When we start with one routine activity, we are encouraged to do the same activity daily for a week and notice all of the sensations. And in week 2, the participants are encouraged to choose a new routine activity. After week 2, we encourage participants to continue this in their lives by choosing a new activity per week to focus on or they can choose to revisit a past practice. This practice can be anything from a walk, shower, sweeping the floor, doing laundry, typing, filing, meetings, or anything else.

8 METAPHORS

Each MBWE session begins with a metaphor that is linked to the theme of the session. Metaphors are helpful in understanding the complex world and have a way of helping us to relate to our daily experiences. Every week, the teacher reads out or describes the metaphor. In some sessions, she follows up with inquiry questions to generate insights from the metaphor while allowing for silence in other sessions.

The suggested metaphors can be found in appendix 5. Here is the entire list of the metaphors used in the MBWE program including those used at the beginning of the sessions:

- The pilot
- Cow's milk
- Young woman or old woman
- A car without a steering wheel
- Like a torchlight
- Shoot and look or look and shoot
- Camera and its lenses
- Are you a passenger?
- Animals within rhino
- Clouds in the sky
- Rope and snake
- Rivers and ocean

The above metaphors can be replaced with other metaphors that are relevant to the session theme and learning outcome.

9 POEMS

Poems are helpful in understanding about our life experiences, concepts, something, someone, and also our mind, emotions, and thoughts. Poetry has a unique way of linking concepts together and expressing ideas in a succinct manner. In mindfulness, we use poems to contemplate on a practice, life, and our experiences that can enhance our wellbeing.

In the MBWE, the teacher can choose to read out the poem, *The Guest House*, or place it on a flip chart or distribute the poem as a handout or place it in the journal. Once the participants or the teacher have read out the poem, the teacher can choose to do a paired or small group discussion on the meaning of the poem. After the discussion, the teacher opens a plenary discussion about insights on thoughts and emotions from the poem. An alternative is to go directly into the plenary discussion without the small group discussions. Teachers are encouraged to use the poem to explore experiences, thoughts, emotions and also the difference between resignation and acceptance. The intention is to explore what acceptance looks like and feels like in daily living.

Although, *The Guest House* by Rumi, is used in the MBWE, we have added a few more for your consideration so that you can chose one that may suit your audience. The following poems can be found in appendix 6:

- *The Guest House* by Jalaluddin Rumi
- *Two Wolves – A Cherokee Parable*
- *Thoughts* by Walt Whitman

- *Three Gifts* by Confucius
- *Lotus* by Rabindranath Tagore
- *The Blind Men and the Elephant* by John Godfrey Saxe

10 EXERCISES

We have a few exercises throughout the eight-week MBWE to help deepen the insights generated from the practices. The suggested exercises and the step-by-step facilitation methods are found in appendix 7. We briefly present the purpose and salient features of these exercises in this section.

Wellbeing and Mindfulness

We know that mindfulness contributes directly to one's wellbeing. While there are many models of wellbeing, we use the Integrated Wellbeing Model (IWM) as it is a comprehensive model that integrates both hedonia and eudaimonia. You can read more about IWM in Chapter 2 and its application during inquiry in Chapter 5.

The teacher briefly presents the five components of the IWM to the participants followed by a floor activity around the IWM. The participants are invited to physically move themselves to the areas of wellbeing that they are most satisfied with and have a discussion with the other participants. Once the discussion is over, the teacher does a debrief on their emotions and thoughts resulting from the conversations. The process is then repeated for areas that they are least satisfied with or areas that they would like to focus more on. This is followed by an inquiry by the teacher.

Negativity Bias and Positivity

In order to notice the reactions we have to both pleasant and unpleasant experiences, the participants are invited to journal over two weeks as part of their homework in sessions 2 and 3. The teacher shares an example in each session to help participants understand the homework requirements. These are then reviewed the following week in small group conversations to look for patterns and insights and then discussed in the plenary where time permits. This practice brings along more awareness to the thoughts-feelings-body sensations connection. In session 3, when the home practice review of pleasant experiences is explored, the teacher then shares how our brains can be trained to be flexible in bringing attention to what is working in our lives. In session 4, when the unpleasant experiences are reviewed, the teacher links them again to the negativity bias of the brain and describes how our brains can be trained to bring acceptance to the negatives.

Brain and Mindfulness

To better understand how the brain functions and how mindfulness practices impact the brain, the teacher facilitates a game called 3–6–9 clap for 5 minutes. The participants form a large circle where everyone can see everyone. Each participant shouts the numbers from 1 to 60 (or 100 depending on the group size) as they move down the circle. There is a catch to this game. The rule is that when the numbers 3, 6, or 9 appears in the number sequence, they should only clap and not shout out the number. The moment they shout out the number accidently at 3, 6, or 9, the game restarts. This goes on until they reach the number 60 or until the 5 minutes is up. Whenever we conduct this game, we notice that some participants become really frustrated, while others strive hard to complete it, and yet others try and direct the rest of the group. Groups that succeed within the 5 minutes are usually overjoyed.

Once the game is completed, the teacher discusses how our brains have been programmed to react through the 3fs (fight, flight, and freeze) and how they can be trained to respond, instead of reacting, if acceptance could be brought to stimuli. With mindfulness, one is able to pause, ground oneself, and then respond rather than be impulsive and react.

Paper Folding Activity

The paper folding activity is a fun way to help participations learn how neuroplasticity works and how we can create new paradigms through mindfulness training. Participants are each given one piece of A4 or letter-sized paper and asked to fold the paper five times with their eyes closed. The teacher demonstrates before asking the participants to do it on their own. She then asks them to unfold the paper back to its original size. And then she gets them to repeat the task of folding it again with their eyes closed. After the second round, she invites them to open their eyes and asks them which round was easier and why they found the second round easier. Just as the lines that were already formed made it easier to fold the second time, practicing mindfulness creates neuropathways in the brain. The more we practice mindfulness, the deeper the neuropathways become. Each time we practice mindfulness, we create new pathways of sensing, thinking, feeling, and behaving that can create new paradigms.

Meaningful Engagements Exercise

We may have many meaningful daily engagements. However, we may not be noticing them or it could be that our lives have more depleting then energizing activities. In this exercise, participants are first asked to review their daily activities and to evaluate them as uplifting or depleting in the daily activities exploration sheet. Once they have completed, the teacher invites them to share their insights of their daily activities. This is followed by a second activity of exploring what is pleasurable, meaningful, or what they are good at in the pleasurable and mastery type activities sheet. From this list, they are invited to commit to one or two of the activities to bring them into their daily life to enhance their wellbeing. The teacher shares the choices that we make in our lives and how we can make conscious choices toward having more of the uplifting and meaningful engagements even if it is just for five minutes a day.

Perspective Taking

In the perspective taking exercise, the participants are invited to explore a variety of situations in which their emotions were triggered and to explore the event, their sensations, emotions, thoughts, and alternative perspectives. This is similar to rational emotive behavior therapy (REBT) by Albert Ellis but rather than *actively* disputing the thoughts, we are interested in exploring alternative ways of looking at the same situation. In a way, it is a form of *gentle* disputing. The teacher starts by asking the participants for a recent event that has triggered some strong emotions in them and uses that event to walk through the entire process. The teacher is encouraged to come to the session with two or three examples of their own in case the participants are not ready to open up.

Just before the teacher invites the participants to explore alternative perspectives, she invites the participants to share how their thoughts and emotions for each situation were helpful or unhelpful. This awareness itself is helpful in navigating through life. This is followed by the didactic teaching on how we have the flexibility to interpret events purposefully. Rebecca Crane (2017) says that we can learn how to better relate to others, rather than depending on past experiences with them, and learning that we are after all, not just our experiences. She further admits that thoughts are just thoughts and not a representation of reality. A word of caution is required here to be mindful that *we are not claiming that thoughts are unreal but rather that they are not representative of the reality that we perceive.* This is why we can have multiple perspectives of the same situation and that with flexibility, we can interpret events purposefully. Rather than being colored in our lens of life through memories or emotions, we make a conscious choice to be present in this moment and respond to a situation.

My Monthly Wellbeing Calendar

If we fail to plan, we plan to fail. The teacher encourages each participant to create their own mindfulness and wellbeing calendar as part of their homework in session 7. They are encouraged to include mindfulness practices and meaningful engagements in the calendar. The encouragement is to have one formal mindfulness practice per day and if this is not possible due to work commitments or others, to consider an informal practice on the busy days and formal practices on days where there is more space in their schedule. Participants are encouraged to plan according to their lifestyle taking into consideration work or study time, traveling time, family time, relaxation time, exercise time, stressful periods, etc., as they plan the calendar. The teacher also discusses with participants the downside of not planning the practice of mindfulness.

When the participants return for session 8, they discuss their calendar plan with one another and further adapt it if necessary. The teacher asks them to explore following the plan for one month and then plan the next month's calendar after they have explored what worked for them. They can consider adding these to their paper or digital calendars and also create reminders.

Mindful Letter to Self

As part of the final session, participants are asked to write a mindful letter to themselves. The purpose of the letter is to remind oneself of the insights into their journey, to motivate themselves to continue, to share with themselves the valuable lessons that they have learned, and also to visualize how they will be in three months' time. This letter is then kept by the teacher and mailed to the participants after three months. Many participants have shared feedback with us that they were pleased to receive the letter and to reflect on some of the learnings that had taken place. A few had also said that it motivated them to restart some of the practices that they had stopped by then.

In this chapter, we have presented the facilitation of mindfulness, the didactic components, and exercises in the MBWE. The specific instructions, scripts, and guide can be found in the appendices. In the next chapter, we will be presenting the method of facilitating the inquiry to generate insights into wellbeing and happiness.

REFERENCES

Bishop, S. R., Lau, M., Shapiro, S., Carlson, L., Anderson, N. D., Carmody, J., . . . & Devins, G. (2004). Mindfulness: A proposed operational definition. *Clinical psychology: Science and practice, 11*(3), 230–241.
Crane, R. (2017). Mindfulness-based cognitive therapy (2nd ed). Routledge.
Kabat-Zinn, J. (2005). *Coming to our senses: Healing ourselves and the world through mindfulness.* Hachette UK.

Rogers, C. R. (1995). *A way of being*. Houghton Mifflin Harcourt.

Segal, Z. V., Williams, J. M. G., & Teasdale, J. D. (2013). *Mindfulness-based cognitive therapy for depression*. Guilford.

Wolf, C., & Serpa, J. G. (2015). *A clinician's guide to teaching mindfulness: The comprehensive session-by-session program for mental health professionals and health care providers*. New Harbinger Publications.

CHAPTER 5

Inquiry and the Generation of Insights

That question you asked about noticing neutral and positive experiences got me thinking differently. You know that I always focused on the pain and tensions in my body and sometimes I was even irritated with this aged body. However, over the weeks, your questions on neutrality, common humanity, acceptance . . . allowed me to appreciate my Self.

–Matthew

In Chapter 1, we had briefly presented the purpose of inquiry and its function in the generation of insights. In Chapter 3, we had presented the Mindfulness-Based Wellbeing Enhancement (MBWE) session plans which included the structure of the program and the specific layer of inquiry employed in each segment of the session plans. In this chapter we will give more depth into the process of inquiry and how a mindfulness teacher steers the interactive dialogue in the direction of gaining personal insights about wellbeing and the happiness paradigm. Our specific focus would be to demonstrate how inquiry and insights can be generated about wellbeing, specifically in the MBWE program. We have organized the content into three broad areas which are knowledge, attitude, and skills.

1 KNOWLEDGE

In this section we will share the purposes and the broad process of inquiry. For easy reference, we reproduce the pedagogy of the MBWE below (see Figure 5.1).

The Inquiry Process

The outcome of inquiry involves personal intimacy with awareness and the knowledge one has about happiness and wellbeing. The former is entirely

DOI: 10.4324/9781003322955-6

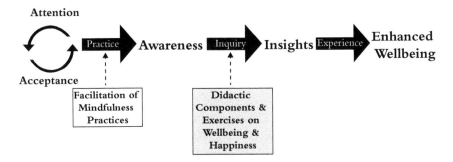

Figure 5.1 The pedagogical process of MBWE

dependent on the personal practice of the participants and the latter depends on their prior knowledge, life experiences, values, and specifically in this case, the skillful facilitation of the didactic components and inquiry by the mindfulness teacher. If the practices do not raise their awareness levels, the participants will find the process of inquiry to be very tiresome and boring. If the didactic teaching components are something already known to them, as in that they are *not* generating new insights or deepening their current insights, one would also lose interest in the practice of mindfulness. In our experience, we had noticed that when teachers are not able to facilitate inquiry with skill and presence, participants lose their trust in the efficacy of the practice and the inquiry segments, and also impute uselessness to the whole mindfulness-based program (MBP) and mindfulness.

As we supervise teachers-in-training, we spend most of our energy and time in mentoring them to facilitate inquiry effectively. It is like developing the mental muscles and creating new neuropathways to be curious, and at the same time following a broad and flexible structure. More often teachers give in to their habitual inclinations with regards to their thoughts which are primarily driven by their colloquial speech patterns. Biases, beliefs, and self-reinforcing behavior compound these habits.

We believe that the best way to learn how to facilitate the process of inquiry is to keep practicing it and by reflecting on one's own self-inquiry. We have also found video-recording oneself facilitating inquiry segments can also be very helpful in reviewing it. Thirdly, having a supervisor to review your recordings and guide you would be most ideal.

With that let us now turn our attention to the participants' engagement with mindfulness practices and inquiry. After the consistent practice of mindfulness, participants will gradually notice their experiences, during and after each practice. These experiences are diverse and varied, around:

- having thoughts about past, present, and future experiences
- recreating the memories and thoughts that they like and rejecting those that they do not like

- noticing sensations revolving around pain and ignoring the pleasant and neutral
- rejection of sensations, emotions, and thoughts, and neglecting the ones that are wholesome

One of the significantly distinct approaches of mindfulness is to bring awareness to one's experiences as opposed to solely attempting to process them cognitively. This is one of the key differences between the cognitive-behavioral traditions of change and the mindfulness approach. This unique approach of mindfulness is best exemplified through the process of inquiry. The first stage of the MBWE pedagogy, as with other MBPs, is the practice and the second stage is the inquiry process where participants are engaged in an interactive dialogue with three important intentions (see Table 5.1).

Table 5.1 Three-layered structure of inquiry in the MBWE

Layer	Outcome	Intentions of the inquiry
1	Noticing	1. To draw out and explore what they are *noticing* during the practice in terms of: • sensations • emotions • thoughts • urges/impulses 2. To be curious about how *attention* and *acceptance* are brought to what is being noticed (especially emotions and thoughts)
2	Discovery	1. To discover how mindfulness is different from the usual way of paying *attention* 2. Being aware of how the mind *interprets* every sensation, emotion, thought, urge, and situation 3. Recognizing the value of ethics and focusing on what works
3	Integration	1. Connecting the discoveries to the *enhancement of wellbeing* through specific wellbeing interventions (e.g. IWM) 2. Gaining insights on how consistent mindfulness practices enhance wellbeing, through the lenses of the *happiness paradigm*

It is at layer 3 where insights are gathered by the participants although this process is cumulative starting from layer 1. These become the key insights from participating in the MBWE. The didactic components presented in Figure 5.1 are used in the MBWE to support the inquiry. It strengthens the arrival at insights through reflection, investigation, evidence, and interpretation.

Each formal practice, informal practice, and exercises would have its specific method of inquiry, while adhering to the three layers. Inquiry can also be conducted horizontally and vertically with the three layers (Woods &

Rockman, 2021). Horizontal inquiry reveals the diverse experiences within an individual as well as across a group of people in the same room (see Figure 5.2). The second aspect of horizontal inquiry also facilitates the discovery of common humanity in the room. Vertical inquiry refers to the depth of experience that can be explored.

Figure 5.2 Horizontal and vertical inquiry

Both of these directions of inquiry employed in each of the layers can be very helpful for a teacher to draw out experiences that lead to the generation of insight. The horizontal and vertical inquiries can be facilitated in different ways at each of the layers. We will demonstrate with some examples in the skills section of this chapter.

The three layers of inquiry are also deployed at different stages of the eight-week MBWE (see Figure 5.3). While we do not advocate a rigid

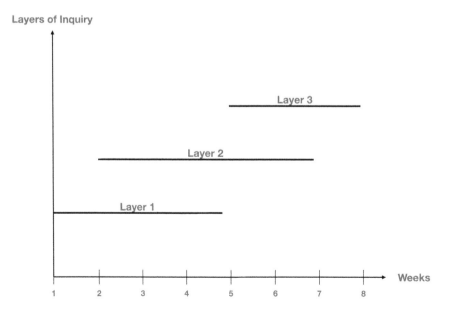

Figure 5.3 Progressive deployment of three-layered inquiry

structure to the facilitation of the layers of inquiry, we have realized, through our supervision work, that novice teachers often struggle with employing each layer progressively and intuitively. As such, Figure 5.3 provides some guidelines on how to use each layer over the eight weeks.

From a pedagogical perspective, each participant is unique and their insights are developed at their own pace and maturity. Participants sometimes discover the

- same insights at the same time
- same insights at different times
- different insights at the same time
- different insights at different times

We often tell our trainee teachers that we need to cultivate non-striving with this expectation, that everyone has to generate insights as we expect them to be so. This neither allows us to be present nor does it acknowledge that people are different and that they would find what they need when they do. This is also closely related to the attitude of trust in mindfulness and its process.

Challenges and Difficulties

Rob Brandsma (2017) lists three challenges that teachers face when facilitating inquiry, which are reactivity, lack of control and not answering questions. Reactivity refers to the habitual reactivity of having the need to answer questions when asked by the participants. We have noticed this in our own teaching experience as well as when supervising trainee teachers. One example is our reaction to silence. After asking a question, participants may need time to think. This may take 3 seconds or maybe 30 seconds. One habit that I (KK) have noticed in myself was the urge to fill up the silence with my voice. Silence was something that I was uncomfortable with in my early years of teaching. In those moments, I would immediately ask another question, or elaborate the question or make a statement to fill that silence. I learned over time that silence is okay and that silence can aid reflection. It also allows us as teachers to be patient with ourselves and our participants.

The teachers' lack of control over what responses would emerge from the participants could possibly create anxiety or even the need to regain control of the teaching by lecturing instead. We have watched teachers-in-training who would ask questions hoping to receive a particular response. And when that does not happen they start lecturing or explaining concepts. It is important to let things be and *when destabilized, we can always go back to a layer-1* inquiry question *and deepen it vertically.*

Third, it is very difficult for teachers to not answer questions. Often we feel the need to answer questions when posed. Not answering a question could be a challenge for several reasons. It may show vulnerability and the need to be in the role of an expert having answers to all questions. Most of the time, it is best not to answer any question that is raised during inquiry unless necessary. As we would always say to trainee teachers, "Your role is to shine the spotlight on the experiences of the participants. And during the instances when the participants turn the light on you, your role is to shine the light back at them." For example,

Participant (P):	Can you tell me if what I did was right or wrong?
Teacher (T):	Perhaps could you share your thoughts about it?
P:	I think it is right because I could accept those difficult thoughts. I didn't fight it.
T:	I am curious to know how *acceptance* plays a part in your happiness and wellbeing.
P:	I can learn to be less reactive and respond to situations with clearer intentions.

We would like to add two more challenges to this list, namely cognitive load and unpredictable responses. Novice teachers might experience the challenge of having too much in their working memory when teaching MBPs. With the increased cognitive load, teachers still have to multi-task to stay within time, manage coordination in the room, and facilitate the curriculum among others. The mental bandwidth for inquiry and staying present could add even more load onto the working memory. Therefore, it is important that we cultivate self-compassion and recognize that inquiry skills get better with practice and regular facilitation with different audience groups. We have heard from many teachers how the facilitation of the MBWE got easier and easier each time, as they became more familiar with the protocol and could naturally be more aware with the participants.

Unpredictable responses are usually responses that are not anticipated in the room. Here are a few examples:

I hate meditation.

I thought this is going to be easy, but now I am finding it challenging.

I don't think you know the answer to my question, from the way that you are choosing not to answer it.

Learning to accept that "I do not know" and being vulnerable to acknowledge that in the room is an invaluable insight in itself. Learning to accept both favorable and unfavorable responses is important for wellbeing. Sharing these insights would be a great opportunity for teachers to walk the path of wisdom instead of just talking about it.

Generation of Insights

Through the three-layered inquiry, we guide participants to generate insights into their wellbeing and happiness. While each participant would gain their own unique insights, all of them would have a common theme which is wellbeing and happiness. Participants would recognize how *attention, acceptance, and awareness through mindfulness practice, coupled with didactic teaching with exercises, can enhance their wellbeing* (see Figure 5.4).

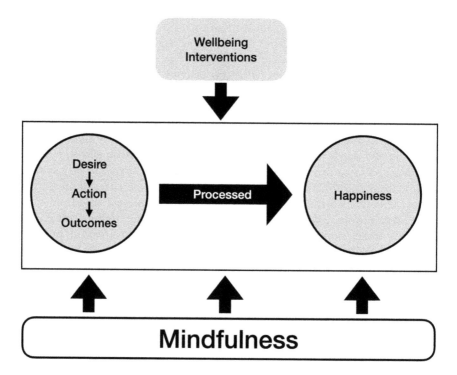

Figure 5.4 Impact of mindfulness and wellbeing interventions on the happiness paradigm

How participants process the outcomes of life has a huge impact on their happiness. Using the cognitive-behavioral traditions approach, it is helpful to see how mindfulness impacts our cognitions while processing outcomes (see Figure 5.5).

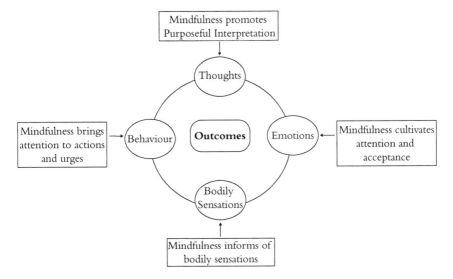

Figure 5.5 Impact of mindfulness on cognition

Mindfulness impacts wellbeing by impacting all the stages of cognition and being able to shift unhealthy paradigms to healthier ones, via the happiness paradigm:

Attention to the positive + Acceptance of the negative + Purposeful interpretation

The primary areas of focus in the MBWE are the domains of thoughts and emotions. The domains of sensations and behavior are secondary though it would be wrong to deem them to be unimportant. It is through noticing our sensations and urges that we slowly start cultivating mindfulness (cf. layer-1 inquiry). And from layer 1 to layer 2, we gradually shift our focus to the thoughts.

We have listed a few examples of insights that we have gathered from our MBWE participants:

• Happiness can become a trait
• There are two types of happiness: hedonia and eudaimonia
• I have a choice over the desire that I want to realize
• Happiness is an internal experience, enabled by objects of desire
• I can bring acceptance to the results of my action
• My happiness is dependent on how I interpret my experiences
• Aligning my desires and wants with what I believe in makes me happy

- Thoughts are not facts, therefore I can shift my viewpoints or take different perspectives
- The pre-goal attainment effect is greater in duration than the post-goal attainment affect
- Paradigms can be changed with selective and flexible attention
- Happiness is only partially controllable, and therefore I can have more reasonable expectations
- Thoughts rise in my awareness and they come and go
- I have less control over the thoughts that emerge in my mind, but I can interpret them differently with wisdom

Mindfulness literature often interprets suffering as stress and depression. However, some scholars attribute stress and depression to cognitive thinking flaws meaning that unless a shift takes place in their paradigm, depression and stress cannot be overcome. In fact, it is important to also recognize how lowered levels of wellbeing often create stress. For example, not paying attention to the positive, rejecting the negative and interpreting situations through negative lenses often exacerbate or create stress, anxiety and depression according to eminent theorists such as Aaron Beck and Martin Seligman.

Having the knowledge of inquiry process and the layers, and knowing the challenges in inquiry, help a teacher to know when and how to deepen the inquiry toward insights.

2 ATTITUDE

The attitude of the MBWE teacher is very critical to the effectiveness of inquiry. In fact this is an aspect of embodiment for teachers, where they embody the seven attitudes of mindfulness that we briefly discussed in Chapter 1.

Patience – one cannot rush the generation of insights like the way we cannot rush the growth of on infant or child. Insights are generated in their own time for every participant. This requires patience on the part of teacher to be able to let the inquiry take its own course over the eight weeks by staying present in spite of having a curriculum to adhere to.

Beginner's mind – the inquiry cannot be pre-planned to the letter. I (SR) remember supervising a novice teacher who told me that she had memorized the inquiry questions. And to her horror, she realized that she was totally lost every time a participant responded to her questions with different responses from her expectations such that she could not ask the next prepared question. Allowing ourselves to cultivate a beginner's mind would then help us to let each inquiry segment to be a new experience with a sense of curiosity.

Acceptance – acceptance can be best understood as non-reactivity to the participants' responses (and non-responses). We allow silence, non-reactivity to participants' negative experiences with a practice and giving ourselves the space to respond to what is happening in the room in response to our question. It is like the way the ocean receives the waters of countless rivers. Responding when required with a present-moment focus is acceptance.

Letting go – as teachers, we model letting go from our way of being, by demonstrating that we may not be attached to a fixed way of doing things. We are flexible to change the way we facilitate the inquiry. For example, we could use a paired conversation, or a small group discussion, or sometimes a plenary (large group) format, or we could sometimes let go of a focused inquiry by telling them that sometimes it is okay to not to arrive at answers.

Trust – like the way we trusted our exploration of mindfulness when we first encountered it, we model it in the room by making that opportunity available to everyone present. We trust the experiences of participants as they share theirs as opposed to doubting what is being shared. We embody trust by trusting what is being shared in the room and we demonstrate that verbally and non-verbally through our body language and appropriate facial expressions within a given culture.

Non-judging – a judgment can sometimes look like an evaluation, an analysis, or even disputing the responses of the participants. It is important that we seek to *understand* what is being said rather than judging it. Understanding what a participant is saying can be a very empowering feeling for her. This requires us to suspend our judgment, criticism, and blame. In fact, judging ourselves in the process of inquiry for not doing an effective job is as unhelpful as judging a participant.

Non-striving – we often see a sense of struggle when novice teachers try their hand at facilitating inquiry because it is unlike any other experience we usually have in our lives, unless you are a mental health or coaching professional, who is used to asking questions and making fewer statements. The struggle is real and it gets more intense as we continue struggling. Non-striving is not putting excessive effort into trying to come up with questions for the inquiry process. Instead we allow a sense of relaxed control like the way you guide a kite with minimal control once it takes flight.

In addition to these seven attitudes for a teacher, McCown et al. (2011) have added three more.

Not an expert – the first being *not an expert* by cultivating "non-knowingness," a philosophical attitude. The attitude of being not a knower allows both the teacher and the learner to suspend specific agendas during every inquiry segment in the MBWE. While the teacher knows that we need to get somewhere, he or she allows the possibility of not getting there, with acceptance and grace.

Cultural sensitivity – the second attitude is the need to adapt the inquiry when cultural and individual resistances appear in the room. Although we will defer this discussion to Chapter 7, we are compelled to state that sometimes an inquiry may not have to be facilitated entirely as a verbal dialogue. Teachers need to abandon this compulsion when necessary. Embodying mindfulness would also then mean that we are sensitive to different cultures. We have noticed that in some cultures people of one gender may not be comfortable having a conversation with someone of a different gender from the one that they identify with. Cultural differences like these would have to be anticipated and allowed in the room as long as they do not lower the wellbeing of others in the room.

Openness – the third attitude is remaining open to all types of outcomes during the inquiry. Sometimes the inquiry segment would be

- Better than expected
- Worse than expected
- As expected
- Opposite to what was expected

Remaining open to these four types of outcomes is itself an embodiment of mindfulness.

Woods et al. (2019) add two more attitudes which are compassion and curiosity.

Compassion – Woods and colleagues state that compassion grows when we allow and meet "each moment, even if difficult or painful, without judgment" (p. 101). Compassion is certainly very important for a teacher because the people who signed up to be in the MBWE program definitely wanted something that they did not already have. And they walked into the room expecting that the teacher is going to be beneficent in facilitating the journey of discovery for them. It is an implicit acknowledgment of vulnerability and humility that deserves the compassion of teachers. This compassion, that comes from not being an *expert* dispensing wisdom to the participants, but rather from a fellow *companion* who is on her own journey, shining her light in the dark alleys of the inner journey.

Curiosity – the second attitude is curiosity which allows the deepening and expansion of the inquiry, horizontally and vertically. It is like a torchlight that allows the brightening of its light as well as shining it in places that we do not usually see. As we walk through the dark alley, the teacher shines the light not only on the ground but also on what is on the sides and above or even taking a pause to make a deeper exploration at particular points on this inner journey.

As can be seen from the above, there are at least 12 attitudes that a teacher can cultivate toward becoming an embodied mindfulness teacher.

3 SKILLS

The philosophical approach to inquiry in the MBWE program is also slightly different from other MBPs. In this section, we will be presenting and demonstrating the methods of facilitating the process of inquiry in the

MBWE through the three layers. We have to qualify that from our experience it is not as easy to learn the art and science of facilitating inquiry by only learning from a book. We have seen trainee teachers struggling with inquiry during their practice sessions in spite of having listened to us lecturing and demonstrating the process; reading on it in books and journals; attending other courses on inquiry; and having experienced it themselves from their MBWE/MBSR/MBCT teachers. We would recommend that readers who plan to teach the MBWE, to attend formal training sessions where they can practice their inquiry skills and receive feedback from supervisors and peers. If you happen to be a certified mindfulness teacher trained to deliver a specific MBP, then we invite you to shift your philosophical dial to a "wellbeing" focus rather than the intentions of the MBP you are trained in.

Stages of Inquiry Process

The process of inquiry involves three successive stages. The inquiry would usually begin right after a mindfulness practice or an exercise. The three stages are:

- **Stage 1:** The teacher asks the participants a question.
- **Stage 2:** There is an engagement with the question by the participants.
- **Stage 3:** An **interactive dialogue** ensues between the teacher and the participants.

In stage 1, the teacher poses a question (either layer 1, 2 or 3) to the participants. And then the teacher sets up the participants for stage 2, by choosing one of three options (refer to Table 5.2), for the engagement with the inquiry question. A specific time is set for the discussion and is clearly communicated to the participants before stage 2 commences. The three options for the engagement with the inquiry question are:

- **Individual reflection:** each participant would reflect in silence on the specific question.
- **Paired discussion:** two participants would engage in discussion of the specific question.
- **Small group discussion:** small groups of threes, fours, or fives discuss the specific question.

The choice of types of engagement at stage 2 can be decided on couple of factors, as indicated in the Table 5.2 below:

Table 5.2 Types of engagement with inquiry

Types	Time	Safety	Advantages	Disadvantages
Individual reflection	Least time needed	Safe and no pressure	• More genuine • Promotes vertical inquiry	Experiences are not shared and heard so no guiding of ideas or clarification of misconceptions/ doubts, etc.
Paired discussion	More time consuming to go pair by pair	Safe	• Any one person can represent the pair in sharing • More depth in sharing • Promotes vertical and horizontal inquiry	• Might be slow and boring for some if there are too many paired discussions • The more vocal in the pair might dominate conversations
Small group discussion	Time consuming to go group by group but less time consuming than the paired conversation	Requires trust in the group to develop safety	• Each group is heard • More experiences are shared • More ideas are covered than the large group sharing • Promotes horizontal inquiry	• Might be slow and boring for some • Some experiences or ideas might be repetitive

After the end of stage 2, stage 3 commences when the teacher invites everyone to engage in a large group (plenary) dialogue. The teacher then facilitates an interactive discussion involving one or multiple layers of inquiry depending on what emerges in the room and the curriculum.

Sequence in Exploration

Similar to the cognitive-behavioral traditions of modern psychology, the process of inquiry explores four important dimensions of cognition, presented in the diagram below (see Figure 5.6):

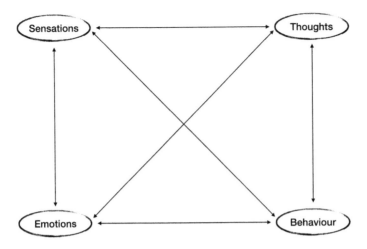

Figure 5.6 Inquiry into the four dimensions of cognition

In spite of knowing that there could be a causal relationship among the elements of cognition, i.e. in the order of thoughts → emotions → sensations → behavior, we allow the possibility of seeing connection in a multi-directional fashion. The reason being that we are not necessarily looking for a structure in the way participants see the connection between one or more of the elements. Rather it is more important that participants use these elements to connect with their own wellbeing through their own wisdom and experience while journeying through the layers as they converge into insights (see Figure 5.7).

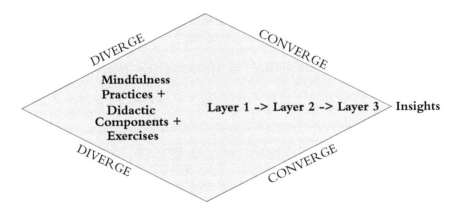

Figure 5.7 Generation of insights

In the next section, we will be presenting the art and science of facilitating the three layers of inquiry. While it is easy for us to present the science by providing the method and examples of questions, we need to acknowledge one limitation. It is easier to teach the science than the art of inquiry as the latter requires a present-moment centeredness coupled with an intuitive response which is developed through practice. An artist can never re-create the same artwork with exactly same brushes or strokes. Two similar paintings may look similar from afar, but they are actually different when you look at them closer. The art of facilitating inquiry is similar and yet different each time you employ it.

We reiterate at this juncture that learning to facilitate inquiry requires mentorship and practice. What we are presenting in the next section would be primarily the science of inquiry in the MBWE and we leave the art of it for you practice and learn from experience and mentorship.

Layer-1 Inquiry

At the first layer of inquiry, the outcome is *noticing* and hence the questions that are asked would allow participants

1. to draw out and explore what they are *noticing* during the practice in terms of:

    - sensations
    - emotions
    - thoughts
    - urges/impulses

2. to be curious about how *attention* and *acceptance* are brought to what is noticed (especially emotions and thoughts)

Though participants are invited to appreciate the cognitive elements through their own experience, there is a pedagogy that guides the layers of inquiry. McCown et al. (2011) state an important principle in the process of inquiry,

> Often an inquiry dialog can lead to confusion rather than clarity. At such a point the teacher may suggest that the participant move back into a formal mindfulness practice for further pre-semantic exploration of sensation, thought and emotion.
>
> (p. 129)

This astute observation tells us an important principle in the process of inquiry, which is to return to the experience of practice i.e. layer-1 inquiry when there is confusion or doubt in the room. Further within the exploration of the elements of cognition, there also appears a pedagogy for exploration and it starts with the grossest experiences among the elements. Sensations become the starting point for the process of inquiry, as illustrated below in the form of a staircase (see Figure 5.8).

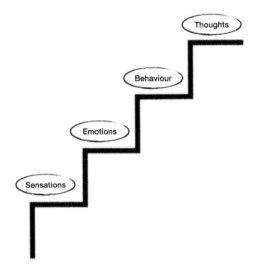

Figure 5.8 Inquiring into the elements of cognition

As you would have inferred by now, the layer-1 inquiry would start with sensations and then proceed upwards. Here is a sample dialogue:

Stage 1

    T: What sensations did you notice during the body scan practice? Discuss in groups of threes for five minutes.

    [Stage 2: Participants discuss the question in groups]

Stage 3

    T: Let's explore the sensations that you noticed and discussed in your groups. Who would like to share?

    P: I noticed a sharp pain in my right ankle.

    T: Were there any *emotion* around that sensation?

    P: I felt a little frustrated with the fact that it distracted me from the rest of the practice.

T: Were there any *urges* around that emotion?
P: Yes, I felt like stopping the practice but I persisted through.
T: And then any *thoughts* around that urge?
P: I felt guilty about feeling that way and tried to push that thought away.
T: Thank you for sharing that.

Sometimes, participants may jump the question to arrive at an emotion or even the urges. In such a situation, we escort the exploration back to sensation. Here is a sample dialogue.

T: Let's explore the *sensations* that you noticed and discussed in your groups. Who would like to share?
P: I was very *frustrated* during the practice.
T: I am curious to know what caused that.
P: It was a distraction.
T: Where was that distraction in the body, if it were to be so?
P: Yeah, at my right ankle. It was a sharp *pain*.
T: Were there any *urges* around that emotion?
P: Yes, I felt like stopping the practice.
T: And then any *thoughts* around that urge?
P: I felt guilty about feeling that way.

As you would have noticed, there are many ways that teachers can steer the direction of inquiry, as illustrated in Figure 5.6. In the two examples above, the inquiry was conducted vertically (refer to Figure 5.2 for context). It is important to note that at layer 1, as it is with any of the other layers, we can explore the horizontal exploration of inquiry. Here is an example:

P: I was very *frustrated* during the practice.
T: I am curious to know what caused that.
P: It was a distraction.
T: Who else in the room had a similar or different experience?

Or you could also take horizontal direction of inquiry in the opposite direction by asking:

T: Where was that distraction in the body, if it were to be so?
P: Yeah, at my right ankle. It was a sharp *pain*.
T: Were there any other parts of the body where you noticed *pain* or *discomfort*?

Horizontal inquiry helps us to explore internal and external explorations. When people report a similar experience, it points out the common humanity that is there in the room. When people report diverse experiences, it shows that people are also different or responses to the same practice can be different.

It is like a dance between diversity and unity that takes place during the inquiry process. There is one more type of layer-1 inquiry that is distinct to the MBWE, which is the exploration of the neutral and the pleasant in the four elements. For example,

T: Where was that distraction in the body, if it were to be so?
P: Yeah, at my right ankle. It was a sharp *pain*.
T: Were there areas around the ankle where there were *no pain* and *everything was fine*?
P: My toes and the rest of the foot were all *good*.
T: How about the area between your knee and your ankle?
P: All *good*.
T: Did you notice any *emotions* arising as a result of what is working well?
P: No.
T: Having this realization that the rest of the limb is working fine, except for the right ankle, are there any *emotions* that you are feeling right now?
P: Well, I am *thankful* for things that are going well too.
T: Are there others in the room who are having a similar perspective of perhaps a sense of *gratitude* for what is going well in the body?

Having gotten adequate responses from a few people in the room, we can move to the next phase of the layer-1 inquiry where we explore how people brought *attention* and *acceptance* toward these elements. This next step is crucial to the inquiry process as it magnifies what has been already experienced through the guided mindfulness practices. Here are two examples of exploration into *attention* in two opposite directions i.e. attention to the *negative* and the *positive*.

T: Could you describe the sharp *pain* that was felt at the right ankle?
P: I am not sure if it was a muscle strain or the tendon. Every time I moved my ankle a little the pain gets allayed. But it doesn't go away.
T: Where was it exactly at the right ankle.
P: [*Pointing to specific part of the right ankle*] . . . right here.
T: Were you able to let the pain *be* as you were bringing attention to other parts of the body?
P: It was difficult but it wasn't impossible.
T: What was not impossible?
P: I was able to *notice* other parts of the body.
T: Which parts?
P: The knees, hips, tummy, shoulders, and so forth.
T: So you were able to direct your attention to those parts weren't you?
P: Yes, I could.
T: What were the *sensations* that you noticed in those parts?
P: They were *relaxed* with *no pain or tension*. My shoulders were *relaxed* which was interesting to notice.

You could also explore in the same manner toward emotions, urges and thoughts. For example,

> T: Could you describe on a scale of 1 to 10, 10 being extremely strong, how strong was that emotion?
> P: It was 6.
> T: I am curious, how so?
> P: Because I could feel my heart thumping but I wasn't impelled to act in any way though.

In the sphere of thoughts and urges, the following are examples of questions:

> T: What were the *thoughts* about?
> T: Were those *urges* something that you were comfortable with or not?

The second aspect of this phase is exploration of *acceptance* toward the negative. Here is an example:

> T: Where was that distraction in the body, if it were to be so?
> P: Yeah, at my right ankle. It was a sharp *pain*.
> T: *Without rejecting* the pain, were you were able to *direct attention* to other parts of the body?
> P: Yes.

In summary, we explore the dimensions of *attention* and *acceptance* toward the four elements as shown in Figure 5.9.

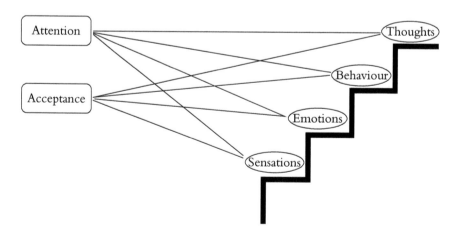

Figure 5.9 Directing attention and acceptance to the four elements of cognition

At each of the elements, we facilitate the inquiry, vertically and horizontally, by exploring:

1   Attention to the various types of elements
2   Attention to the often-neglected experience of the neutral and positive, and
3   Acceptance to both the negative and the positive

At the end of the layer-1 inquiry process, we move to the next layer depending on how adequate we feel the discussion has been in generating insights and the stage we are at in the MBWE curriculum.

Layer-2 Inquiry

The outcome of a layer-2 inquiry is *discovery*. Participants are invited to look at what was noticed in the layer-1 inquiry and explore how they are different from the usual way of paying *attention*, practicing *acceptance* and *interpretation*. At this layer, the participants' intimacy with *awareness* can be very empowering in the process. And we need to be aware that the didactic components, exercises and suggested readings would also be supporting the exploration at this layer, for the participants.

We could open the second layer inquiry as follows:

T: We have been practicing a couple of mindfulness practices for a few weeks. What has been *different* in the way you pay attention?
T: We continue to bring *acceptance* to the discomforts and pay *attention* to that which we usually neglect, which are the things that are going well. I am now curious. How has the way that you *pay attention changed* over the weeks?
T: I am curious, how has the way you brought acceptance *changed* over the weeks?
T: What has *changed* from the way you use to eat/walk/do things, etc., and how are you doing it now?

We can deepen the exploration with different types of responses presenting different ways of purposeful interpretation. Here is an example of a dialogue:

P: I am quick tempered. Now I am noticing the emotions as they rise.
T: How so?
P: I now notice the change in my breathing when my temper rises.
T: And then . . .
P: I take a pause and withdraw myself from the situation that is triggering my moods.

T: How is this *different* from before?
P: In the past I would just lash out when my temper rose. Now it is *different*.
T: Thanks for sharing that. Is there anyone else who had a somewhat *similar* experience?

Through the dialogue we uncover the difference from how it was before. In the above dialogue the participant spoke about *behaviors* and the teacher immediately engaged in horizontal inquiry by asking if anyone else had a similar experience thus appealing to the common humanity in the room.

Here is another dialogue that focuses on the positive and negative:

T: What *other* situations in your life could this pause be brought into so that it becomes *purposeful* to you?
P1: Perhaps before I make a life-changing decision.
T: Perhaps you can give us some examples of such life-changing decisions.
P1: Like deciding on a life partner, a job, or even moving to another country.
T: What are some *different* thoughts that this pause might *create*?
P1: Maybe is this really what I want or need? What am I looking for with this new job?
P2: Perhaps, is it money that I want or is it happiness?
T: You are seeing something deeper as to how these attentional capabilities impact our choices in life and being happy. How *about* if these situations *do not manifest* the way we want them to?
P3: I would try again.
P4: Maybe I would try an alternative means to achieve it.
T: Certainly this *flexibility* is helpful in life. Anyone else who would like to share . . .?
P1: Maybe I can accept the situations without rejecting them?
T: What *emotions* would there be in such situations if *acceptance wasn't there*?
P1: Frustration, disappointment . . .
T: We discussed how mindfulness brings *acceptance*. Could *acceptance* be brought to those emotions?
P1: Yes.
T: How would it help?
P1: I can take a pause, think, and reset. It clears my mind of the expectation for a specific result.
T: How is this *different* from the usual way that we relate to life situations?
P1: I used to reject them and then lose sleep over them.
P2: I would keep complaining. Now I understand that things are not entirely in my control.
P3: Way more peaceful than before.

T: How could *attention* to situations that are going well in our life pos-
     sibly *help* us?

P1: I can perhaps also notice what is going well in my life as well like you
     know my family is healthy and we get to travel once or twice a year.

P2: Appreciate people and things that support me.

P3: Maybe learning about my strengths and what I value?

From the above dialogues, you can see how we are gradually extending the
way we brought attention and acceptance differently to the elements to other
life situations beyond internal experiences. By doing this, people discover that
what was discovered within can help in *behaviors* and *interpretation* as well. You
would have also realized how the *happiness paradigm* is discovered by participants in their own ways through the inquiry.

Let us now turn our attention to bringing *awareness* into the inquiry process. *We would only do this once participants in the room have discussed the differences
in the way they paid attention and brought acceptance in life.* It is important to
acknowledge that awareness is the most abstract mechanism as it can be inex-
plicable and therefore confusing. To reiterate what was discussed in Chapter 1,
awareness is not subject to agency, as in choiceless, like light that reveals objects
without getting in touch with it.

Here is how we could possibly bring the discovery of *awareness* as though
it is being unveiled. Because awareness is abstract, we would usually depend
on metaphors and analogies.

T: We could possibly be seeing now that we are becoming aware of *what
     is* without changing them in any way. Allowing thoughts, sensations to
     just be in awareness like the way clouds are in skies. The clouds come
     and go, but the sky remains as it is without holding on to the clouds.
     What are your thoughts about this analogy?

T: Awareness is like the true north; it does not change its direction.
     Because it doesn't change, everything else depends on awareness. Sim-
     ilarly, it is in awareness that we see our thoughts, emotions, sensations,
     and urges. How would you relate this to your own experience?

T: Awareness is like the light of a torch. When the torch is off, you don't
     see the objects. When it is dim, we don't see things clearly but we have
     some glimpses. When it is bright enough, we see things clearly. How
     would you relate this to emotions, thoughts, urges, or actions?

Some responses we have heard at this juncture are:

P1: I never saw it this way. Yeah, my thoughts just come and go in my
     mind. I have no control. I did not cause it directly. It happens just like
     that. Why do I then own it?

P2:   My happiness and sorrows are all just thoughts. I can choose what to pay attention to like the way I choose which bus to board and to ignore the buses that do not go the destination I want to go to. Regardless they are just there in my awareness.

P3:   I feel lighter to know that awareness is not in contact with my thoughts, be it happiness, stress or misery. I never saw it this way. I am the sky, not the clouds.

With this, you would have noticed how the layer-2 inquiry allows participants to discover a new way of relating with their cognition and wellbeing.

We have encountered that with some participants the outcome of layer 3 is automatically discovered in this layer itself. If that happens, we do not obstruct it at any point of the inquiry process. We allow that to happen naturally.

Layer-3 Inquiry

The outcome of layer 3 is *integration*. Participants discover how mindfulness enhances *wellbeing* through specific *wellbeing interventions* (e.g. IWM) and the *happiness paradigm*. Insights are gathered by the participants from the inquiry at this layer and participants connect to the reasons that they had signed up for the MBWE. The effort required by the teacher to facilitate at this stage is easier than the other layers though it is very crucial because this is where they generate meaningful and purposeful insights that would possibly guide them in the rest of their lives. Our questions at this layer could be:

T: With all of the discussions and realizations, how has that *impacted your happiness or wellbeing*?

T: How does this *wisdom* you have gained about yourself *support your wellbeing*?

T: How does mindfulness *contribute* to your *wellbeing and happiness*?

T: How can these realizations *make our life whole*?

T: What are the *benefits* of becoming intimate with *awareness* itself?

In our experience, the responses can fall on the baseline or above it (see Figure 5.10). Sometimes you hear people reporting restorative benefits and results such as:

- reduction of stress
- reducing anxiety
- reducing the frequency of depressive moods

Figure 5.10 Types of outcomes

Other participants usually report that they became happier, more purposeful, and enhanced self-awareness thus showing the appreciative benefits of mindfulness. These include becoming aware of:

- their disposition for happiness: hedonia or eudaimonia
- their wants, likes, and dislikes
- their values and strengths
- their beliefs and knowledge
- happiness being the prime goal of life and the other goals are its levers
- being happier

There is also a third possibility which is that there is no impact at all. We have yet to encounter such participants though it may be possible. I (KK) remember a class that I led where a participant brought her spouse telling him that he needed mindfulness and she kept repeating that at various junctures of the eight-week program. In a casual conversation after a class, he shared with me that he was there because his wife wanted him to be there and not of his own accord. Sometimes people report no impact due to the lack of personal commitment or motivation. The locus of choice has a huge impact on motivation and commitment to practice.

We can deepen the inquiry at this layer by asking participants to identify the areas of impact in their lives using wellbeing interventions. For example, in the MBWE we use the Integrated Wellbeing Model (IWM) intervention and ask participants during the last session to share the areas in which they have noticed a positive impact (refer to Table 5.3).

Table 5.3 Elements of the Integrated Wellbeing Model (IWM) intervention

	Aspect	Elements
1	Spatial self	• Space and environment that we are in • Interaction of the body with the environment
2	Physical self	• Engagement with physical activity • Physiological health
3	Emotional self	• Emotional experiences • Emotional resilience • Emotional intelligence • Emotional regulation
4	Intellectual self	• Wisdom and knowledge • Values • Attitude and strengths • Locus of control • Decision making • Religiosity and spirituality • RelationshipsPersonality
5	Eudaimonic self	• Purpose • Meaning in life

At this stage, participants would see how mindfulness impacted wellbeing via the happiness paradigm and wellbeing interventions.

Closing an Inquiry

How do we close an inquiry at any of the layers? One way that we have found to be very helpful is to organize what was discussed and share it back with the participants as a summary. Here are a few examples:

> Layer 1 – many of us in the room noticed the discomforts during the mindful movement practice. We also saw that with flexible attention, we could also notice what was working well. Emotions are often connected to our thoughts. Mindfulness brought attention to both the negative and the positive and a sense of acceptance to all of our experiences. Each one of us had different experiences as well and that is okay. With that let us now turn to . . .

> Layer 2 – we saw how our minds can learn the skill to take alternative perspectives through mindfulness practices. And make choices with minimal effort around what conduces wellbeing. Being intimate with

awareness allows us to create a healthy distance between the Self and what the Self experiences. Let us now explore a practice . . .

Layer 3 – it was heartening to see areas of positive impact via your practice of mindfulness though it was different for each one of you. Mindfulness not only restores your balance but also allows you to direct your attention to what is valuable to you. Let's now . . .

These are ways that you can close an inquiry segment in the MBWE depending on which layer you are at and what was already discussed in the room. Depending on the week and the group dynamics, you may also consider requesting any of the participants to summarize the insights.

Supportive Inquiry Skills

Now let us turn our discussion to a few supportive skills that help us in being effective in facilitating the process of inquiry.

• **Asking open-ended and close-ended questions** – asking open-ended questions and close-ended questions at appropriate points helps the participants to direct their attention. At the beginning of an inquiry, at any layer, we generally ask open-ended questions to diverge and explore the experience such as:

What was experienced during this practice?
What emotions were there?
Please share with us more about . . . ?

Close-ended questions help us to navigate through dense information to arrive at clarity. At appropriate times, you may ask close-ended questions such as:

Where was that pain?
Which was easier to notice: the painful or the neutral sensations?
You felt disappointed with the practice today?

We recommend that we stay away from the "why" questions unless required as they are invasive and sometimes may mean an implicit judgment. Ask more of the *how, what, when, where, who,* and *how* questions instead.

- **Common humanity** – common humanity acknowledges that we are connected by both the joys of being human as well as the unpleasant. It is important during inquiry to continuously lean on horizontal inquiry to show that we are more similar than we think we are.
- **Familiar vocabulary** – as much as we stay away from semantical complexities, it is important that as a MBWE teacher, we build a vocabulary of positive emotions. Often, we realized that people are more familiar with their negative emotions as compared to the positive. We recommend becoming more aware and familiar with the vocabulary of positive emotions such as gratitude, joy, hope, awe, and eagerness. It helps participants to effortlessly cultivate a vocabulary for the positive.
- **Say less, ask more** – we often repeat this dictum "less is more" to trainee teachers. Personal insights are better generated through questions than statements. Statements are more effective in trying to present something already conceptualized. So say less and ask more.
- **Active listening** – active listening is described as being engaged in the listening instead of being distracted or disinterested. This skill requires curiosity. We often say that this would mean that *we listen to understand rather than to respond*. Remain curious and desire to understand what is being shared in the room as only then can we make an informed response.
- **Not responding to technical questions** – from time-to-time participants ask technical questions about mindfulness, its evidence, and neuroscientific dimensions among others. While we respect and recognize that participants are curious to understand these technical aspects, we want to respectfully stay away from getting into a lecture or unplanned didactic teaching that might take time away from the practices. We recommend that teachers give a short answer if you have it and postpone a deeper exploration outside the class through an email, sending reading materials, or using any other mutually agreed platform with more information. And if you do not know the answer, it is important that to say that you do not have it, but are willing to check it and respond later if necessary. Embodied mindfulness allows us to acknowledge that we do not have to know everything to be happy.
- **Receiving feedback** – sometimes participants give feedback during the sessions even when unasked for. Positive feedback is always easier to accept than negative feedback. We can respond to both negative and positive feedback with a simple thank you. Further, we may also respond to negative feedback by saying that I am a constant "work in progress" because we all are. Thank them so that we can take this feedback constructively to help us improve our teaching.
- **Advice giving** – often we see beginner teachers struggling to stay away from advice giving. It is good practice for us to stay away from advice giving because advice presupposes many things such as the teacher being an expert, the assumption that the same solution for me could be for you,

and that people do not have their own means to find answers and solutions. We could possibly stay away from advice giving and allow people to find their own answers and solutions through inquiry.

- **Metaphors and analogies** – the use of metaphors and analogies is very powerful in conveying abstract ideas. Summarizing and organizing what was discussed in the room through metaphors and deepening inquiry into them can be an effective way to generate insights.

In this chapter, we have described how inquiry is crucial in generating insights. If you wish to dive deeper into the different ways inquiry can be effectively facilitated, we recommend the work of Rob Brandsma (2017) who has devoted much effort in presenting these skills. We want to reiterate a point that we mentioned at the beginning of this chapter, which is that the most effective way to learn the art and skill of facilitating inquiry is by practicing and being mentored.

In Closing

With this chapter, we have completed part I of this book, which has presented the foundations of mindfulness and wellbeing and has introduced the MBWE protocol along with the method of teaching it. We hope that more professionals teach this protocol to different populations, cultures, and settings and share their insights with us so that people can discover enhanced wellbeing through mindfulness.

REFERENCES

Brandsma, R. (2017). *The mindfulness teaching guide: Essential skills and competencies for teaching mindfulness-based interventions* (1st ed.). New Harbinger Publications.

McCown, D., Reibel, D., & Micozzi, M. S. (2011). *Teaching mindfulness: A practical guide for clinicians and educators.* Springer.

Woods, S. L., & Rockman, P. (2021). *Mindfulness-based stress reduction: Protocol, practice, and teaching skills.* New Harbinger Publications.

Woods, S. L., Rockman, P., & Collins, E. (2019). *Mindfulness-based cognitive therapy: Embodied presence and inquiry in practice.* Context Press.

PART II

CHAPTER 6

Enhancing Group Learning in Mindfulness-Based Programs

My therapist taught me mindfulness, one-on-one, for 10 weeks. I actually prefer the group setting as I could share more of my insights. I could also learn from others . . . my self awareness has increased over the weeks and I believe I am more compassionate to others than before.

–Rodrigues

Mindfulness in the past was either practiced in solitude or in small groups. Today, we see large gatherings where hundreds or thousands of people practice mindfulness online as well as onsite. Specifically, right from its inception, mindfulness-based programs (MBPs) have been conducted as a group intervention rather than an individual intervention. As Rebecca Crane puts it, the group process is a definitive feature of MBPs, "given the centrality of the group within the learning process, it can be seen that the skill with which the group process is managed is of paramount significance" (Crane, 2017, pp. 156–157).

Although all MBPs are usually conducted in groups, mindfulness teachers often use the same facilitation methods with all populations and classes. Rarely have we found diverse facilitation methods in MBP curricula. One reason could be the standardization of the MBP protocols that prevents teachers from making significant adaptations. We have shared how to adapt the poems or metaphors and additional facilitation tools in Chapter 4. And in Chapter 7 you would find how MBPs can be adapted for participants from different cultures. While most MBPs are group based, some participants may not be suitable for a group program, and we have shared ways in which the mindfulness-based wellbeing enchancement (MBWE) can be adapted to individual coaching in Chapter 4.

In this chapter, we aim to address a few of these issues and empower teachers to be able to facilitate a group to enhance experience-centered learning. In the process, we will be drawing insights from the fields of group counseling

DOI: 10.4324/9781003322955-8

and psychotherapy to inform the way we can enhance learning in MBPs, while respecting the evolving tradition and practices of MBPs.

1 THE GROUP

What is the purpose of a group? The answer varies depending on the objective of the group which can be social, therapeutic, and educational, or a combination of these or more. For example, in a therapeutic group, the focus is on treatment by processing the members' experiences, thoughts, and emotions within the group; while a task group focuses on the successful completion of a specific task which impacts a company or community.

Groups can be an open or closed group. In open groups, new members can join the group at any point and existing members can be replaced. However, in closed groups, the number of members and the members themselves are fixed and the doors are shut once the group is formed. And this intact group journeys together from the first session to the last. While members in a closed group, can choose to leave at any time, they are never replaced. In the case of MBPs, the groups are always *closed groups* as members are recruited, selected, and confirmed to be part of the group over the eight-week period and no new members are ever allowed into the group after the second session. In the case of an MBP, the group meets for eight consecutive weeks for a duration of 2–3 hours depending on the program. There is also a half or full day of mindfulness which can be anything from 4–6 hours. This 4–6-hour session is not common in most therapy groups unless it is an intensive process group. In terms of time duration, MBPs are considered to be short-term groups as there is a set termination date and there is no extension beyond the set date.

There are many misconceptions about groups. We discuss some common ones here:

- **Everyone would feel comfortable being in a group:** this can be very far from the truth. While it is helpful for many, it is not suitable for everyone. For example, for people who have experienced trauma, individual sessions are more helpful than being placed in a group to reduce possible secondary trauma. This is the reason for the inclusion and exclusion criteria discussed in Chapter 3.
- **Everyone must leave the group with the same benefits:** genuine interactions are encouraged with a focus on sharing experiences of self rather than looking for similarities. Group learning happens with both common and distinctive experiences. Over the years of conducting therapy groups and MBWE groups, I (SR) have witnessed more members sharing different benefits rather than the same ones. In the MBWE, some find more meaning in their lives, while others experience lowered stress levels

or improved relationships. Some common benefits have been enhanced self-awareness and being happier.

- **Groups are not suitable for people who are anxious in crowds:** groups are in fact a safe space to practice speaking with others. Our experience has been that when we create a safe space for people to interact casually in pairs and small groups, they gradually become more comfortable speaking in the plenary sessions. It is necessary that we should not be overly focused on the "task" of practicing mindfulness but rather focus on allowing each person to feel comfortable and safe in the presence of each other. This can be done systematically in the way that we facilitate discussions through a variety of activities which take into consideration the culture of the group. For example, body contact ice-breakers may not be suitable for a mixed gender group or elderlies in some cultures. Many have said that respectful and sensitively designed ice-breakers have helped them to connect with others and they start to share more of their experiences in the group.

2 PROS AND CONS OF GROUP LEARNING

Groups offer a unique learning experience. From the table (see Table 6.1), you would notice that that are more advantages, than disadvantages, for teaching mindfulness in groups. Though MBPs are unique, they share the same advantages and disadvantages that are applicable to all types of groups.

Table 6.1 Advantages and disadvantages of group learning

Advantages	Disadvantages
Represents the microcosm of the society that we live in	Not suited for everyone and therefore require higher functioning individuals
Negotiated self-discovery and enhanced self-awareness through interaction with others	Does not support people who have a deep fear of speaking in front of a group
Enhanced other-awareness	Lack of confidentiality
Improved interpersonal relationships	Shared attention of the facilitator, less personal attention
A sense of belonging to a community and promotes social mindfulness	Group pressure for conformity
Unlearning and learning from one another through the acceptance and exposure to multiple perspectives	Personality clashes
Encouragement and support to continue practicing mindfulness	
Cost effective	

We encourage that teachers be aware of the pros and cons of a group and take this into consideration in their intake process and be willing to explore individual coaching if necessary.

3 GROUP TYPOLOGY

There are many types of groups and we have summarized some key ones in the table below (see Table 6.2) for your easy reference. Of course, there can be hybrids, and the list is not exhaustive.

Though MBPs are usually considered to be not therapy groups or psychoeducation groups, they do certainly fall between *psychoeducational* groups and *process* groups in their characteristics. MBP groups are psychoeducational, though mindfulness teachers are not expected to be subject-matter experts and subscribe to non-knowingness, quite unlike the role of the leader in such groups. And similar to a process group, all members are required to share their own individual experiences as authentically as possible and to support one another. In a way, MBPs are a *hybrid psychoeducational process-oriented group*. The group's freedom, belonging, and resonance (McCown et al., 2011) are features of the process-oriented group while adherence to the eight-week program with a curriculum comprising didactic components and homework is closer to psychoeducation.

The mindfulness-based stress reduction (MBSR) class that I (SR) attended consisted of about 40 members. Thankfully the mindfulness teacher was also a skilled psychotherapist who happened to be familiar in facilitating groups so she could manage the group effectively. However, to be able to really meet the needs of the group, we recommend that the group size should be between 5 and 20 participants, which is close to the size of a psychoeducational group. The teacher then could still give individual attention to the participants when needed while attending to the needs of the group as a whole.

4 GROUP DEVELOPMENTAL STAGES

How the group develops over the weeks is very much dependent on the leadership, the group members, their cohesiveness, environment, setting, the level of structure, and flexibility among others. Here we summarize the developmental stages of a group (see Figure 6.1) by Bruce Tuckman (Tuckman and Jensen, 1977) from formation to adjourning.

Based on the developmental stages, we recommend ways in which the mindfulness teacher could adapt her leadership style in accordance with the stage where the group is at (see Table 6.3).

Generally the group is more dependent on the teacher at the beginning, undergoes some level of resistance (if any) in sessions 2 or 3, and slowly

Table 6.2 Types of groups

Type of group	Goal	Role of leader	Recommended size	Duration
Task group	Specific, measurable, achievable, relevant, and time-bound (SMART) goals to improve efficiency or to complete an identified task or goal with established process	Focus on the here and now, set clear goals, manage agenda, lead the group to focus on and complete the common goals and tasks. May include writing reports and assessments	8–15 members	Closed once the task is complete
Psychoeducational group	Educational, growth oriented, preventive, and remedial	Identify key areas of deficit, create a curriculum around identifying and resolving the deficits, share new knowledge through didactic or experiential methods of facts, process their thoughts and challenges in moving forward and motivate members to integrate new skills into their daily living. The leader needs to have subject knowledge, expertise, and to be able to teach members how to solve problems, and learn new skills and assign homework to the participants	8–20 members; some groups can have up to 40 members	Fixed number of sessions – can be anything from 5 to 15 sessions depending on the curriculum
Psycho-therapeutic group	Remedy for mental disorders and severe and/or chronic psychological challenges for personal and interpersonal challenges of living	Work on deeper intra and inter psychological challenges and maladjustments including reconstructing unhealthy personality patterns and looking into childhood issues and trauma	8–10 members	Long term – usually lasts for a couple of years

(Continued)

Table 6.2 Continued

Type of group	Goal	Role of leader	Recommended size	Duration
Counseling group	Prevention, self-awareness, growth, and remedy for the challenges faced	Work on the here and now and improve personal and interpersonal relationships. There may be specific topics that the group works on or the goals emerge as the group interacts	8–12 members	Short to medium term lasting for a couple of months
Support group	Self-help for chronic conditions	May or may not have a leader. The group shares their personal journey, encourages and supports one another, and shares knowledge to help each other on the change journey	8–15 members	Medium or long term
Process-oriented group	Personal growth and development	Focused on the here and now and to enhance self-awareness to improve personal and interpersonal relationships. There is usually no topic, agenda, and very little structure. Sometimes there is a theme of focus. The leader takes a more facilitative role and the group is generally in charge of the session and guides the sessions through their connections, reflections, interactions, and insights	5–10 members	Medium or long term

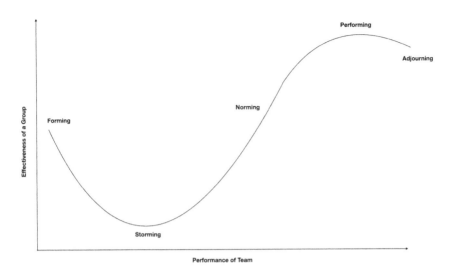

Figure 6.1 Developmental stages of a group

Table 6.3 Leadership style based on stages of group development

Stage	Description
Formation	The group gets oriented with one another and with the teacher. The group may be uncertain and confused about goals, structure, and the process. The teacher needs to be more active here to lead the group with guidelines, structures, and ground rules. Trust level is usually lower at this stage. We recommend that the teacher welcomes each person to the session, connects with members as they enter the room, includes ice-breakers and also starts proceeding with conversations in pairs or groups of three before plenary conversations to build psychological safety and trust
Storming	Here the group may struggle with leadership; tensions and frustrations may arise from the home experiments/homework, and they may want more answers, advice, or direction from the teacher. The teacher should acknowledge and normalize their challenges as valid and work through them by integrating their concerns with the practices into their teaching and use inquiry to help them express their concerns with the practices
Norming	At this stage, the group accepts the teacher's leadership and trusts the teacher, the members, and the process. There is greater consensus and increased co-operation to explore the practices, reflect on the challenges, and appreciate sharing of the group. More plenary conversations can be explored here. There is a sense of acceptance of being part of the group and being invested in each other's growth. The teacher can build on more vertical and horizontal inquiry at this stage

(Continued)

Table 6.3 Continued

Stage	Description
Performing	Here the group is more flexible, more helpful to one another, and there is greater openness in sharing and more shared responsibility in the process. While the teacher guides the group through the curriculum, she engages the group to support the learning by engaging in their experiences, insights and content. The teacher provides fewer teaching materials and focuses on the participants' individual and shared learning. The instructions for the mindfulness practices can be more spaced out with less guidance, and layer-3 inquiry can be beneficial with a focus on common humanity in the room
Adjourning	There is usually a sense of sadness and anxiety around separation, mixed with positive feelings toward members and the teacher and learning to be without the group. The teacher can support participants with these feelings by linking them to the attitude of letting go and being curious about the future. She also prepares the group in sessions 6 and 7 about sustaining the practice without the group and again in session 8 when she reviews and closes the group with the possibilities of attending drop-in sessions or mindfulness retreats to continue the practice

develops more trust, cohesion, and becomes comfortable with interdependence from sessions 4 or 5 onwards. Developing trust is one of the most crucial task of the leader as it impacts the development and dynamics of the group. For each stage, there are specific tasks that the teacher should engage in to help the group develop trust and to move smoothly to the adjourning stage. Of course this is a guide as some stages may occur concurrently. The task functions also shift from orientation to problem solving to acceptance as the weeks progress. Tucker's model gives us a general understanding of what the group might experience and to be ready to respond with awareness accordingly.

5 GROUP LEADERSHIP STYLE AND EMBODIMENT OF THE TEACHER

Lewin et al. (1939) and White and Lippitt (1968) identified three leadership styles that are relevant even today and also to mindfulness teachers. These are:

1. **Authoritarian leader:** this style of leadership is generally more autocratic and power rests with the leader who behaves in a highly directive manner and gives advice, interprets, and directs movement of the group. The members are dependent on the leader and the leader expects conformity and we can call it a very *guru*-oriented style of leadership.

2. **Democratic leader:** this is a more group centered and egalitarian style, where the focus is more on group cohesion and participation. The leader is more facilitative and less controlling. There is greater collaboration and shared responsibilities with the intention of promoting self-awareness.
3. **Laissez-faire leader:** this is the most passive form of leadership where the group is responsible for its direction and growth while the leader helps when requested.

Which style is most suitable for a mindfulness teacher? Ideally, it would be the democratic style of leadership as the mindfulness teacher is more facilitative than autocratic. Berg et al. (2017) stated that there is a strong relationship between the style of leadership, satisfaction level, group psychological safety, cohesiveness and group efficiency among others. They further state the group leader's functions to be the following five, which we feel are directly applicable to a mindfulness teacher,

- being able to care for the group by being genuine, compassionate, and warm
- providing for and facilitating emotional stimulation through free expression and deep reflections of their personal experiences
- meaning attribution of the content, process, and experiences thus raising their self-awareness
- executive functions of managing the content, connections, and dynamics of the group with a structure and yet being flexible in the moment to the here-and-now experience of the group
- the use of self which refers to the presence of the leader which aligns with the embodiment of mindfulness by the teacher

The teacher needs to be able to focus on both the content and the process of the group to have a productive group dynamic and this is specifically mentioned in domains 1, 3, 5, and 6 of the MBI-TAC, which will be briefly discussed in Chapter 8. The group is a system and is impacted by the interaction of the leader, members, and the group as a whole.

There are times when the mindfulness teacher may have to change her style to an authoritative one depending on the culture of the participants, though this is an exceptional adaptation when needed (discussed in Chapter 7). One such situation where an authoritative leadership style is needed is when a participant(s) causes imminent harm to another participant(s) by word or deed. The teacher needs to take a stand and intervene to protect and support participants. This is required when actions or verbal and non-verbal expressions:

- cause imminent harm to someone and oneself
- obstruct the potential to know and gain knowledge
- causes distress, sorrow, and injury to someone

Corey (2016) states that part of being authentic and sincere in the growth of others is to give feedback and challenge members to look deeply into their lives as honestly as possible and examine their beliefs and actions. The teacher needs to be confident, resilient, and versatile to know when to shift her leadership style depending on the situational and cultural needs.

6 THERAPEUTIC FACTORS OF MBPS

Irvin Yalom and Molyn Leszcz, pioneers of group psychotherapy, have written extensively about the 11 therapeutic factors, which they call "an intricate interplay of human experiences" (Yalom & Leszcz, 2020, p. 1) in a group. Out of these 11 factors, only eight seem to be directly relevant for MBPs. The three factors that are not directly relevant are corrective recapitulation of the primary family group, imitative behavior, and catharsis. We will not discuss these three factors since they are not of any direct relevance.

Table 6.4 provides a summary of the eight therapeutic factors which we encourage every mindfulness teacher to consider when teaching. All of these factors are interdependent and occur at different stages of the eight-week program. The segregation is only arbitrary.

Table 6.4 Therapeutic factors in MBPs

Factor	Description
Group cohesiveness	There is a strong sense of trust in the teacher, the process, the practices, and the group as a whole. The teacher brings a sense of value and belongingness to the group by creating a psychologically and physically safe environment. The teacher's embodiment of mindfulness and attitudes are of paramount importance here.
Interpersonal learning	Through the inquiry, participants are encouraged to share about their thoughts, feelings, urges, bodily sensations, and insights. Participants gain personal and interpersonal insights through the sharing.
Instilling hope	The teacher supports and encourages participants to explore different mindfulness experiments every week of the session and as part of their weekly homework to instill hope implicitly, bringing compassion and kindness to those who may find mindfulness difficult. Through the inquiry and sharing, participants encourage one another by the shared experience of common challenges and growth. This develops optimism toward their own growth, and focus on practicing, rather than comparison with each other's progress.

Factor	Description
Universality	The teacher guides the participants to notice that they have similar experiences in the areas of challenges, urges, habits, feelings, and thoughts. Common humanity is recognized in the room. The teacher invites others who have similar challenges to share and be willing to be vulnerable with each other. Through the interactions, they acknowledge that they are not alone in the struggles. In fact, this insight promotes social mindfulness by the recognition that each has needs, struggles, and desires and that we each play a part in each other's lives.
Imparting information	The sharing of knowledge by the teacher, especially during the didactic components of the MBP, about the brain and other wellbeing concepts, and the conversations with fellow participants help to gain knowledge and insights into oneself and others. This knowledge is helpful in recognizing how we can relate with the MBWE's happiness paradigm.
Altruism	The mindfulness teacher encourages participants to support one another in the growth process by sharing their real experiences, without comparing each other's experiences. This is one of the reasons why we have "not giving advice" as a guideline in session 1. We also realized that members have a positive view of themselves when they build on each other's stories and when they extend help to one another. Social mindfulness dimensions are also explicitly taught in the MBWE to further promote altruism.
Socializing techniques	The group provides an environment where each participant learns to interact with each other with respect and by focusing on sharing more about self rather than commenting on others. There is also the guideline of "silence is okay" to allow space for reflection and to accept that no response is fine too.
Existential factors	The teacher guides the participants to focus on the present moment; to be aware of the reality of living, bringing a sense of acceptance to life experiences, directing attention to what is working well and to interpret experiences from one's purpose and meaning in life rather than to be trapped in existential anxieties.

These eight factors are implicitly there in all MBPs and are very powerful mechanisms for change. We believe that MBPs have the potential to create a transformative change within participants by making these factors more explicit in its curriculum. These factors can also address the criticisms waged at the first generation MBPs, as discussed in Chapter 8.

7 WORKING WITH A GROUP

Working with a group is very different from working with an individual. We have discussed the preparation for the MBWE sessions and how to facilitate it in Chapters 3, 4, and 5. In this section, we discuss the attitudes and behaviors that support group learning in any MBP:

- **Embodiment and attitudes of the teacher**

  We discussed leadership skills earlier and we wish to add that the embodiment of the teacher and her attitude is of utmost importance when working with a group or in individual coaching. The teacher's personal practice, authenticity, and lived experience among others impact the group's dynamics, insights, and outcomes. A teacher cannot fake it and make it, as it does not work. We have dedicated more space for this discussion in Chapter 8.

- **Setting up a conducive environment**

  The teacher is encouraged to set up the room before the participants arrive. This includes having the right amount of lighting, checking on the temperature of the room, and arranging the mats where everyone can see each other and reflecting equal status and power if possible. We have shared some possible ways to set up the room in Figure 6.1. You may have to make adaptations depending on the space that you are in by trying to achieve a circular or semi-circular seating, if possible, or make adjustments to negotiate with the space. The teacher also needs to ensure that the writing boards are cleaned and ready for use if necessary.

  The teacher should also have their facilitation tools ready before the participants arrive e.g. mat, cushion, chime, stop watch, scripts, journals, water, attendance sheet, and writing materials. When the participants arrive, the teacher should focus on welcoming and being present with the participants.

- **Welcoming the group**

  When the participants arrive for the first session of the MBP, they might feel uncomfortable as they do not know each other or the teacher. It is recommended that the teacher greets the participants at the door or near the entrance before inviting them in to sign their attendance, and to take a seat. Once everyone is in the room, we formally welcome them and introduce the space, informing where the washrooms and fire safety exits are among others. We then turn to the ice-breaker activities. The ice-breaker activities should be positive, engaging, safe, and relational. We finally move to self-introductions to support the forming stage of the group and the teacher too is encouraged to share information about herself.

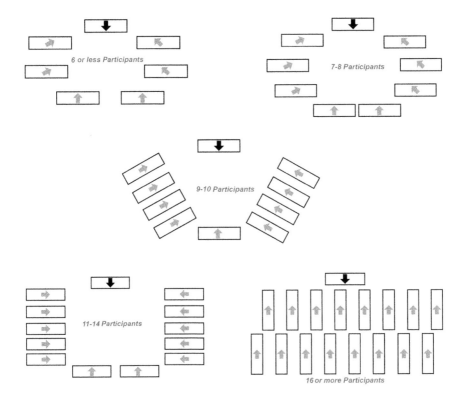

Figure 6.2 Types of room layouts

- **Stating clearly the purpose of the group**

    The teacher has to ensure that the group is clear about the purpose of the MBP. Sometimes participants come into the session expecting to learn theories and concepts rather than practice together while others may expect immediate therapeutic outcomes. This is why it is important for the teacher to set the expectations by starting with a short practice within the first 30 minutes of the session. The teacher should also reiterate, when needed during the eight weeks, that the focus will be on experience and insights rather than theory or therapy. Having said that, to ensure that it is an inclusive program, we can add reading materials especially for participants who may be curious about the theory of mindfulness. These can be in the form of recommended books, articles, journals, podcasts, and videos.

- **Multi-generational learning preferences**

    We cannot ignore the impact of the multi-generational audiences we encounter in the room. We have noticed very distinct learning styles among different generations. With the baby boomers (born between 1946 and 1964), we have seen a preference for face-to-face learning and live interactions. This group is also known to prefer reading from books and having open discussions and dialogues. Generation X (1965–1980) prefers active/experiential learning and active group discussions. They are most suited to onsite sessions. However, we know of many who are willing to learn and adapt to online learning as well as we keep the technological requirements basic.

Generations Y and Z (1981–2012) would have an inclination toward technology-based learning. Learning through apps, virtual-online, and self-paced learning are something up their alley. They are generally more versatile and are open to onsite and online learning or even a hybrid program. We know that online programs work, if properly designed, as we have been delivering many online sessions for adults and teenagers since the COVID-19 pandemic.

- **Co-creating the ground rules or guidelines**

  For the group to function well together, it is important to have common understanding and expectations of one another. We encourage teachers to share some guidelines with the group and also to invite the group to add to the list. This is usually written on a large sheet of paper and placed in the room in each session. Some examples of guidelines are relationships with devices, maintaining confidentiality, not to give advice to one another, to share one's own experience, and that speaking is optional.

- **Ensuring that each member is heard**

  It is of utmost importance that participants' voices are heard right at the beginning of the group. We can do this by having conversations in pairs or groups of three followed by large-group discussions to create psychological safety in the group. This allows members to talk to one another, share ideas freely, listen to one another, and feel connected in the group. For example, we usually ask participants to share what brought them to the MBWE. Usually when participants speak at the beginning of the sessions, they are more willing to participate and engage over the weeks. During inquiry segments, we encourage teachers to listen to each person speaking without interruptions and to model this behavior for others to learn to listen patiently to one another.

- **Helping participants feel connected and accepted in the group**

  It is human nature to want to be accepted and heard in a group. The teacher needs to be careful not to have favorites in the group or gravitate toward the more vocal members during discussions. The teacher's body language, facial expression, voice, and the words of encouragement among others impact the sense of belongingness within the group. We encourage teachers to invite the members to speak without forcing them to speak. I (SR) remember when I was facilitating the final session of the MBWE, two of the participants, who were close friends, shared that the "speaking is optional" guideline helped them feel connected, comfortable, and encouraged to be in the group. They shared with the group that they were both more "introverted and wanted to speak" when they were ready. In fact, I remember hearing more of their voices from session 4 onwards as compared to the earlier sessions.

- **Enhancing understanding by asking questions and connecting concepts**

  Sometimes when members share their experiences, we may not fully comprehend their private world or experience. We can use many strategies to aid the comprehension and deepen the appreciation of what is being shared by,

  - Listening attentively to the person when they are sharing by having eye contact, leaning toward the person, nodding or using verbal encouragers as we listen
  - Repeating and paraphrasing our understanding of what was said especially so when some participants in the group appear confused
  - Connecting and summarizing what several participants have shared on similarities or differences in experiences
  - Engaging the rest of the participants by asking for their insights based on what one or two participants had shared
  - Asking open-ended questions to clarify or deepen the understanding and the experience

- **Starting and closing the sessions each week**

  Each week, after the brief welcome, we encourage teachers to start the session intentionally. In the MBWE, we start the session with a metaphor to get the group thinking about the theme of the week and to engage the participants.

  We close the session by sharing the home experiments for the week, clarifying any doubts that the group may have, sharing any information that is needed in anticipation of the next session and make any announcements. You could also consider closing with a short practice or poem.

- **Termination of the group**

  In the final session, we wrap up the eight-week journey with a course evaluation and a closing circle. The closing circle is where the participants reflect on their eight-week journey with the group. We usually recommend having some guiding questions or statements to help the group. Depending on the group size and dynamics, this can take anything from 15 minutes to 30 minutes. From our experience facilitating the MBWE in groups, there is sharing of gratitude, high points, life-changing experiences, meaning, happiness, and also sadness of no longer being in the group. We listen and accept all of the experiences. As part of the closing, we also encourage the participants to continue their mindfulness journey through daily practice, attending retreats, and short workshops. We know of some who meet monthly and continue their practices together, like a community of practice.

The above are some of the attitudes and behaviors that we encourage mindfulness teachers to adopt to enhance the learning experience for participants in an MBP.

8 EXCEPTIONS TO GROUP SETTINGS

We argue that not all participants are suitable for being placed in a group-learning setting as they may not feel safe in a group, or may pose a risk to themselves and others, and also may not benefit from it (Berg et al., 2017). Candidates who have been diagnosed with certain types of mental health problems are more suited for individual coaching with a person trained in both mindfulness and psychotherapy. For example, participants diagnosed with PTSD, or experiencing severe anxiety, and crisis could benefit from one-on-one mindfulness coaching instead. This information could be obtained from the candidate's intake form submission for us to make informed decisions on suitability. This would also include verbal monopolizers, sociopaths, overly aggressive, extremely hostile, self-absorbed people, and those who are out of touch with reality though these may not be evident during the intake process (Berg et al., 2017).

How can we be more inclusive, in spite of these challenges that may fit the exclusion criteria? Insisting that all MBPs be conducted in a group setting in fact excludes people who may really need it and yet are unsuitable for a group environment. The solution could be to provide mindfulness training for them in different settings such as,

- Individual coaching
- Small groups of not more than five participants
- Medium-sized groups of not more than ten participants

However, it is *required* that their mental health provider approves their participation in these settings to ensure their wellbeing is our top priority. You can revisit the exclusion criteria discussed in Chapter 3, if needed.

In Closing

The first salient feature of this chapter was the potential that the therapeutic factors from the field of group counseling and psychotherapy could inform MBPs. The second was on how teachers could consciously bring more awareness to Tucker's model of group development, ethics in teaching mindfulness, and working with groups to allow these to inform their teaching. In the next chapter, we will present how MBPs could be adapted for different cultures to further enhance the learning experience.

REFERENCES

Berg, R. C., Landreth, G. L., & Fall, K. A. (2017). (6th ed.). *Group counseling: Concepts and procedures*. Routledge.

Corey, G. (2016). *Theory and practice of group counseling* (9th ed.). Cengage Learning.

Crane, R. (2017). *Mindfulness-based cognitive therapy* (2nd ed.). Routledge.

McCown, D., Reibel, D., & Micozzi, M. S. (2011). *Teaching mindfulness: A practical guide for clinicians and educators*. Springer.

Lewin, K., Lippitt, R., & White, R. (1939). Patterns of aggressive behavior in experimentally created "social climates." *Journal of Social Psychology, 10*, 271–299.

Tuckman, B. W., & Jensen, M. A. C. (1977). Stages of small-group development revisited. *Group & Organization Studies, 2*(4), 419–427.

White, R. K., & Lippitt, R. (1968). Leader behavior and member reaction in three "social climates." In D. Cartwright & A. Zander (Eds.), *Group dynamics: Research and theory* (3rd ed., p. 57). New York: Harper & Row.

Yalom, I. D., & Leszcz, M. (2020). *The theory and practice of group psychotherapy* (5th ed.). Basic Books.

CHAPTER 7

Cultural Adaptations

I am thankful that you added a folktale that I had grown up listening to and connecting it to mindfulness. It just opened doors to new possibilities in my life which I had never seen before.

–Yuxuan

We remember participating in a mindfulness summit that was held in India, the birthplace of Buddhism and Hinduism, two religions often cited to be the sources of mindfulness. The summit commenced inaugurally with a group of Tibetan Buddhist monks building a sand mandala. It was a spectacle for many delegates, including ourselves, as these monks meticulously built the mandala with total attention and devotion. The next day, they had a ritual for destroying the sand mandala which was so arduously built. Everyone who might have watched this for the first time was completely absorbed.

Right after that moment, both of us wondered how this would go down in Singapore, a secular multicultural society. We would possibly be seen as propagating religion in a secular conference. What is acceptable in India may not be so in Singapore and in some parts of the world. For example, the singing bowl which is accepted in some cultures as a symbol of mindfulness and a tool for mindfulness teachers, can be regarded as a religious accessory in others. This brings us to the discussion on how culture influences the way we assimilate mindfulness into our lives. We know that people select techniques and practices based on cultural heritage, worldviews, and values (Boniwell & Tunariu, 2019).

You will see in Chapter 9 that though mindfulness was born in Asia, it was adapted by Americans for Americans, especially within a predominantly white American culture. Evolution, like this one, is something common in all human cultures and civilizations, and adaptations would continue to happen in America and other parts of the world. Given that mindfulness has its roots in Asia and has been practiced there for the longest time, bringing MBPs to

DOI: 10.4324/9781003322955-9

Asia may sometimes seem like we are selling ice to the Inuit. However, we need to qualify that mindfulness as a secular, clinical, self-help, and brain training tool is something new to Asia as mindfulness has always been embedded within religious and soteriological practice.

Even in the very birthplace of secular mindfulness, North America, cultural adaptations have been needed especially when MBPs were brought to non-white American audiences such as the African and Native American communities (Proulx et al., 2018). Many black Americans are Christians and MBPs were not consciously designed with biblical principles. Researchers found black Americans interpreting stillness and meditations as opportunities for "hearing God." Could Native Americans who have traditionally relied on indigenous healing methods, infuse mindfulness into their traditional healing practices and their native cultures? African Americans have memories of physicians who have knowingly harmed them. Could these memories emerge and create distrust toward MBPs as being something oppressive especially when led by a white teacher? What are its ramifications? In another study, African Americans found mindfulness to be effective in reducing stress and stress related health challenges but participants preferred that its presentation be adapted in its content and facilitation with more cultural and spiritual affinities (Woods-Giscombé & Gaylord, 2014).

Evidence outside of North America also tells us a similarly story. MBPs that were found to promote grit, worked differently among participants from individualist and collectivist cultures (Raphiphatthana et al., 2019). It was found that mindfulness strengthened grit in participants from an individualistic culture more significantly than those from a collectivistic one. In another study with the Haitian population, the individualistic and amoral self-focus found in most MBPs was rejected by the participants (Hoffman, 2019). In response, these participants, during the program, naturally adapted their focus to the collective wellbeing of the country. In another study, it showed that white British participants were more likely to be aware of their physiological states, emotions, and deep level cognitions as compared to the Chinese participants (Chen & Murphy, 2019). When MBPs were led by a white teacher for a minority population, there were lower levels of engagement mainly due to leadership challenges, language difficulties, and affordability (Hazlett-Stevens, 2020). Interestingly, some cultures also interpreted mental health issues such as anxiety and depression differently. For example, minority cultures often experienced increased levels of psychosocial stress.

These findings tell us that by assuming we are solving a universal problem of suffering with MBPs, we may have overlooked diversity factors. When we do not adapt MBPs, we run the risk of implicitly and unconsciously encouraging non-American and non-white people to become like white American or British communities. This phenomenon may also plant the seeds of the belief that "West is Best" as opposed to cultivating a cross-cultural approach to practice and teaching (Huang et al., 2017). Instead of enhancing wellbeing, we could possibly create the very suffering that MBPs were created to alleviate. This new type of suffering could be internal-conflicts, cultural dissonance, and microaggression.

Given the potential that adaptations have, we invite MBP teachers and developers to be open to new pedagogies and intentionally meet people *where they are* instead of displacing their cultural selves. As Holly Stevens (Hazlett-Stevens, 2020) says,

> Some cultural groups might be best served by novel Mindfulness-Based Intervention curricula developed from within their given culture before examining intervention effectiveness within that cultural context.

1 CULTURE

To make these cultural adaptations, we need to first understand what culture is and what are its dimensions. Culture is popularly defined as patterns of shared behavior that are transmitted across generations by a group of people or society. These shared behavior patterns can be better understood through their dimensions. Several models of dimensions have been proposed by researchers though there is no unanimity. When appreciating these models, we do need to recognize that they contain both etic and emic perspectives. An etic perspective of culture takes the universal and similar dimensions across different cultures. The emic perspective, on the other hand, views the specific distinctions of those dimensions. For example, many cultures may consider marriage to be an important institution though the types of marriages such as monogamy and polygamy could be different in cultures. The former presents the etic and the latter, the emic perspective. In the case of the MBWE, the explicit assumption is that wellbeing is something that is universally relevant and desired by all cultures. However, the way each culture views, prioritizes, and assimilates wellbeing could possibly be different. In fact, the evidence that we have for MBPs thus far is also from an ethnocentricist perspective.

One of the assumptions that the first-generation MBPs make, on which most second- and third-generation MBPs are modeled, is that stress and depression are universally seen as something negative. Ronald Purser (2019) and Robert Sharf (2016) offer another perspective by arguing that stress is overrated and a manufactured phenomenon that has been unduly promoted. Depression, for example, in the Sri Lankan context can be something positive when viewed through the lenses of the Buddhist culture. In fact, within the Hindu culture, depression is often seen as an indicator that one should reflect on their lifestyle and possibly an opportunity to re-evaluate life priorities, or even a sign that one is ready for transition into monastic life.

Therefore, it is important that we shift from the ethnocentricist view of suffering and wellbeing, and adopt a more culturally relativistic approach when it comes to MBP adaptations.

When making adaptations to MBPs, we need to identify the "what" and "how" of doing it. And what model could we use to make these adaptations given that there are a couple of them? In our informal experiments over the years, we have found the Hofstede's six dimensions of national culture very useful. Hofstede's extensive research across many countries has found six dimensions to be valid, which are:

1. Masculinity vs femininity
2. Uncertainty avoidance index
3. Power distance index
4. Individualism vs collectivism
5. Long-term orientation vs short-term orientation
6. Indulgence vs restraint

Masculinity vs Femininity

In this dimension, masculine cultures have a preference for recognition, earnings, challenges and the drive for success. On the other hand, Feminine cultures prefer relationships, cooperation, modesty, and quality of life. These preferences are not gender centered. Gender roles are known to be less fluid and more distinct in masculine cultures as compared to feminine ones.

Uncertainty Avoidance Index

This dimension refers to a culture's tolerance of ambiguity, where participants avoid change and things that are unexpected and unknown. Participants who score a high degree in this index prefer strict guidelines, clear instructions, and expect to be told exactly what to do. Evidence for any results would be of paramount importance and they would have a low tolerance of ambiguity. A low degree in this dimension would mean that participants are accepting of situations, ideas, thoughts, and innovation. This dimension is strongly related to how cultures view and cope with anxiety.

Power Distance Index

Power distance refers to how the minority or less powerful members of a culture accept power and authority and how they expect power to be distributed unequally. A high degree of this dimension would mean that participants prefer a hierarchy and clear leadership. A lower degree indicates a preference for people to challenge authority and to distribute power more equally among members.

Individualism vs Collectivism

Individualist cultures have loose ties with others that indicates a strong connection with oneself or with one's family. They are more concerned with the "I" than the "we." Values, rights, and focus on personal and familial needs are important to them. Collectivist cultures are those that consist of groups of tightly knitted relationships. Loyalty and support are hallmarks of this culture. Communication is direct in individualist cultures and indirect in collectivist ones.

Long-Term Orientation vs Short-Term Orientation

A long-term orientation indicates that such a culture would value pragmatism, persistence, thriftiness, and capacity for adaptation. Long-term growth is encouraged versus short-term gains. Short-term orientation values immediate needs gratification, quick results, and unrestrained spending. There is a preference for traditions and the present rather than the future.

Indulgence vs Restraint

This dimension refers to the degree of freedom given to people to fulfill their desires. Indulgence refers to the high level of liberty to gratify one's desires. Restraint refers to the strict control that cultural norms have on an individual to regulate themselves in the fulfillment of their desires.

2 ORIGINAL CULTURES OF THE MBPS

Before we share how adaptations could be made to MBPs, it is important to note that first-generation MBPs were developed by and for a homogeneous population (predominantly white in North America and the UK). Hofstede's six dimensions (Hofstede, 2011) for these populations can be found in Figure 7.1. From the chart, we can readily see that both the UK and the North America have very similar cultures.

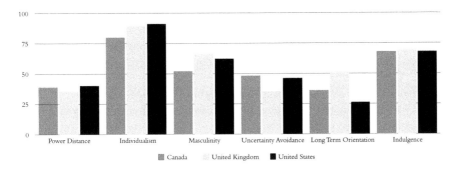

Figure 7.1 Cultural dimensions of Canada, the United Kingdom, and the United States

However, when you compare Singapore with the United States, you get to see a very different picture (see Figure 7.2). There is greater power distance in Singapore and hence authority, such as that of the teacher, is naturally respected. It is a collectivist society with higher levels of interdependence and as such, group learning is valued. There is also lower uncertainty avoidance, greater restraint, and control among the people, and they value long-term orientation and investment. They are likely to be more open to the eight-week, or longer, programs for their wellbeing. You could perhaps now see why MBP adaptations are very critical to their effectiveness.

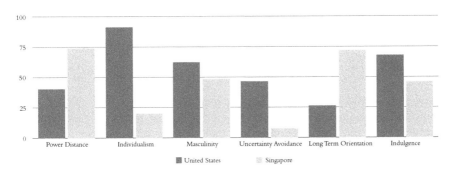

Figure 7.2 Cultural dimensions of the United States and Singapore

3 CONSIDERATIONS FOR ADAPTATION

Let us now look at the elements of MBPs that could and should be adapted. In doing so, the two components of MBPs, the essential and variable (Crane, 2017), that will be presented in Chapter 8, would also have to be considered. Essential components are the ones that are non-negotiable such as the formal and informal practices, inquiry, didactic components, and exercises. Variable components can be adapted based on the culture, audience, and the intentions and outcomes of the MBP which include for example the duration of each session. Cultural adaptations for the essentials is discouraged as we run the risk of losing the integrity, and may even compromise, the effectiveness of an MBP. What we aim to show in this section is how specific adaptations could be made to MBPs without compromising their integrity.

One of the biggest challenges for mindfulness teachers is their own beliefs and evaluations of cultures that are alien to them. Sometimes in our grand vision of wellbeing, we could possibly become ethnocentric in our expectations. While it is important that we allow cultures to self-negotiate their means to wellbeing, yet the teacher presents the theory, exercises and practices as possibilities instead of solutions. For example, we could meet a culture where women are subordinated to men. Instead of desiring to emancipate these women in the room, by perhaps educating the men there, we could just meet them in the present moment as they are, as this is their current reality and perhaps something that is appreciated in the culture. We need to let go of our own lenses of judgment and appreciate their perspectives of wellbeing. If any change is required, we let them discover *that* through their insights about wellbeing. The teacher's personal values could potentially stand in the way of the MBP pedagogy if they encounter situations that oppose it.

Cultural adaptations are made by honoring the present reality without striving to change it. The role of teachers is to pave the way for insights to be generated, not to create them based on their own values, beliefs, and life experiences. Self-awareness, acceptance, letting go, and adaptability are virtues in this case.

Diversity

The first consideration is the participants' diversity. We have encountered both homogenous and heterogeneous cultures in the room. The elements of homogeneity and heterogeneity could include these multiple areas:

- Hofstede's six dimensions
- Beliefs: faith and ideological subscriptions
- Pre-existing cultural relationships with meditation

For novice teachers, when experimenting with adaptations, it may be helpful to work with participants of a homogeneous culture rather than a heterogenous one. We have learned that it is easier to make adaptations for the former than the latter. It is important to first become familiar with adaptations for a homogeneous audience before moving to ones that we are unfamiliar with. For example, one of our trainee teachers requested to do her eight-week practicum with a group of people of a different culture from hers and a culture which she had very limited experience of. She came from a space of compassion as she felt they had a strong need for mindfulness. However, when we asked her a couple of questions about her adaptability, she became aware that she was not ready for a group that differed in religion, ethnicity, and spoke predominantly in Singlish (a variety of English spoken in Singapore) which she was not familiar with. This is why we recommend novice teachers to start with the familiar before embarking on the unfamiliar. The unfamiliar requires more careful preparation, deeper study, and adaptation.

4 HOFSTEDE'S SIX DIMENSIONS OF CULTURE

The impact of the six dimensions of culture is huge on any MBP. Depending on the values of the dimensions, mindfulness teachers can adopt different facilitation techniques to allow participants to relate to the content. In this section, we will discuss how the elements of MBWE and MBPs could be adapted based on Hofstede's six dimensions and other factors. If you are working with participants of a particular nationality, Hofstede's research (Hofstede, 2022) can be useful in generating the six dimensions for every country. We present four case studies of adaptations.

Case Study 1

In the sample (see Figure 7.3), you will realize that the values are very similar to the cultures from which the MBPs were born. In such situations, we have found that very few adaptations are needed. To begin with, the teacher should first look for the lows and highs in each of the dimensions to guide one's adaptations.

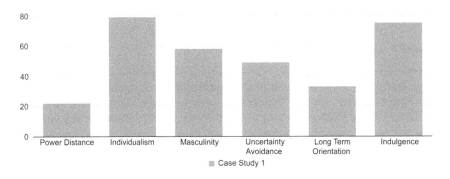

Figure 7.3 Case study 1

In this sample, the relatively low long-term orientation could mean that the participants may expect immediate results during the MBP program and the sustainability of the practice after the MBP would also need more support. When questions about the expectation of immediate results pop up in the room, the teacher could possibly respond with deeper inquiry questions at layer 2. This will help to deepen the appreciation of the momentary changes that are sometimes neglected in favor of expecting "big" results. The high level of individualism in this sample would not hamper the recommended facilitation of the MBWE or any MBP. The low power distance would mean that the leadership style of the teacher would be one of a democratic facilitator rather than an authoritative one, similar to being a fellow companion. The high level of indulgence would also mean that the participants are likely to recognize their positive emotions, and physiological states among others. This could also mean that they could also possibly resist negative emotions. It would be good to direct the inquiry to the acceptance of the negative if that emerges in the room.

Case Study 2

In the sample in Figure 7.4, the three dimensions that stand out are power distance, individualism, and indulgence.

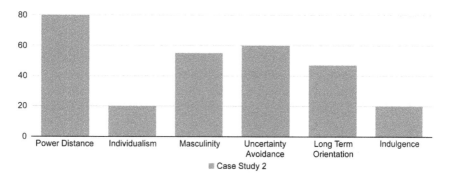

Figure 7.4 Case study 2

The leadership style of the teacher would require a significant shift when working with this culture. Teachers are expected to be authoritative and take an active role in "telling" people what needs to be done. As much as mindfulness teachers do not play the role of subject matter experts, this culture would place an unconscious expectation that you should be one. In this scenario, the teacher would have to balance the *ask* with a little *tell*, when needed.

You can probably expect more questions from this culture, given that the uncertainty avoidance is higher. Teachers would have to provide brief answers to questions asked before "shining the light back at them." Here is an example how it can be done:

P1:   During my practice, I experience unwanted thoughts that come up. How do I handle those thoughts?

T: Thoughts are like clouds and they come and go. Some may look like dark clouds and some of them, white and bright. We treat those dark clouds like the way the sky would, allowing them to just *be*. Mindfulness helps us to discover this potential that we all have. [*silence for a few seconds*] I am curious to know what emotions you noticed when those unwanted thoughts emerged.

Given that indulgence is low in this culture, people may not see that they have the liberty to decide on what works for them and may follow societal norms and restrain themselves. Their lives may be seen as being dependent on others and they may have challenges recognizing positive emotions. When inquiry is directed at positive emotions, they may not remember them as they are less important in this culture. It would then be helpful to spend more time in layer-1 inquiry, especially about the range of neutral and pleasant sensations and emotions.

The low individualism indicates that this is a collectivist culture. In such situations, small-group discussions could be very helpful in helping them to see how insights could be shared realities. Introducing small-group discussions and acknowledging the common humanity in the room can be very helpful in their assimilation of mindfulness.

Case Study 3

In Figure 7.5, much adaptation is required but we will focus only on those that we had not covered in the previous case studies.

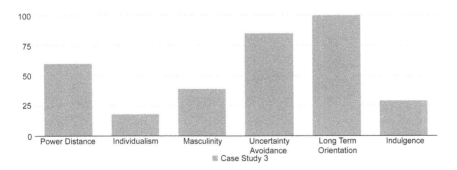

Figure 7.5 Case study 3

The low levels of masculinity would mean that they appreciate a quality of life that emphasizes wellbeing as compared to striving for wealth and achievements. The participants are likely to have an immediate resonance with wellbeing. The pro-social elements of MBWE would be something that would find a groove among the participants who are of this culture.

With a high level of uncertainty avoidance, participants may find the inherent design of the MBWE not acceptable. The MBWE, as with any other MBP, does not have a specific predetermined or predictable outcome. One significant adaptation that can be made here is to have more didactic teachings that connect their experiences to the outcomes. We could also consider giving more reading materials and research evidence to alleviate anxiety. The home practices could also be more structured by facilitating a process that allows the participants to plan what to practice at which times of the day. When inquiry questions take an unpredictable direction, it may cause confusion or even anxiety. In such situations, it may be helpful to share how the MBP is structured, how it is going to be conducted, and the teacher's role beforehand. Abstract ideas can also be challenging for such a culture and it would be recommended that the didactic components are shared in an organized and structured manner.

A very high long-term orientation would mean that the sustainability of mindfulness in their life and its long-term benefits are critical to their assimilation of mindfulness. For example, sessions 7 and 8 of the MBWE, where the sustenance plans are being facilitated, would be critical to this culture in planning for perseverance and incorporating mindfulness into daily living.

Case Study 4

In Figure 7.6, we shall focus only on masculinity.

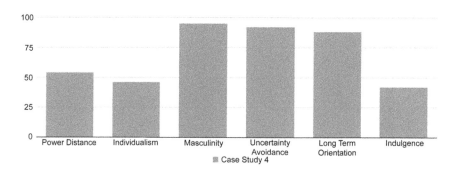

Figure 7.6 Case study 4

A high level of masculinity could mean that competition and success would put participants in the striving mode and possibly viewing mindfulness to be another task in their "to-do" list. The emphasis on the present moment and the attitude of non-striving throughout the MBP could help in allowing the participants to stay grounded while practicing mindfulness. It is also important to emphasize that the present centered attention is confined to mindfulness practices per se, and not to the plans we make in our personal and professional lives, which deal with planning for the future. Otherwise, people may find mindfulness to be something not pragmatic. We have noticed such responses with business leaders when they encounter the *present-moment* discourse.

With the four case studies, we have shown some possibilities of how adaptations could be made in the room with participants of homogeneous culture. We have created a simple guide, though not exhaustive, summarizing what needs to be considered when preparing to deliver any MBPs with homogeneous audiences (see Table 7.1).

Table 7.1 Summary of adaptations for each cultural dimension

	Dimensions	Low	High
1	**Power distance**	• Likely to prefer the teacher to be a democratic facilitator • Asking questions would work with this audience	• Participants may expect the leadership style of the teacher to be more authoritative while balancing facilitation • Need to balance *asking* with *telling*
2	**Individualism**	• More pair and small-group discussions are helpful to see how insights are shared realities • Helpful to actively acknowledge common humanity	• No significant change is required to the recommended facilitation guide
3	**Masculinity**	• No significant change is required to the recommended facilitation guide	• Periodic emphasis on the present moment and non-striving could help in allowing the participants to stay grounded
4	**Uncertainty avoidance**	• No significant change is required to the recommended facilitation guide	• May expect teacher to answer questions when asked. Helpful to give short answers before asking questions • Provide more supportive reading materials after sessions • Be more directive with less flexibility • Share the structure of the MBP beforehand

(Continued)

Table 7.1 Continued

	Dimensions	Low	High
5	**Long-term orientation**	• No significant change is required to the recommended facilitation guide	• Sustainability of mindfulness in their life and its long-term benefits are critical to their assimilation for mindfulness
6	**Indulgence**	• Participants are likely to be unable to acknowledge positive emotions and take control of their actions easily • Helpful to guide them to notice neutral and positive emotions in daily life	• May actively resist negative emotions and may find it easier to notice positive emotions • Helpful to guide them to practice acceptance of negative emotions in daily life

How about when working with a heterogenous group? It is definitely less clear cut. When working with a heterogenous audience, the six dimensions of culture would have to be used flexibly depending on the behaviors exhibited in the room. With a present-moment focus, teachers may have to notice each and every participant's behavior in the room based on the six dimensions and respond accordingly and respectfully. With such a mixed audience, you may need to use adaptations, suggested in Table 7.1, for each of the dimensions and gauge the response you receive. While this may not be predictable, as in the case of homogenous audiences, this does require a present-moment response and even course corrections. It would be a classic situation of different strokes for different folks.

Faith-Based Adaptations

As we have seen from research, participants negotiate their beliefs with what is taught in the MBPs. We see more second-generation MBPs in recent times that bring religious and spiritual teachings explicitly into their curricula. In the same way, faith dimensions could be brought into the content of the MBWE provided that the participants in the room belonged to the same faith tradition and a clear communication has been made that this is a faith-based MBP.

Several MBWE components can be adapted so that their wellbeing can be approached and appreciated through the lenses of their faith. The first area of adaptation is the metaphors and poems. Teachers could easily replace the metaphors and poems with ones that are already known and honored by faith traditions. Stories from the scriptural canon can also be used as substitutes.

When doing so, it is important that these stories, parables, and metaphors are chosen based on the session themes, and not randomly selected.

The second area would be to identify specific teachings or excerpts from the scriptural canon, or from respected teachers, that bring across the value of the four mechanisms of mindfulness. Using those key passages, verses, parables, and stories from religious literature can be used in the didactic segments of the MBWE. As you make these broad adaptations, the fundamental pedagogy of the MBWE should not be compromised.

The other opportunity for adaptation is also finding scriptural anecdotes, quotes, and teachings that support the three elements of the *happiness paradigm*, which can be used as metaphors or in the didactic segments.

Happiness paradigm = Attention to the positive + Acceptance of the negative + purposeful interpretation

As you adapt the MBWE for people of faith traditions, it is important to have a subtitle to the program title to convey that a faith dimension has been introduced into the otherwise secular MBWE. This is to ensure that we do no mislead anyone into thinking that this is a secular program. For example, you could title it as "Mindfulness-Based Wellbeing Enhancement: The Taoist Way." One important condition when making such adaptations is to ensure that a trained mindfulness teacher who subscribes to the faith tradition delivers it. It is also recommended that this teacher be mentored by a supervisor who is familiar with designing MBPs and, if possible, familiar with the faith.

It is of utmost importance that we honor the worldview that these faith traditions teach as it is very much bigger than the MBWE. In no way does the MBWE replace, substitute, or erase any of the religious tenets. Instead, an adapted MBWE, supports the intentions of a faith tradition. It is like the way a type of footwear may support your walk to a destination, but the destination remains unchanged, i.e. wellbeing and happiness. In fact, from our original secular MBWE program, we already noticed that the MBWE is supportive, rather than restrictive, of faith-based interpretations. Here are some excerpts from our participants:

> My five daily prayers have become more meaningful rather than mechanical. I also realized that mindful movement is so connected to the salat and now I am able to pay more attention to each movement.
>
> –A Muslim participant

> I really appreciate the parts on positivity and it aligns beautifully with my faith of focusing on people and helping others with compassion.
>
> –A pastor

Dharana and Dhyana are so common for us Hindus. I appreciate that mindfulness has aligned with my practices and also taught me to be not distracted during my mantra chanting and pujas.

– A Hindu participant

A word of caution when adapting the MBWE for faith traditions, is the possibility that the intentions of wellbeing could possibly be replaced by soteriological goals. If soteriological goals happen to be the goal, then we would recommend that a new MBP be created for this purpose as the intentions would be different from the intentions of the MBWE. The outcomes of the MBP if changed, is no longer the same MBP as the practices and didactic segments would also have to change accordingly.

5 CROSS-CULTURAL SENSITIVITY

Cultural sensitivity is defined as the awareness and acceptance of others' cultures. I (KK) remember going to a yoga class in the mid-1990s. And there came a lady clad in a sari (a South Asian drapery). I could not imagine my yoga teacher teaching yoga in a sari. My image of a yoga teacher, then, was a man or woman in activewear like yoga pants and a t-shirt. Here was this lady in a sari, performing the signature sun salutations, with a speed and flexibility that put a young man in his twenties to shame.

We have expectations of dress code, gender, dining etiquette, and manners. I (SR) met a non-Asian master executive coach in a retreat a couple of years ago and she was very inquisitive about my culture and me. She had never closely interacted with a person of Indian descent in her 50 plus years of existence. In case you did not know, South Asians traditionally eat their food with their bare hands, usually with the right hand. She was curious if I ate the same way and when I confirmed with a resounding "yes," she immediately cringed. Her response to me was a lecture on how our hands are dirty and I should use cutlery. It got interesting as she was using her hands to eat the chicken wings a little later during dinner. I believe her intentions were genuine though they lacked awareness and acceptance of cultural differences.

A similar situation may happen with your participants. Allowing people to be comfortable in their skin is an important sign of acceptance and respect. Like my (KK) encounter with my yoga teacher, sometimes traditional clothes may be assumed to be inappropriate. It is important that we inform our participants that there will be stretching and that loose clothing is helpful during such practices and leaving it to their best judgment on what works for them rather than *telling* them what they should be wearing. It is also important that we model this cultural sensitivity in our dressing as well, in an appropriate manner.

Another important dimension is when delivering sessions in a language other than English. We have attempted to translate our English instructions into local languages where possible. And this required a great deal of effort as the translators and interpreters of the instruction scripts and didactic content had to be proficient bilingually, as well as understand the intentions of mindfulness. We remember translating the word "mindfulness" into Chinese and our team were at loggerheads as to which of two words identified, would be the best translation for it. We took six months translating the content and getting the views from several of our team members, who not only knew the language, but were also culturally immersed in its use as well as being trained to teach mindfulness. As much as translations are much needed for people who are not familiar or proficient in the English language, it is necessary that we do it not as a translation exercise, but rather with the immersion in culture and context of a language. More importantly, the subtle nuances that mindfulness teaching has, would have to be brought into the translation.

It is also important that we factor in the needs of participants with a faith subscription that requires them to observe daily prayers at specific times of the day. In several of our MBWE sessions, we have had requests for opening the rooms earlier so that they could say their prayers before the classes. We could possibly ask if the participants have any special requirements or needs during your sessions, and especially for the self-retreat, which may occupy the whole morning, afternoon, or evening.

Lastly, it has become a common practice that mindfulness teachers use the Tibetan singing or meditation bowl as a bell to signify the beginning and end of a formal mindfulness practice. Although these bowls are of recent origin, and not from Tibet, as they are usually deemed to be, they are modeled after the *rin* temple bells of Japan. These singing bowls exude religiosity or spirituality and this identity may cause confusion when delivering a secular MBP like MBWE. We suggest that mindfulness teachers use more neutral bells, such as chimes, which can be very helpful in ensuring that the program is secular in every possible way.

As you can see from our discussion, secular mindfulness was originally created and taught in the North American culture. In this chapter, we provided a framework and case studies of cultures that were different from the original culture of the Mindfulness-Based Stress Reduction and Mindfulness-Based Cognitive Therapy programs, and how adaptations can be made. We invite you to experiment with these adaptations and continue to learn from them as they continue to inform your wisdom.

REFERENCES

Boniwell, I., & Tunariu, A. D. (2019). *Positive psychology: Theory, research and applications*. McGraw-Hill Education.

Chen, S., & Murphy, D. (2019). The mediating role of authenticity on mindfulness and wellbeing: a cross cultural analysis. *Asia Pacific Journal of Counselling and Psychotherapy*, *10*(1), 40–55.

Crane, R. S. (2017). Implementing mindfulness in the mainstream: Making the path by walking it. *Mindfulness*, *8*(3), 585–594.

Hazlett-Stevens, H. (2020). Cultural considerations when treating anxiety disorders with mindfulness-based interventions. In *Handbook of cultural factors in behavioral health* (pp. 277–292). Springer.

Hoffman, D. M. (2019). Mindfulness and the cultural psychology of personhood: Challenges of self, other, and moral orientation in Haiti. *Culture & Psychology*, *25*(3), 302–323.

Hofstede, G. (2011). Dimensionalizing cultures: The Hofstede model in context. *Online readings in psychology and culture*, *2*(1), 2307–0919.

Hofstede, G. (2022, June 24). *Home – Hofstede Insights Organisational Culture Consulting*. Hofstede Insights. Retrieved from www.hofstede-insights.com/

Huang, Z. M., Fay, R., & White, R. (2017). Mindfulness and the ethics of intercultural knowledge-work. *Language and Intercultural Communication*, *17*(1), 45–57.

Purser, R. (2019). *McMindfulness: How mindfulness became the new capitalist spirituality*. Repeater Books.

Proulx, J., Croff, R., Oken, B., Aldwin, C. M., Fleming, C., Bergen-Cico, D., . . . & Noorani, M. (2018). Considerations for research and development of culturally relevant mindfulness interventions in American minority communities. *Mindfulness*, *9*(2), 361–370.

Raphiphatthana, B., Jose, P. E., & Chobthamkit, P. (2019). The association between mindfulness and grit: An east vs. west cross-cultural comparison. *Mindfulness*, *10*(1), 146–158.

Sharf, R. H. (2016). Is mindfulness Buddhist? (and why it matters). In R. Rosenbaum & B. Magid, (Eds.). *What's wrong with mindfulness (and what isn't): Zen perspectives* (pp. 139–152). Wisdom Publications.

Woods-Giscombé, C. L., & Gaylord, S. A. (2014). The cultural relevance of mindfulness meditation as a health intervention for African Americans: Implications for reducing stress-related health disparities. *Journal of Holistic Nursing*, *32*(3), 147–160.

CHAPTER 8

Effectiveness of Mindfulness-Based Programs

I never knew about the possibility of adverse effects especially when mindfulness is taught by untrained teachers.

–Scott (Mindfulness Teacher-in-Training)

In our area of work, we often get consulted by organizations and schools who are very interested in bringing mindfulness into their institutions. One popular question we are asked is "How do we know if the mindfulness program will work?" We view this question as coming from a genuine intention of wanting to ensure that a mindfulness-based program (MBP) is optimal and effective. It is therefore important that we, as practitioners and professionals, know how to approach this with honesty and with the genuine intention of beneficence and to support people in achieving their desired goals. In this chapter, we will discuss on the effectiveness of MBPs and in the process present design considerations that could guide in creating, adapting, and testing MBPs.

1 EFFECTIVENESS OF MBPS

How can we know that an MBP is effective given that there are so many factors involved in designing and facilitating it? Rebecca Crane (2017) has offered a framework through which we can appreciate the effectiveness of an MBP (see Figure 8.1).

We can frame the effectiveness into three broad categories, namely the teacher, program, and the intention. We will discuss each of these components in the following sections.

DOI: 10.4324/9781003322955-10

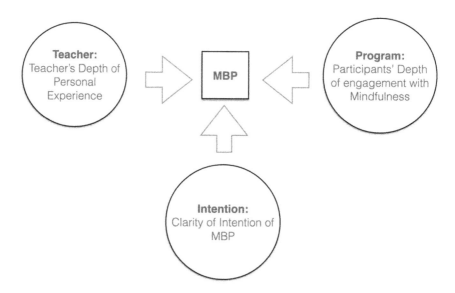

Figure 8.1 Factors that influence the effectiveness of MBPs

1.1 The Teacher

The role of the teacher is given much emphasis in mindfulness literature. With the growing interest in training as a mindfulness teacher, and possibly the exponential growth in the number of mindfulness teachers globally, much has been written on teacher competence because this depends on the teachers' depth of personal experience as well as the ability to teach.

Ruth Baer (2003) suggested that better designed studies on mindfulness are needed. However, the importance of the teacher's role in ensuring that MBPs are delivered effectively was not emphasized. Kabat-Zinn (2003) responded to her article, emphasizing the importance of the role of mindfulness teachers in MBPs. To quote him,

> In our experience, unless the instructor's relationship to mindfulness is grounded in extensive personal practice, the teaching and guidance one might bring to the clinical context will have little in the way of appropriate energy, authenticity, or ultimate relevance, and that deficit will soon be felt by program participants.
>
> (p.150)

This shows the importance of personal practice in the case of teaching mindfulness, unlike other professions where personal experience or practice is not as important nor critical to the effectiveness of the intervention. We have met therapists and coaches who vouch for the efficacy of process over the *wielder* of the process and exhort people to trust the process with less consideration for the therapist or the administrator of the process. We liken this to professional roles where the effectiveness of the intervention does not depend on the personal experience with using the intervention on oneself. For example, a doctor who administers smoking cessation pills need not have to be a smoker or a user of the pills. Likewise a coach or therapist may use modalities that they themselves have never used or experienced for themselves. In contrast, mindfulness teachers would have to have experienced mindfulness for themselves and *embody* mindfulness through committed and sustained practice. In his response to Baer, Kabat-Zinn further emphasizes the following to be contingent on the effectiveness of an MBP:

- Authenticity of teaching depends on the instructor's formal lifetime practice
- Teachers and participants attending classes and retreats after completing the MBP
- Teachers' immersion within their own lived experience that allows them to respond appropriately and specifically to the participants' questions
- Teachers not only depending on book knowledge and concepts, because *awareness* cannot be presented through constructs

Kabat-Zinn warns that without personal practice and embodiment, MBPs

> run the risk of becoming caricatures of mindfulness, missing the radical, transformational essence and becoming caught perhaps by important but not necessarily fundamental and often only superficial similarities between mindfulness practices and relaxation strategies, cognitive-behavioral exercises, and self-monitoring tasks.
>
> (p.150)

The *experience* of the teacher is therefore the foundation of the effectiveness of any MBP. We want to emphasize that immersion in *awareness* is therefore a critical component. Teachers lean on this experience as they teach the participants, though they may come from different cultural, religious, or ethnic backgrounds. They negotiate this with their own individual experiences with awareness, in spite of their backgrounds, like the way oceans behold the waves without any resistance. It is *indeed* about the embodiment of mindfulness that is critical.

The second aspect is the teacher's ability to teach. To fulfill the need for assessing mindfulness teachers, in 2018, the Bangor University together with several UK universities came up with *Mindfulness-Based Interventions: Teaching Assessment Criteria* (MBI:TAC). This was developed so that trainee teachers could review their competence to teach an MBP curriculum. The MBI:TAC is perhaps the only teaching assessment criterion currently available for mindfulness teacher certification. Interestingly, Kabat–Zinn was not part of this initiative. There have been three versions of the MBI:TAC so far, with the most recent version published in 2021. The MBI:TAC lists six competencies for a mindfulness teacher:

1. Coverage, pacing, and organization of session curriculum
2. Relational skills
3. Embodying mindfulness
4. Guiding mindfulness practices
5. Conveying course themes through interactive inquiry and didactic teaching
6. Maintaining the group learning environment

These competencies are very helpful in assessing the competence of teachers. Among these competencies, we have found *embodying mindfulness* to be the most challenging to assess and demonstrate. Why? This is a result of personal practice and something that varies from person to person depending on how intimate one is with awareness itself. Without embodiment, all the other competencies are not as useful, in our opinion. It is embodiment that brings value to all the other competencies and not vice versa. We encourage all teachers to read the MBI-TAC during their training and also revisit it occasionally to refresh their memories and familiarise with the competencies.

1.2 The Program

The program refers to the design and content that promotes the participants' depth of experience with mindfulness (see Figure 8.1). The engagement with mindfulness involves active participation in each of the sessions in the MBP and the subsequent personal home practice by the participants. This program component also refers to the way an MBP is designed or adapted.

Any MBP would have two distinct components, the essential and the variable (Crane et al., 2017) as briefly stated in Chapter 7. We have adapted these components to present a more holistic approach to MBP in the Table 8.1 below:

Table 8.1 Essential and variable components of MBPs

Essential components	Variable components
Informed by the confluence of mindfulness and other scientific traditions	The core essential curriculum elements are integrated with adapted curriculum elements and tailored to specific contexts and populations
Underpinned by a model of human experience	Variations in program structure, length, and delivery are formatted to fit the population and context

Essential components	Variable components
Develops a new relationship with experience through mindfulness mechanisms and insights	
Supports the cultivation of positive qualities and the regulation of negative qualities	
Engages the participant in sustained mindfulness training with an experiential inquiry-based learning process and in exercises to develop insight and understanding	

The essential components would include components of MBPs such as formal practices, informal practices, inquiry, didactic components, and exercises. The variable components would be the adaptations that are required based on the intentions of the MBP as well as the audience in the room. These variable components could include the program duration, length of each session, and maximum number of participants among others. Almost all of the different types of MBPs would have the formal practices as a non-negotiable feature. We have already discussed how adaptations could be made in Chapter 7 based on culture and other contexts.

Furthermore, the variable components can be negotiated through several structural components that hinge on the participants' depth of experience with mindfulness. Below you will find a few considerations that are helpful in making adaptations to the MBWE, and other MBPs, if needed.

Period of Engagement

We have encountered two variations of the usual eight-week engagement. The first is the introductory session that could last for an hour to possibly three or four sessions lasting an hour each. These are classes that aim to get people to dip their toes in mindfulness.

The second type is a very intensive engagement where participants attend a whole-day workshop, as shown in the sample below:

9.30 am – Introductions	1.15 pm – Mindful walking
9.50 am – What is the program about?	1.50 pm – (Exercises/didactic)
10.20 am – Defining mindfulness	2.10 pm – Dialogue
– Raisin practice	2.30 pm – Sitting meditation
– Body scan	3.20 pm – Seated mindful movement
11.30 am – Mindful movement	3.35 pm – Setting home practices
11.50 am – Awareness of breath	3.50 pm – Lovingkindness meditation
12.15 pm – Dialogue	4.00 pm – Goodbyes
12.30 pm – Lunch in silence	

Technically, we would not consider these two types as MBPs, though they are intensive. We see a strong correlation between the results of mindfulness and the period of engagement. In a 2020 systematic review of 56 studies, conducted at workplaces with about 2,700 participants, it was found that the average period of engagement was 7.5 weeks with the average total number of hours to be 17 hours i.e. 7.5 sessions × 135 mins (Vonderlin et al., 2020). In another 2021 review of 28 studies on workplace adaptations, it was found that the average length of engagement was 8 weeks with an average weekly session length of two hours (Johnson et al., 2020). Based on these studies, we can certainly be reassured that the longer the period of engagement with mindfulness practices, the better the effects (see Figure 8.2).

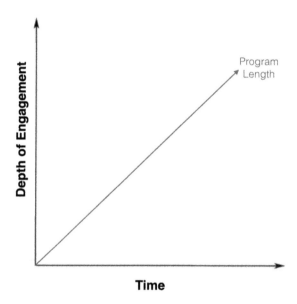

Figure 8.2 Depth of engagement with mindfulness training

What would be the minimal period of engagement for an MBP to produce results? Though from our study, we found that research suggests that a duration of at least 5–8 weeks of engagement with mindfulness would produce positive results, we are of the opinion that this question is not very helpful because the length of engagement does not guarantee committed practice by participants. The purpose of the MBP, as we see it, is to *cultivate lifetime practice of mindfulness* through the insights and outcomes of the MBP. We see the end of an MBP as the beginning of a lifelong practice of mindfulness. Therefore, the principle behind shortening an MBP should be addressed through asking ourselves the question, "How much time would I need to sufficiently facilitate the goal of *cultivating the lifetime practice of mindfulness?*"

Modes of Deliveries

With the increased availability of technology and internet connectivity, more MBPs are conducted online with instructor led sessions. We remember attending a five-day retreat online and we went away with a positive experience. We see an increasing trend of mindfulness training providers letting go of the need to deliver onsite sessions, and adding more online sessions, especially since the COVID-19 pandemic. Our experiences of delivering sessions online inform us that we need to account for the fatigue that online sessions cause. This is mainly due to distractions in the environment, multi-tasking, and tiredness. Studies have confirmed the negative effects on physical and psychological health due to online engagements.

We also see a trend of people desiring online sessions as they would reduce commuting and preparation needed for attending sessions. Having said that, we also see a continued interest among people for onsite sessions as well, as a preferred option. We need to acknowledge that MBPs have long been delivered as onsite sessions and most of the evidence we have is from such sessions, although we see growing evidence for the efficacy of online sessions. We therefore encourage online sessions to be concise and introduce regular breaks when needed.

Venue of Program

We have noticed that venues have a significant effect on participants. I (KK) remember attending the Mindfulness-Based Stress Reduction program in a classroom at a local university. At times, the temperature was either too warm or too cool for my comfort. There are various factors to be considered when choosing a venue and sometimes as teachers, we may not have much choice over the venue and its settings, such as when it is hosted by an institution. The primary considerations when deciding on a venue would be comfort, how welcoming it is, cultural sensitivity, and safety. Some factors to be considered are:

- Noise levels in the vicinity
- Safety and accessibility of the venue

- Accessibility for people who are differently abled
- Temperature controls in the room
- Types of floor surfaces
- Adequate space in the room for the number of participants
- Space to be culturally neutral

The above is definitely not an exhaustive list but we may need to adapt the program depending on the above factors. We have noticed from our participants' evaluations that all of the above, and possibly more, would affect the participants' experience in the room. It is important that we reduce distractions and discomfort while they learn to appreciate mindfulness in the sessions.

Locus of Choice

Locus of choice, indicates whether the participant had voluntarily joined the program or whether they were conscripted (see Figure 8.3). This has a significant effect on how people engage with the program.

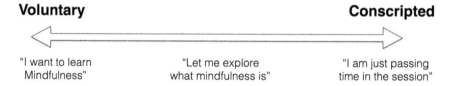

Figure 8.3 Locus of choice scale

We have seen a fair share of people who were involuntarily or unwillingly enlisted into the program and this happens more often when an institution hosts the program. Often a few components of the program will have to be adapted in such a way that we can promote more curiosity in the room to reduce possible resistance. There would be a need to *soften* the experience with more innovative ways of piquing their curiosity. Sometimes, we do lighten the mood in the room with more fun exercises and games to discover the intentions of the didactic components instead of facilitating it the way recommended in the curriculum. With a younger population, this can become a challenge as sometimes they do not know why they are "forced" to attend a mindfulness program. We therefore have an adapted MBWE for younger audiences which includes a different set of metaphors, poems, exercises, and informal practices though the intentions are the same. We would encourage you to refer to books and resources meant for these audiences to explore the various modalities that can be used to introduce and sustain mindfulness.

1.3 Intentions

Every MBP has a specific intention and we cannot understate the power of intention within each participant engaging with the program. Just like the MBWE, which has the specific goal of enhancing wellbeing through mindfulness, every MBP has a unique intention. It is with this intention that participants sign up for the program. The alignment of participants' intentions with the intention of MBP creates clarity for the participants, the teacher, and the curriculum designer of any MBP.

We have also noticed that sometimes participants suffer from stress and anxiety when we share the home practices at the end of each session. Although, we always encourage self-compassion and not create stress, or induce any form of guilt during these moments, we still do not lose sight of the pedagogy of the MBP. The home practices remain unchanged though we promote self-compassion and acceptance even if they failed to undertake them.

As shown in the Figure 8.4, an MBP typically begins by gradually increasing the intensity of the practices and hits a peak somewhere in the middle. After crossing the peak, we gradually empower the participants to discover their own commitment to practice that allows them to sustain it comfortably.

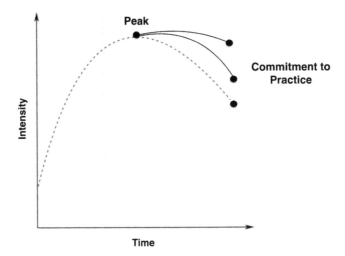

Figure 8.4 Intensity curve of MBPs

By the time participants reach their final session, they will have known what has worked and what has not, and based on those insights, they would make a commitment that would work for them. As mindfulness teachers, we would have to facilitate the process to allow them commit to a practice(s) that would be sustainable for them, by remembering that the goal of an MBP is to *cultivate the lifetime practice of mindfulness.*

2 OUTCOMES AND EVIDENCE

Related to the intention of MBPs are the outcomes. One of the most unique phenomena of mindfulness compared to other contemplative approaches would be its abundant evidence. The American Mindfulness Research Association has been recording the number of published papers on mindfulness since 1980 (see Figure 8.5). In 2021, 1,362 papers were published and the numbers are rising year after year which is an indication of the impact and increase in evidence.

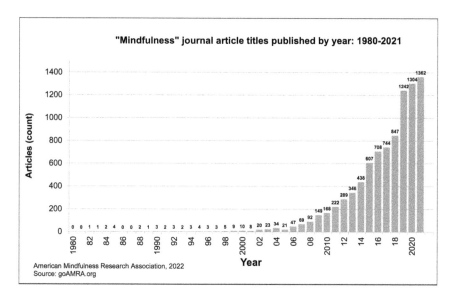

Figure 8.5 Mindfulness journal article titles published annually: 1980–2021

Edo Shonin and William Van Gordon (2016) found ten unique results of mindfulness. These are:

1. Structural brain changes
2. Reduced autonomic arousal
3. Perceptual shift
4. Increase in spirituality
5. Greater situational awareness
6. Values clarification

7. Increase in self-awareness
8. Addiction substitution
9. Urge-surfing
10. Letting go

These ten results, and from our survey, we have found many benefits and positive outcomes, beyond the narrow scope of reducing stress and depression, that can be organized into the following areas:

- Learning capabilities
- Innovation and creativity
- Parenting
- Improving relationships
- Self-awareness
- Interpersonal functioning
- Empathy and compassion
- Performance – personal and professional
- Happiness
- Emotional balance

From the trend in Figure 8.5, we can certainly expect to see a positive trend in the increase of research and interest in mindfulness in various areas of human development and living.

3 MEASURING MINDFULNESS

We are in a world where the quantification of impact matters. In the same fashion, mindfulness results too would have to be quantified. To meet this need, researchers from different parts of the world have created questionnaires that can measure the impact of mindfulness. These self-reported questionnaires are either single faceted scales, reporting a single outcome, or multi-faceted scales, reporting multiple outcomes. These questionnaires can be administered to participants before and after an MBP and the difference is usually studied. We have had the experience of using several of these questionnaires with participants from this part of the globe. We have made a compilation in Table 8.2 of many of the known questionnaires.

These questionnaires can be used to measure the outcomes of MBPs depending on what aspects of mindfulness we wish to measure. It would be helpful to know that almost all of the questionnaires measure trait mindfulness, except for the SMS, AMPS, and TMS, that measure state mindfulness. It is also important to be aware that sometimes MBPs do not yield positive results, or deliver weak results, for reasons that we will discuss in the pages to come.

Table 8.2 List of mindfulness questionnaires

Title	Number of items	Outcomes(what it measures)
Single facet scales		
1 Mindful attention awareness scale (MAAS)	15	Attention, informed by a sensitive awareness of what is occurring in the present
2 Freiburg mindfulness inventory (FMI)	14	Regulation of one's attention
3 Cognitive and affective mindfulness scale (CAMS)	12	Captures a broad conceptualization of mindfulness with language that is not specific to any particular type of meditation training
Multiple facet scales		
1 Kentucky inventory of mindfulness skills (KIMS)	39	• Observing • Describing • Acting with awareness • Accepting without judgment
2 Five facet mindfulness questionnaire (FFMQ)	39	• Observing • Describing • Acting with awareness • Non-judging of inner experience • Non-reactivity to inner experience
3 Philadelphia mindfulness scale (PMS)	20	• Present moment awareness • Acceptance
4 Toronto mindfulness scale (TMS)	13	• Curiosity • Decentering
5 Applied mindfulness process scale (AMPS)	15	• Positive emotional regulation • Negative emotional regulation • Decentering
6 State mindfulness scale (SMS)	21	• Objects of mindful awareness • Qualities of mindful awareness
7 Southampton mindfulness questionnaire (SMQ)	16	• Observation • Non-aversion • Non-judgment • Letting go

4 THE BRAIN AND MINDFULNESS

Another method of measuring the effects of mindfulness is by the studying the brain. With the invention of fMRI machines and other similar equipment, the effects of mindfulness on the brain can now be visibly seen through brain scans. Since the late 1990s, we are seeing more neuroscientific evidence for mindfulness and meditation. Leading this field are researchers such as Sarah

Lazar and Richard Davidson. Without having to share an overwhelming amount of information, we would like to list the areas of the brain that mindfulness impacts (Tang et al., 2015):

- Anterior cingulate cortex
- Multiple prefrontal regions
- Medial prefrontal cortex
- Striatum
- Amygdalae
- Posterior cingulate cortex/precuneus
- Insula

Moreover other researchers have also captured the emergence of new neural networks within the brain with mindfulness practice. We need to qualify that the field of neuroscience continues to grow and we know little about how the brain works as new theories are being developed debunking older ones. However evidence from research thus far gives us some interesting phenomena on how mindfulness impacts the brain and we discuss a few of these here.

- Amygdalae – these regions are responsible for emotional responses, sometimes popularized as the flight-freeze-fight response. The Amygdalae are also associated with negativity bias which automatically directs our attention to negative events and makes decisions from a position of fear. Mindfulness decreased gray-matter density in the Amygdalae, which suggests a positive impact on anxiety, stress, and other related symptoms. The flight-freeze-fight responses would be less active or tamed with mindfulness.
- Prefrontal cortex – this region of the brain oversees activities such as decision-making, regulating emotions, and abstract planning. Mindfulness improves the prefrontal cortex functioning and increases its activity. Gratitude is also associated with this part of the brain where increased activity was found in fMRI scans. It was also found that repeated emotions of gratitude motivate people to support others by relieving their stress and stressors. The prefrontal cortex can also be trained to direct attention to the positive with mindfulness training.
- Hippocampus – this is the seat of memory and learning. Mindfulness was found to increase cortical thickness in the hippocampus thus enhancing memory performance and learning.
- Default mode network (DMN) – This network of the brain is responsible for autopilot behavior such as mind wandering, planning, remembering the past, self-reference, and thinking about others. Mindfulness reduces the DMN activity thus bringing a more present centered cognitive activity.

- Insula – a complex part of the brain that is connected to other parts of the brain and is responsible for interoception. Mindfulness strengthens the insula connection thus increasing self-awareness and dispositional mindfulness. The insula is also known to be the compassion center of the brain. Therefore, it has been hypothesized that mindfulness can increase compassion.

It is important to be aware that the neuro-effects of mindfulness tend to be different in short term, long term, and lifelong meditators and it is important to be mindful of these when vouching for the neuroscientific evidence of mindfulness (Zeidan, 2015).

5 ADVERSE EFFECTS OF MINDFULNESS

Discussions about the adverse effects of mindfulness are rare in mindfulness literature. While the adverse effects of *meditation* have been documented, we have not seen much literature about mindfulness until approximately five years ago. When discussing the adverse effects of mindfulness, it is important to note that *there have been adverse effects with all well-established approaches to health and wellbeing, including psychotherapy, pharmacotherapy, and physical exercise* and therefore it is not as significant in the case of mindfulness (Baer et al., 2019).

Research (Shapiro, 1992) conducted with long-term Vipassana practitioners, found that 62 percent of the subjects reported at least one of three adverse effects in the areas of intrapersonal, interpersonal, and societal dimensions. A cross-sectional study of meditators who attended an intensive and long-term mindfulness meditation retreat, reported that over 60 percent of the meditators experienced at least one negative effect (Farias & Wikholm, 2016). Recently in 2021, it was reported that about 70 percent of the subjects who practiced mindfulness reported some form of adverse effect (Britton et al., 2021). The adverse effects of mindfulness as reported in these papers are listed below:

- increased anxiety
- depression
- full-blown psychosis
- increase the awareness of difficult feelings
- exacerbation of psychological problems
- depersonalization
- derealization
- grandiosity
- autoscopy

- increased negativity
- increased disorientation
- addiction to meditation
- adverse societal effects
- negative emotions
- transient distress

These adverse effects are likely to be found in participants with pre-existing depression, bipolar disorder, or psychosis. On another note, participants with comorbid conditions, severe symptoms as well as other vulnerabilities, were seen to benefit from MBPs (Baer et al., 2019). It was also found that most of the adverse effects were caused by *intense* retreats and *very* brief interventions rather than MBPs (Atalaya, 2019; Lustyk et al., 2009).

Anna Lutkajtis (2018) surmises that another cause of these adverse effects could be due to limitations of Western psychology. The philosophy of deconstructing the nature of the psychological self, a phenomenon prevalent in Eastern and Eastern-influenced contemplative traditions, is alien to Western psychology. Hence, these effects are often confused with dissociative psychopathology. Another cause identified is the poor teaching by mindfulness teachers who were not healthcare professionals or not adequately trained (Doblin, 2012; Van Gordon et al., 2017).

What could we do to prevent and reduce the occurrences of adverse effects? The first and foremost requirement is a proper intake process which includes inclusion and exclusion criteria, as discussed in Chapter 3. The second requirement is to ensure that the mindfulness teachers are trained adequately. The third is to work with MBPs that have sound conceptual foundations of mindfulness with clarity of their intentions (Baer et al., 2019).

6 POPULAR CRITICISMS OF MBPS

In the last decade, scholars of repute have strongly criticized MBPs. These comments, however, have targeted primarily the first-generation MBPs, namely Mindfulness-Based Stress Reduction and Mindfulness-Based Cognitive Therapy (though other MBPs may not be immune from them either). We believe that, in the spirit of mindfulness, we should not be averse to criticism and instead allow critics to inform our wisdom. Through feedback, we can learn to make changes if required. In this spirt, we have listed the salient comments from several sources in Table 8.3:

What can we learn from these criticisms? Ashin Wirathu, a Myanmar Buddhist monk, is an apt example at this juncture. Despite being a Buddhist monk, and having possibly meditated for some time, he participated

Table 8.3 Criticisms of MBPs

Sources	Salient comments
Mindlessness: *The Corruption of Mindfulness in a Culture of Narcissism* (2017), by Thomas Joiner	• The culture of narcissism has made authentic mindfulness diluted, distorted, and pernicious • The problem is how mindfulness is promoted rather than how it is practiced • The non-judgmental self-focus of mindfulness promotes narcissism, solipsism, and self-indulgence • Most of mindfulness research is overhyped
McMindfulness: *How Mindfulness Became the New Capitalist Spirituality* (2019), by Ronald Purser	First-generation MBPs: • help people to adjust to the very conditions that caused their problems • turn a blind eye to societal causes and capitalistic exploitation • overrate stress and privatize the problems of people • do not promote ethical behavior as it does not automatically rise from bare attentional practices • have commodified and sold mindfulness like products in the market • used mindfulness for self-serving and ego-enhancing purposes that run counter to both Buddhist and Abrahamic prophetic teachings
Mindfulness and Its Discontents: Education, Self, and Social Transformation (2019), by David Forbes	MBPs: • reinforce neoliberalism • uses mindfulness to gain self-centered skills in stress reduction, self-promotion, self-enhancement, hedonic happiness, and corporate profits, and productivity over common good • lack moral foundation and have appropriated its original meaning • should become more civic or social to end poverty, wealth and income inequity, racism, sexism, homophobia, and xenophobia
What's Wrong with Mindfulness (And What Isn't): Zen Perspectives (2016), edited by Robert Rosenbaum & Barry Magid	MBPs: • have appropriated mindfulness from Buddhism and commodified it in Western culture – spiritual materialism, capitalism • promote narcissism and its neuro-effects are overrated • blur the ethics and morals of the mindfulness teacher • promote "bare attentional" practices which are not the mindfulness of Buddhism • do not operate on the precondition that the practitioner has renounced hope that happiness is possible in the material world, and therefore it is not the mindfulness taught in Buddhism • made depression a problem when in Buddhism it is viewed as something positive as it allows the abandonment of hope for happiness in the world

Sources	Salient comments
The Mindful Elite: Mobilizing from the Inside Out (2018), by Jaime Kucinskas	• Success of secular mindfulness was due to the watered down, Westernized, and capitalist infused society, quite contrary to the commitment of Asian Buddhist monastic traditions
	• Early leaders of mindfulness used their access to and power within powerful institutions to gain legitimacy for their agenda
	• The leaders also overtly promoted the acceptable aspects and hid the controversial aspects of their mindfulness agenda
	• The leaders changed the positioning of Buddhism to spread mindfulness
	• The mindfulness movement continues to be elitist driven and does not allow access to people who may not be economically, socially, and culturally advantaged
	• Mindfulness conferences continue to be expensive and dominated by well-educated people with doctorates. The leaders of these movements and the beneficiaries continue to be predominantly white. Only 9 percent of the contemplative leaders in the author's sample were Asian despite Buddhism's roots in Asia. Blacks and Latinos each formed less than 3%.
	• Mindfulness programs in institutions continue to be palliative rather than transformative

in creating anti-Muslim rhetoric and inciting violence against Muslims in Rohingya. This violence had affected thousands of Muslims. Therefore, we cannot vouch for lovingkindness and peace as guaranteed effects of mindfulness. Enhanced awareness, emerging from mindfulness practices, does not automatically generate ethics. It is for this reason that the didactic components in MBPs are well placed to direct attention to wholesome ideas that are ethically sound. This has been one of the biggest gaps raised by the critics.

Next, though the first-generation MBPs, such as the MBSR and MBCT, have been the prime target of these critics, we need to be wary about appearing to be on the McMindfulness bandwagon. Further mindfulness, when delivered as a secular MBP, should not be a means to propagate Buddhism or other Asian religions (Hinduism, yoga, etc.) through the back door. Moreover, we also need a more social, civic, ethical, and wisdom-centered approach to mindfulness which can moderate current criticisms of mindfulness. Teachers need to exercise caution when vouching for the effects of mindfulness by presenting the outcomes as possibilities instead of promoting or selling it with a guarantee. We need to tap into common humanity as a resource to impact society through MBPs. It needs to be culturally sensitive, adaptive, and inclusive. This would also mean that we do not privatize human problems and instead balance them with awareness of social causes of problems. It is our belief that the MBWE addresses most of these criticisms, and possibly newer MBPs should make a concerted attempt to implement these positive changes to its curriculum.

7 ETHICS OF TEACHING MINDFULNESS

The ethics of teaching mindfulness is centered around doing no harm or reducing the potential of harm to oneself and others. This comprises of two important components for mindfulness teachers, which is one's personal ethical behavior and one's professional conduct.

A mindfulness teacher's personal conduct is important, and this requires the bringing of awareness to one's behavior and relationship with oneself with the intention of beneficence and doing no harm. One's embodiment and awareness would also allow teachers to self-negotiate within the sphere of collective values and norms espoused in diverse cultures.

A teacher's professional conduct revolves around bringing awareness to one's professional conduct and relationships with others with the intention of beneficence and doing no harm before, during, and after participation in an MBP. We have listed a few important guidelines for mindfulness teachers in this regard. Mindfulness teachers

- should not use mindfulness for harmful purposes – for example, providing training to staff in a company where the employer has policies which create stress and then uses mindfulness training to teach them to cope with the very stress
- should promote diversity, equity, and inclusivity
- should teach mindfulness with a sole and clear intention to generate wellbeing
- should not propagate any religion, religious agenda, political agenda, economic agenda, etc.
- should not cause imminent harm to anyone and oneself
- should make mindfulness training available to all without any discrimination. The exclusion criteria for MBPs should be solely for the purpose of preventing harm
- should promote and act with compassion, empathy, and kindness
- model the accommodation and respect for all cultures
- should promote non-aggressive and peaceful ways of change making
- should not engage in unethical marketing or overstating and exaggerating the positive effects of mindfulness

As we conclude this chapter, we would like to make the following recommendations, should you wish to create a new MBP with a specific intention or outcome.

- gather existing evidence that suggests the attainment of the outcome through mindfulness and its mechanisms
- possess the competence and experience in the domain of the outcome or intention
- deliver the specific MBP one is trained in several times before creating a new MBP
- be favorable to obtaining feedback and validating the effectiveness of the MBP
- create new didactic components and exercises in support of generating insights around the intention or outcomes
- introduce a more social, civic, ethical, wisdom-centered approach to mindfulness training

In this chapter we have presented the effectiveness of MBPs through their program design, teacher competencies, evidence for its outcomes, and criticism. In Chapter 9, we will be discussing the untold history of mindfulness.

REFERENCES

Anālayo, B. (2019). The insight knowledge of fear and adverse effects of mindfulness practices. *Mindfulness*, *10*(10), 2172–2185.

Baer, R. A. (2003). Mindfulness training as a clinical intervention: A conceptual and empirical review. *Clinical Psychology: Science and Practice*, *10*(2), 125.

Baer, R., Crane, C., Miller, E., & Kuyken, W. (2019). Doing no harm in mindfulness-based programs: conceptual issues and empirical findings. *Clinical Psychology Review*, *71*, 101–114.

Britton, W. B., Lindahl, J. R., Cooper, D. J., Canby, N. K., & Palitsky, R. (2021). Defining and measuring meditation-related adverse effects in mindfulness-based programs. *Clinical Psychological Science*, *9*(6), 1185–1204.

Crane, R. S. (2017). Implementing mindfulness in the mainstream: Making the path by walking it. *Mindfulness*, *8*(3), 585–594.

Crane, R. S., Brewer, J., Feldman, C., Kabat-Zinn, J., Santorelli, S., Williams, J. M. G., & Kuyken, W. (2017). What defines mindfulness-based programs? The warp and the weft. *Psychological Medicine*, *47*(6), 990–999.

Dobkin, P. L., Irving, J. A., & Amar, S. (2012). For whom may participation in a mindfulness-based stress reduction program be contraindicated? *Mindfulness*, *3*(1), 44–50.

Farias, M., & Wikholm, C. (2016). Has the science of mindfulness lost its mind? *BJPsych Bulletin*, *40*(6), 329–332.

Johnson, K. R., Park, S., & Chaudhuri, S. (2020). Mindfulness training in the workplace: Exploring its scope and outcomes. *European Journal of Training and Development*, *44*(4–5), 341–354.

Kabat-Zinn, J. (2003). Mindfulness-based interventions in context: past, present, and future. *Clinical psychology: science and practice, 10*, 144–156.

Lustyk, M. K., Chawla, N., Nolan, R. S., & Marlatt, G. A. (2009). Mindfulness meditation research: Issues of participant screening, safety procedures, and researcher training. *Advances in Mind-Body Medicine, 24*(1), 20–30.

Lutkajtis, A. (2018). The dark side of Dharma: Why have adverse effects of meditation been ignored in contemporary Western secular contexts? *Journal for the Academic Study of Religion, 31*(2), 192–217.

Shapiro Jr, D. H. (1992). Adverse effects of meditation: A preliminary investigation of long-term meditators. *International Journal of Psychosomatics, 39*(1–4), 63.

Shonin, E., & Van Gordon, W. (2016). The mechanisms of mindfulness in the treatment of mental illness and addiction. *International Journal of Mental Health and Addiction, 14*(5), 844–849.

Tang, Y. Y., Hölzel, B. K., & Posner, M. I. (2015). The neuroscience of mindfulness meditation. *Nature Reviews Neuroscience, 16*(4), 213–225.

Van Gordon, W., Shonin, E., & Garcia-Campayo, J. (2017). Are there adverse effects associated with mindfulness? *Australian & New Zealand Journal of Psychiatry, 51*(10), 977–979.

Vonderlin, R., Biermann, M., Bohus, M., & Lyssenko, L. (2020). Mindfulness-based programs in the workplace: A meta-analysis of randomized controlled trials. *Mindfulness, 11*(7), 1579–1598.

Zeidan, F. (2015). The neurobiology of mindfulness meditation. In K. W. Brown, J. D. Creswell, & R. M. Ryan (Eds.), *Handbook of mindfulness: Theory, research, and practice* (pp. 171–189). Guilford.

CHAPTER 9

The Untold History of Mindfulness

I've always thought that mindfulness is Buddhist but I have started to appreciate mindfulness a lot more now and am also grateful to so many traditions and teachers who have contributed to my growth and learning today.

–Atiqah (trainee teacher in mindfulness)

A river would usually look different downstream from when it is closer to its source. Fed by the many tributaries along its course, the river becomes unrecognizable primarily from the way it looks by the time it reaches down to the plains. Such is the case with the evolution of mindfulness where it has been fed by different practices and philosophical traditions to the point where it becomes quite unrecognizable by the time it becomes a secular practice.

In this chapter, we will be discussing the *brief* history of mindfulness in ancient and modern times. We will be drawing on salient points from several sources and our own knowledge to answer two big questions, often unasked and unpopular, about secular mindfulness:

- Was Kabat-Zinn's mindfulness Buddhist?
- Was secular mindfulness an invention by Kabat-Zinn?

Though this chapter is not essential for mindfulness teachers, it can still aid in the appreciation of secular mindfulness in its evolution and development especially since there has been misinformation about mindfulness and its roots perpetuated by and originating from high places. We will deconstruct these assumptions from the standpoint of modern evidence and textual sources. In the process of presenting our position, we may disagree with several authors that we have cited and learned from in the other chapters of this book. In no way is this a devaluation of their competence on the subject of teaching mindfulness. We do not wish to throw the baby out with the bathwater.

DOI: 10.4324/9781003322955-11

Due to my (KK) early exposure to mindfulness in the late 1990s through the Advaita Vedanta tradition and my training in Indian philosophy, many doubts emerged about the way secular mindfulness was positioned. I realized this immediately when I participated in the mindfulness-based stressed reduction (MBSR) program and after studying the *Full Catastrophe Living* by Jon Kabat-Zinn. And in 2019, I was invited to Delhi to speak at a conference to show the connection between the often neglected Indic roots of Kabat-Zinn's secular mindfulness. My initial findings were confirmed when I started to see a trend in the recent writings of scholars of Buddhism such as Sarah Shaw and Robert Sharf. Let us now discover this untold story of secular mindfulness.

1 MINDFULNESS IN INDIC RELIGIONS

We might think of mindfulness as one tributary of the human wisdom tradition.
While its most highly articulated roots lie deep within Buddhism,
its essence is universal and has been expressed in one way
or another in all human cultures and traditions.

–Jon Kabat-Zinn

It is important to state that historically all forms of meditation arose in religious traditions. And mindfulness is a *unique* type of meditation among several other types. Mindfulness originated in two Indic religions, namely Hinduism and Buddhism. The original terms for mindfulness were *smrti* (in Sanskrit) and *sati* (in Pali), the latter being the language of early Buddhism. The terms smrti and sati literally mean 'memory' or 'remembering'. However, the Buddha (c. 500 BCE) repurposed the definition of sati into a form of vigilance (Shaw, 2020). Two entire discourses by the Buddha, *Anapanasati Sutta – Discourses on the Mindfulness of Breathing* and *Mahasatipatthana Sutta – Discourses on the Great Foundations of Mindfulness*, are considered the foundational texts on Buddhist mindfulness. Eventually within Buddhism, sati meant a host of practices that revolved around *vigilance, attention, remembrance, mental stability, meditation style, wisdom, discrimination, and a process* (Hwang & Kearney, 2015). It is to be noted that the purpose of mindfulness in Buddhism is for the purpose of advancing the practitioner to the eighth limb of the eight-fold path, *samadhi*.

Prior to the Buddha and until the 1st century CE, ideas and teachings about vigilance and remembrance appear in the Vedic (early Hindu) texts as well. Though the term smrti appears in the Yogasutra-s (4th century BCE to 3rd century CE) in the context of memory, smrti was not the preferred term in the case of Vedic texts. The reference to *vigilance* appears in many of the pre-1st-century texts such as the Katha and Mundaka Upanishads (466–386 BCE) and the Bhagavad Gita (c. 200 BCE) as the Sanskrit term *apramatta*. Another variant of vigilance in Sanskrit is the term *apramada* which appears in the Mahabharata (3rd century BCE–3rd century ce) and the Baudhayana Dharmasutra (500–200 BCE). The difference between the dating on the Vedic texts and the period of Buddha, is due to the pre-Buddhistic teachings not being put into writing until much later, which is the case with most of pre-1st century Indic teachings and traditions.

The mindfulness tradition within Buddhism continued to develop into two focal areas, one on the practice of directing attention to the breath and the other directing attention to insight (Shaw, 2020). The Vipassana and Zen traditions are proponents of the insight path. Most of the MBPs appear to belong to the attentional path of using the breath as an anchor though the written works of Kabat-Zinn exude the influence of the insight traditions as well. Interestingly, such a division of practice and insights is also found in the pre-Buddhistic Vedic texts, the Upanishads, as upasana-s and jnana (Prabhavananda & Smith, 1979; Ishvarananda, 1959).

Alexander Wynne (2007) argues in his book *The Origin of Buddhist Meditation,* that Buddha was informed by the early Vedic teachers and teachings (not the Hindu texts though) in his distinctive formulation of his teachings. A similar view was held by Vishwanath Prasad Varma (1973) in his book *Early Buddhism and its Origins.* They claim that early Buddhism was influenced by the Upanishads and the Vedic practices. Barry Boyce (2011) refers to the same point when he states that mindfulness existed prior to the Buddha. This could possibly explain the similarities in the way sati and apramatta/apramada have been described in both traditions. What we would see after the period of the Buddha, is that both Buddhism and Hinduism utilized the quality of being *vigilant* within their respective soteriological systems. However, it is through the Buddhist teachers that vigilance or mindfulness got its deepest and extensive treatment as a practice.

The translation of the word sati continues to create controversy. Many different English definitions have been proposed. Jeff Wilson in his book, *Mindful America,* had compiled these translations which are conscience, ascertainment of truth, watchfulness, well awake, correct memory, right memory, and right self-discipline. However, it was Rhys Davids' 1886 translation of sati as *mindfulness,* that has become the most popular and preferred one.

The original source of mindfulness goes back to the times of the Vedic tradition and early Buddhism, though it can be found as a practice in other faith traditions.

2 MEDITATION AND MINDFULNESS IN THE ABRAHAMIC RELIGIONS

Meditation and mindfulness can also be found in the Abrahamic religions (Christianity, Judaism, and Islam), and are usually of three types: recitative, visualization, and unmediated (Eifring, 2013). As with almost all religious meditative traditions, rarely do we come across content-less meditations in the Abrahamic religions, such as the bare-attention tradition of the modern Burmese Buddhists. In this regard, meditations in the Abrahamic religions are closer to the insight traditions of Buddhist mindfulness and the Hindu Upanishads, as they employed scriptural insights into their meditations.

The Merkavah (c. 1st century ce) and the Kabbalah (12–16th century ce), mystical traditions of Judaism, are two examples that taught meditation as a spiritual practice. With the rise of monasticism within Christianity between the 4th and 7th centuries ce, the recital of Jesus prayer emerged. This meditative practice was for the purposes of concentration on God, internalizing specific spiritual attitudes, to cultivate mental tranquility, and reduce mind wandering (Johnsén, 2013). More complex forms of meditations were developed in 7th–8th-century East Syrian Christianity, which included practices such as concentration, bodily movements and meditation, and culminating in an illumined mind (Seppala, 2013). The German Christian Meister Eckhart (1260–1328) and the 16th-century Teresa of Avila had also taught very interesting conceptions of "being" and "doing" as meditative prayer (Cooper, 2013; Frohlich, 2013).

The Sufi tradition of Islam is highly replete with meditative practices. Bringing an inward focus and the removal of mental distractions are principles of the Dhikr, a meditation which involves both stillness and movement (Buehler, 2016). Al-Ghazali (1058–1111), one of the most prominent and influential Islamic teachers, in his Ihya Ulum al-Din, presents the virtues of vigilance and awareness, *muraqabah*, which are very supportive in ensuring one's behaviors and actions are intentional (Shaker, 2015). Al-Ghazali's description of the practice is very similar to mindfulness as presented in the Indic religions.

It is a misnomer to assume that meditation and mindfulness are alien to the Abrahamic religions. Similar to Buddhism and Hinduism, contemplative practices evolved in the medieval times among the Abrahamic religions.

3 ROOTS OF SECULAR MINDFULNESS

We believe that any investigation into the roots of secular mindfulness should start with Kabat-Zinn as he is the founder of this whole movement via his MBSR. His words, both the explicit and the implicit, would have to be studied in order to understand what influenced the MBSR. Kabat-Zinn (2011) claims that in 1979, during a two-week Vipassana retreat, he got the inspiration for the MBSR as a flash of insight.

During our search for the roots of secular mindfulness over the past few years, we encountered an interesting phenomenon. Almost every author connected the roots of secular mindfulness to Buddhist origins by presenting an unbroken and continuous tradition from the times of the Buddha until today. Woods and Rockman (2021), claim that MBSR was a product of Burmese Buddhism and Vipassana traditions. They do not state any other influences which was worrying for us. Feldman and Kuyken, in their insightful book, *Mindfulness: Ancient Wisdom Meets Modern Psychology* (2019), state

> Mindfulness and mindfulness training are embedded in most contemplative traditions . . . Although it is possible to outline how contemporary mindfulness draws upon the rich lineage of each of these early traditions [referring to a few other spiritual and philosophical traditions], in this book, we draw primarily on Buddhism and, specifically, Buddhist psychology.

They do not state why they chose to neglect the "rich lineage of the other early traditions." McCown et al. (2011) devote almost 50 pages in their book locating mindfulness within Buddhism that goes as far back as the beginnings of Orientalism with William Jones in the 18th century. To make matters more confusing, Kabat-Zinn in his foreword to the aforementioned book states,

> competency in teaching mindfulness within secular mindfulness-based frameworks is a combination of knowing and not knowing. It helps to know from the inside, through your bones and skin, the general framework of the *dharma*, including the Four Noble (Ennobling) Truths, the Eight-Fold Noble Path, something of the Abhidharma, stories of the certain teachers and teaching stories, and perhaps the teaching lineage of at least one Buddhist tradition.
>
> (p.xxi)

Given these perspectives, it is important to examine the works of Kabat-Zinn to understand what gave birth to the secular MBSR.

Kabat-Zinn's Influences

Kabat-Zinn in his works between 1982 and 2011 explicitly presented several influences of secular mindfulness. They can be broadly categorized into four schools which are Vipassana, Zen Buddhism, yogic traditions (Advaita Vedanta), and Hatha yoga. In Table 9.1 below, we have compiled the influences cited.

Kabat-Zinn clearly states in his papers that there were only four consistent sources of influences for MBSR, known as the stress reduction and relaxation program (SRRP) in its early years. In the next section, we make a concise presentation of these four traditions.

Table 9.1 Influences of Jon Kabat-Zinn

Sources	(1) Vipassana	(2) Zen Buddhism	(3) Advaita Vedanta	(4) Hatha yoga	Other sources
Kabat-Zinn, (1982)	Sattipatana Vipassana or insight meditation of Theravada Buddhism	Soto Zen of Mahāyāna Buddhism	Yogic traditions: J. Krishnamurti, Vimila Thakar, and Nisargadatta Mahara		
Kabat-Zinn, Lipworth & Burney, (1985)	Sattipatana Vipassana or insight meditation of Theravada Buddhism	Soto Zen of Mahāyāna Buddhism	Yogic traditions: J. Krishnamurti, Vimila Thakar, and Nisargadatta Maharaj		
Kabat-Zinn, (1994)	Buddhist mindfulness meditation practice			Hatha yoga	
Kabat-Zinn, (2003)	Buddhism		Yogic traditions: Vedanta of Nisargadatta Maharaj, J Krishnamurti, Ramana Maharashi	Hatha yoga	Eckhart Tolle, Lao Tzu, Chuang Tsu
Kabat-Zinn, (2011)	Joseph Goldstein	Chinese and Korean Zen traditions	Yogic traditions: Vedanta of Nisargadatta Maharaj, J Krishnamurti, Ramana Maharashi	Hatha yoga	

Vipassana

Vipassana, a Pali term, literally means *insight*. The goal of this practice is to develop insight into the nature of reality through the teachings of Buddhism. This tradition was believed to be resurrected by two Burmese monks, Ledi Sayadaw (1846–1923) and Mahasi Sayadaw (1904–1982). These two teachers were known to have adapted Vipassana meditation for Burmese laypeople. The latter was particularly interested in making meditation accessible to the laypersons who were not familiar with Buddhist scriptural canon and in the process founded the "bare-attention" tradition. Scholars are of the view that both of these Buddhist monks had reinterpreted the original meaning of sati found in the Buddhist canon (Sharf, 2016).

Kabat-Zinn's teacher, Jack Kornfield, was a student of Mahasi Sayadaw. Another of his teachers, Joseph Goldstein, learned Vipassana through S. N. Goenka (1924–1979) and U. Ba Khin (1899–1971) who belonged to the tradition of Ledi Sayadaw.

Soto Zen

Soto Zen is a Zen school of Japanese Buddhism that was developed in the 13th century by the teacher, Dogen. This tradition has Chinese roots, as Dogen learned these teachings in China before returning to Japan. This school developed a unique practice called Shikantaza which involves object-less meditation coupled with inquiry. Kabat-Zinn (2011) states that he learned Soto Zen from the Korean Zen teacher, Seung Sahn (1927–2004) in the 1970s.

Advaita Vedanta

Kabat-Zinn cites four Indian teachers, namely Jiddu Krishnamurti, Vimala Thakar, Ramana Maharshi, and Nisargadatta Maharaj, who have directly influenced his conception of mindfulness. He erroneously places all of the teachers under the umbrella of yogic traditions although these teachers are of the Advaita or the Advaita Vedanta tradition. These teachers, especially Ramana, Krishnamurti and Nisargadatta, have also radically influenced the eclectic and secular Neo-Advaita movements in North America. Neo-Advaita is described as having a

> significant effect on the larger culture of liberal American spirituality, particularly with regard to Neo-Advaita's eclecticism, focus on interior transformation, privileging of experiential over conceptual dimensions

of religion, mistrust of conventional religious organizations, ideal of the divinized human, and vision of human unity and solidarity across religious as well as national and ethnic boundaries.

(Lucas, 2011, p. 98)

Neo-Advaita is a modern offshoot of Advaita Vedanta and is often criticized by traditional Advaita Vedanta practitioners and teachers as not presenting a *clear* and *structured* path to free oneself from suffering (Waite, 2011). Popular teachers such as Eckart Tolle, Mooji, Andrew Cohen, and Rupert Spira are examples of contemporary teachers of Neo-Advaita.

Advaita Vedanta is considered to be the oldest Hindu tradition that traces its source to the Upanishads. It teaches that that self is intrinsically whole, undifferentiated and homogeneous awareness. This teaching finds its expression throughout Kabat-Zinn's books. One interesting feature of this tradition is that meditation is downplayed (or even criticized at times) and seen as not being the means to its soteriological goal. There is no evidence that Kabat-Zinn had any contact with any of these teachers. We can presume that these teachers are part of his informal lineage.

Jiddu Krishnamurti (1895–1986) was a charismatic Indian philosopher who taught from his direct experience. His statement "truth is a pathless land" is often considered to be the core of his teachings. He also popularized the term "choiceless awareness" which Kabat-Zinn uses to describe the awareness that arises from mindfulness practices. Vimala Thakar (1921–2009) was largely a follower of Krishnamurti, and taught that spiritual liberation should be coupled with social action.

Nisargadatta Maharaj (1897–1981) is a teacher of Advaita and considered to be an enlightened person. He did not write any book though all of his books were transcribed conversations by his followers. His book *I Am That* is considered to be his magnum opus. He had a significant influence on the Neo-Advaita movement. Jack Kornfield has been radically influenced by this teacher and spent some time with him in Mumbai. When a Buddhist magazine (Shaheen, 2016) asked Kornfield in an interview as to why he would rely on a Hindu teacher to explain the Buddhist conception of emptiness, he stated "I believe that dharma is universal . . . I use whatever expressions best help to awaken us." This position and attitude are also found in the works of Kabat-Zinn. Kornfield lists Nisargadatta as one of his teachers on his personal website.

Ramana Maharshi (1879–1950) taught Advaita Vedanta and is possibly the most prominent teacher inspiring the Neo-Advaita movement. He taught the method of self-inquiry which is to reflect on the question "Who am I?" He was a man of few words and promoted the inquiry into the self through silence, removal of ignorance, and abidance in awareness. Both Jack Kornfield and Joseph Goldstein quote the words of Ramana in their teachings. Kabat-Zinn (2011) states that Ramana's method of "Who am I?" is the core practice shared by Zen traditions as well.

Kabat-Zinn's deep influence of Advaita can be seen in a quote by Nisargadatta Maharaj from the book *I Am That* (Nisargadatta, 1973) that appears in Kabat-Zinn's paper:

> . . . by watching yourself in your daily life with alert interest with the intention to understand rather than to judge, in full acceptance of whatever may emerge, because it is here, you encourage the deep to come to the surface and enrich your life and consciousness with its captive energies. This is the great work of awareness; it removes obstacles and releases energies by understanding the nature of life and mind. Intelligence is the door to freedom and alert attention is the mother of intelligence.
>
> (Kabat-Zinn, 2011, p. 300)

In the first edition of the book *Full Catastrophe Living*, Kabat-Zinn acknowledges several other teachers of the yogic tradition such as Swami Chinmayananda, Ram Dass, and John Lauder. However, in the second edition of the same book, these teachers are not acknowledged.

Hatha Yoga

Hatha yoga is a sophisticated form of religious discipline developed in medieval India originally meant for ascetics. However, Hatha yoga became secularized and eventually became a postural system by the time it became popular in America after the middle of the last century. One significant feature of Hatha yoga is that it is body positive, a feature not found in Buddhism and Advaita Vedanta. Kabat-Zinn acknowledges John Lauder as his Hatha yoga teacher in the 1960s. In a 2021 podcast interview with Wendy Hasenkamp (Kabat-Zinn, 2021), Kabat-Zinn states that

> the body scan, which in part I adapted from what John Lauder was doing at the end of his yoga class, and of course from Goenka's sweeping meditation, U Ba Khin's whole tradition of very micro level scanning through the body, after doing three days of anapana, just breath awareness.

This shows that Kabat-Zinn could have inherited his body-positive attitude from his Hatha yoga teachings. On the contrary, in early Buddhist and Advaita Vedanta teachings, the human body is seen as something repulsive. We can infer that the body scan practice is an invented practice, though its antecedents can be found in Buddhist teachings in the last century (Anālayo, 2020).

A few consistent trends found in Kabat-Zinn's mindfulness can be traced to these four influences which are:

Table 9.2 Mapping of trends against Kabat-Zinn's influences

	Trends	Vipassana	Zen Buddhism	Advaita	Hatha yoga
1	Non-dual or choiceless awareness as a state of being		□	□	□
2	Pedagogy involving inquiry and dialogue	□	□	□	
3	Mindfulness practices being an unaided and objectless meditation	□	□	□	
4	Body-positive attitudes				□
5	Life as something positive instead of suffering			□	
6	This worldly, the present life	□	□	□	□

Zen and Advaita Vedanta share several of these features, in spite of them being different epistemologically and in their ontological appreciations of reality. Leesa Davis (Davis, 2010) records four of these common features as:

- Unfindability analysis – the principal target of unfindability analysis is the practitioner's objectified and reified notions of self in the form of the objectified, individualized "I" that is at the heart of the bifurcating self-and-other (subject/object) structures of personal identity.
- Bringing everything back to the here and now – the experiential effect of "cornering" the student in the absolute present moment in which there is no "room" for conceptual projections of the future or abstractions from the past to take hold and proliferate.
- Paradoxical problems – "develop" the undermining of practitioner adherence to dualisms by exploiting the rising sense of paradox and contradiction that the practitioner experiences when familiarly structured either/or patterns of thought are problematized by non-dual understandings.
- Negation – such negative pointers as non-grasping, no-mind, unborn, non-thinking, and not-knowing (among others) are emphasized in the foundational texts and frequently employed by teachers to refute students' dualistic attachments to reified concepts of self and path.

Kabat-Zinn appears to have noticed these features in his early years of training and made them part of his "universal dharma," though *these common features are not found in the Pre-Zen Buddhism and other non-Zen Buddhist traditions.*

In summary, the sources of secular mindfulness as conceptualized by Kabat-Zinn is plain and simple. Contrary to what has been claimed by many authors, four distinct traditions were fused and secularized to make mindfulness accessible to everyone, thus removing the barriers to it. *These four traditions being Vipassana, Zen Buddhism, Advaita Vedanta and Hatha Yoga.* As Stephen Morris (2022) observed, Kabat-Zinn has certainly combined multiple knowledge traditions that were ontologically and epistemologically distinct, in spite of them having similarities. Kabat-Zinn's innovation and insights deserve more credit than it has been given thus far.

Most mindfulness books do not specifically acknowledge the influence of the Advaita and Hatha Yoga (or sometimes Zen) on neither the MBSR nor secular mindfulness. We have also found books that forcefully connect the limited Buddhist influences of secular mindfulness to the tenets of Buddhism (or Buddhist Abhidharma). Not only that, we have also noticed a trend where Kabat-Zinn gradually loses the vocabulary of the yogic traditions in his speeches and works from the 1990s, though it is implicitly there.

Our findings confirm Sarah Shaw's (2020) observation in her book, *Mindfulness*, that Kabat-Zinn's interpretation of secular mindfulness could have been influenced by his contact with Advaita Vedanta, Zen traditions, and Burmese Vipassana teachers. However, it is interesting how subsequent books and research papers have mostly failed to study the two other influences, i.e. yogic traditions and Hatha yoga, that influenced the MBSR. In summary, Kabat-Zinn's mindfulness is

- not solely Buddhist
- an invention by him
- a combination of different and incompatible traditions
- secular and wellbeing focused given that the soteriological goals have been eliminated from it

4 THE LINEAGE OF KABAT-ZINN

Where did Kabat-Zinn inherit his unique appreciation and understanding of mindfulness which brings together different traditions that are epistemologically distinct? We believe that Kabat-Zinn inherited this from his own teachers. We made an attempt to construct his lineage (see Figure 9.1).

The connection to a lineage can be both formal and informal. The formal connection to a lineage comes from a formal training and direct contact with teachers of a tradition. The informal connection, on the other hand, comes from one's conscious and unconscious intellectual subscription to teachings of a teacher or a school of thought. This could be from reading books, watching videos, and meeting the teachers. We can include Philip Kapleau (1912–2004), Nisargadatta Maharaj, J. Krishnamurti, Ramana Maharshi, and Vimala Thakar

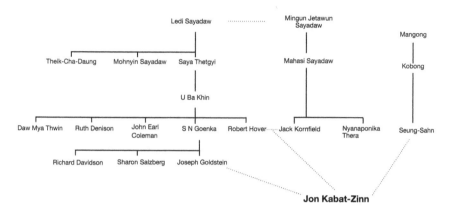

Figure 9.1 Jon Kabat-Zinn's lineage

in this category. Interestingly, Kabat-Zinn declares more of his informal than his formal connections to his lineage in his works.

Books often claim that Kabat-Zinn learned from the famous Vietnamese Buddhist monk, Thich Nhat Hanh (1926–2022). However, Kabat-Zinn (2011) states that he did not meet Thich Nhat Hanh before his book, *Full Catastrophe Living*, was published. Kabat-Zin's early training in meditation in 1973 was from Robert Hover (1920–2008), a student of U Ba Khin in the Vipassana tradition (Anālayo, 2020). Further, he learned meditation at the Insight Meditation Society (IMS) with Jack Kornfield and Joseph Goldstein in the 1970s (Wilson, 2014). Jack Kornfield was known to have incorporated many other spiritual traditions into his teachings such as non-dual Zen, Tibetan Buddhism, and Advaita Vedanta, which were inherited by Kabat-Zinn. Kabat-Zinn learned Zen from the Korean Zen teacher, Seung Sahn, in the early 1970s (Kabat-Zinn, 2011). We can consider these four teachers as Kabat-Zinn's earliest formal connection to the lineage.

5 THE MYTH OF BUDDHIST ORIGIN

> Repeat a lie often enough and it becomes the truth.
>
> (Anonymous)

As discussed above, Kabat-Zinn clearly states in his papers that his secular mindfulness has been radically influenced by non-Buddhist traditions as well as adapted Buddhist teachings (specifically Zen) in a secular way, given that he was (is) not a Buddhist nor a Buddhist scholar. In spite of this evidence, mindfulness literature continues to perpetuate a solely Buddhist origin to mindfulness or deliberately contract an explicit doctrinal connection. Robert Sharf

(2016), Chair of the Berkeley Center for Buddhist Studies, states that secular mindfulness is quite different from Buddhism, and that it is perhaps more Hindu and quite contrary to the goals of Buddhism. We can go on and on ad nauseum about how this partial account of mindfulness gets perpetuated by very reliable and expert mindfulness teachers and scholars. When something gets repeated again and again, it becomes history and truth. Such is the case with secular mindfulness in our opinion.

To us, this effort to reclaim secular mindfulness to Buddhism, and citing appropriation, is similar to how postural yoga in the Western world has been cited as an appropriation. Let us now briefly discuss how this myth of Buddhist origin could have been possibly perpetuated.

We need to acknowledge that Kabat-Zinn's works are bereft of the Buddhist beliefs of rebirth, karma, deities, devotional/magical practices, Buddha being a spiritual being, the non-negotiable authority of the Buddhist canon, and the importance of the community (sangha) (Husgafvel, 2018). In addition, the pessimism found in Buddhism is completely replaced by a positive perspective of life including the body being seen as something positive. Rupert Gethin (2015), Professor of Buddhist Studies of the University of Bristol, claims that the modern mindfulness conceptualizations of non-judgmental acceptance, open-monitoring, and focused attention are alien to Buddhist conceptualizations of mindfulness. A similar idea has also been proposed by Robert Sharf and Sarah Shaw, though the latter entertained the possibility of such modern conceptions with qualifications. Interestingly, these astute views are coming from scholars of religion rather than from mindfulness teachers.

On the other hand, Kabat-Zinn is seen at times to progressively deepen the Buddhist connection with mindfulness after the mid-1990s, as we see an increasing amount of literature accusing him of appropriating Buddhism. At this juncture, we know that Kabat-Zinn's mindfulness was not categorically Buddhist. Let us now briefly look at the history of Buddhism in America which may throw more light in our favor.

Buddhism entered America about 180 years ago through immigrant Asian Buddhists. However, when Buddhism met America, it was transformed into a different religion as its teachings got watered down. Jaime Kucinskas (2019) and Ann Gleig (2019) claim that this transformation took place through the minds and teachings of Americans who assumed that they were teaching a "purer" version of Buddhism steeped in cognitive depth without the superstitions, rituals, and cosmology subscribed to by the immigrant Asian Buddhists. These Americans were usually white Euro-American converts who tended to psychologize the teachings of Buddhism and taught meditation for therapeutic purposes. Wilson (2014) further argues that these Americans,

- reinterpreted Buddhist cosmology
- removed the monastic context
- removed the Buddhist context

- whitened Buddhism – making it relevant to a white population
- constructed a new lineage

This movement eventually became to be known as American Buddhism which is now about 180 years old. This movement was also influenced by the *modernist* Buddhist traditions of Thailand, Japan, and Tibet. American Buddhists, both lay people and the monastics, cherry picked elements that best depicted Buddhism to be modern, humanistic, and scientific. They downplayed ceremonial aspects, chanting, beliefs, and cosmology. For example, Andrew Weiss, an American Buddhist teacher, writes in his book, *Beginning Mindfulness: Learning the Way of Awareness,* that "the teachings of the Buddha, in the earliest and original form, are remarkably free of doctrine" (Weiss, 2004, p.xvi) which is obviously untrue. He further claims that Buddhism does not offer any beliefs to believe in, thus making the religion universal. This attitude was also found among the early orientalists such as the Rhys Davids and Paul Carus. We need to recognize that these attitudes were not recent but have been cultivated over 180 years starting with the early Buddhist teachers and interpreters. Sophia Rose Arjana in her book *Buying Buddha, Selling Rumi* (2020) claims that this same phenomenon has happened in the American soil to Hinduism and Islam when unique forms of Yoga and Sufism were developed. Arjana further states that this phenomenon is a deliberate process of searching into the mysticism within Buddhism, Hinduism, and Islam, and repackaging it as spirituality. Eventually, she states, it gets commodified in the American soil.

American Buddhism, while domesticizing Buddhism, also took the position that enlightenment was not exclusive to Buddhism but is universal, thereby taking the view that the dharma too is universal, a position Kabat-Zinn often shares to justify his secularization of mindfulness. This position has also been legitimized through the interpretations of the Buddhist canon by even monastic Buddhist teachers, according to Gleig.

It is within this movement of American Buddhism that Kabat-Zinn first learned meditation from the teachers at the IMS, namely Jack Kornfield and Joseph Goldstein. Kabat-Zinn's introduction to mindfulness comes from a background of watered down and transformed forms of Buddhism. As much as the IMS was formed to teach Theravada Buddhism, yet it was an American form heavily informed by *modernist* forms of Buddhism from Burma. The difference was that Kabat-Zinn took another step forward by secularizing it. However, as Fronsdal (1995), opines that Western teachers favor a secular approach to mindfulness because the Buddhism's "world-renouncing, literalist, dualistic, male-centered and at times misogynist tendencies" prevents people from accessing its important value:

> Today most Western lay teachers offer an alternative to such orthodoxy. Rather than stressing world renunciation, they stress engagement with, and freedom *within* the world. Rather than rejecting the body, these Western teachers embrace the body as part of the wholistic

field of practice. Rather than stressing ultimate spiritual goals such as full enlightenment, ending the cycles of rebirth, or attaining the various stages of sainthood, many Western teachers tend to stress the immediate benefits of mindfulness and untroubled, equanimous presence in the midst of life's vicissitudes. Rather than emphasizing spiritual and psychological purification, most western teachers focus on the transformation of one's relationship to one's emotions and to one's inner and outer world.

Many teachers confirm that Kabat-Zinn had extracted the religious elements of Buddhism and left it stripped of its soteriological goals. Robert M. Rosenbaum and Barry Magid (2016) and Wilson (2014) state that while Kabat-Zinn separated Buddhism from mindfulness, his teachers at IMS and earlier American Buddhist teachers retained the major elements of Buddhism.

We can therefore surmise (see Figure 9.2), that secular mindfulness becomes another offshoot of American Buddhism, in the same way that the latter was an offshoot of traditional Buddhism.

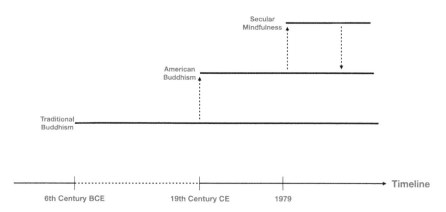

Figure 9.2 Timeline of mindfulness evolution

We see another trend emerging in the last two decades among American and traditional Buddhists who capitalize on the fame of secular mindfulness to zealously connect it back to Buddhism, a phenomenon confirmed by Kucinskas. Though we can see that mindfulness is not Buddhist nor religious, yet scholars, like Wilson, wage several unjustified charges against Kabat-Zinn and mindfulness advocates which includes:

• hiding overt references to Buddhism so that they can bring mindfulness to secular audiences to further their agenda
• making contradicting and confusing statements trying to squeeze themselves out of Buddhism

We believe that these charges arise from the *erroneous* assumption that mindfulness is exclusively Buddhist, an unchallenged assumption that has become accepted truth. This error has been exacerbated by the fact that Kabat-Zinn chose to introduce the term *mindfulness* to his SRRP when he changed its name to MBSR after 1992. Prior to 1992, we do not see any works laying claim to mindfulness. We wonder if these inaccurate representations and unjustified charges would be so if he had chosen to use the terms "meditation" or "awareness," instead of "mindfulness."

With this assumption, another phenomenon emerges within American Buddhism, which is the reclamation of mindfulness into the Buddhist fold. Wilson and Gleig describe this phenomenon as American Buddhism influencing mindfulness first and then later mindfulness influencing American Buddhism itself. We also see the trend of MBSR getting authenticated through a process of legitimization by Buddhist teachers and practitioners perhaps more zealously than even Kabat-Zinn. Kucinskas rightfully observes that Buddhists are now using this as a "placeholder for the whole dharma" because of its lack of specificity. In fact, the *term* "mindfulness" alone seems sufficient to lay claim over it. And in doing so *these authors strategically leave out the other significant influences cited by Kabat-Zinn when tracing the roots of mindfulness. This gets repeated again and again until the myth seemingly becomes a truth.* Rebecca Crane (2017) rightly states that this trend is problematic when bringing MBPs into institutions.

How does Kabat-Zinn respond to these accusations? He responds by suggesting that secular mindfulness "can be" Buddhist, though not solely. The second type of response he gives is that it is secular, by leaning on to his "universal dharma." To begin we need to acknowledge that Kabat-Zinn was trained in medicine and as a mindfulness practitioner. Unlike his teachers, he was neither a Buddhist, nor a Buddhist teacher, nor a Buddhist scholar. He was not interested in the scholarly aspects of mindfulness. He clearly states that his intention in creating MBSR was to heal people, and that too without the proselytizing zeal found commonly in religious teachers. To quote him, "These meditative practices are really meant to recognize and learn to inhabit that domain of being, *as opposed to fragment it into the sacred-secular divide*, the mind-body divide, or the self-other divide" (Baer, 2017). We see this tenor in all his works.

Kabat-Zinn acknowledges his influences clearly in his works without hiding them, although the emphasis could be varied. Sometimes he responds to the charges of appropriation by interpreting Buddhism and mindfulness through the lenses of universal dharma, a popular trend already found in American Buddhism. For example, in an interview in 2015, he claimed that mindfulness has the,

> potential to actually elevate humanity in profound ways that are just completely in accordance with the fundamental teachings of the

Buddha about the nature of suffering and the possibility of the sort of transformation and liberation from suffering . . .

(Shonin, 2015)

And by claiming so, he does not lose the secular stance he takes with his secular mindfulness. Responses like these show to the Buddhist sympathizers, that they could connect secular mindfulness to Buddhist tradition if they wanted to. In the same interview, he states that "I didn't make up the idea that there is such a thing as mindfulness meditation" and that he learned it from a Nyanaponika Thera's (1901–1994) (a Sri Lankan monk of German descent) book *Heart of Buddhist Meditation*. Interestingly, Thera also comes from the lineage of the *bare-attention* tradition of Mahasi Sayadaw, the Burmese monk. This tradition, a *modernist* tradition within Buddhism, teaches that one can attain enlightenment by just training attention. It is obvious that Kabat-Zinn is merely re-stating what has been already there in the American Buddhist meditation movement, which has been profoundly influenced by the Burmese modernist tradition.

The secular position that Kabat-Zinn takes emerges at times when he is not reverential to Buddhism nor the Buddha. He (2011) confesses that in the mid-1980s, he would claim that the Buddha himself was not a Buddhist and that the word Buddha literally meant "an awakened one." He further states that his motivation for MBSR was to show the universality of dharma that helped people live a life well-lived. For example, he considered the streams of self-inquiry asking the question "Who am I?" to be the same in the traditions of Chinese Chan, Korean Zen, Japanese Zen, and the Advaita Vedanta teacher, Ramana Maharshi. Implicitly, Kabat-Zinn was not interested in the technical definitions of what he termed as mindfulness, but was more intentional about how mindfulness helped people alleviate their suffering. He states,

It always felt that the details concerning the use of the word mindfulness in the various contexts in which we were deploying it *could be worked out later by scholars and researchers who were knowledgeable in this area*, and *interested in making such distinctions and resolving important issues* that may have been confounded and compounded by the early but intentional ignoring or glossing over of potentially important historical, philosophical, and cultural nuances . . . as well as a deeper understanding of the dharma itself . . .

As much as he found inspiration from the works of Buddhist monks, such as Nyanaponika Thera, and sought approval for his universal dharma from Thich Nhat Hanh, Dalai Lama, and Benhuan, he was not intending it to be defined so clearly. His conceptions of non-dual awareness and non-duality in mindfulness was linked to his eclectic training from his direct teachers. He further advocates assimilations of other traditions, when he (2011) claims that the early teachers of MBSR were also inspired by the Buddhism, Sufism, Taoism, yoga and Vedanta.

We can certainly conclude from the above discussion that Kabat-Zinn did not invent mindfulness, but *he had certainly invented secular mindfulness.* Further the "tributaries" of the ever expanding "river" of secular mindfulness happens to be non-Buddhist sources thus casting doubts if its teachings are the same as the Buddha and early Buddhism. This could explain why the river downstream looks very different from its sources in the highlands.

In conclusion, we would like to invoke a famous analogy of the chariot that 7th-century Buddhist scholar, Candrakirti, writes in his Madhyamakavatara. He uses the chariot analogy to justify emptiness of the self, by showing that the individual is composite and when broken down, the self ceases to be absolutely real. Comparing this with the chariot, he states the chariot is a *name* given to something which is composite and when the chariot is dismantled, it ceases to be. Similarly, secular mindfulness is like a chariot with its shaft as Soto Zen, the axle as Advaita Vedanta, the yoke as Hatha yoga, the wheels as Vipassana, the carriage as an empiricism, and the reins as Taoism, Sufism, etc. Every one of these traditions has informed and shaped it to be what it is. Assuming secular mindfulness to be Buddhist is as preposterous as believing the shaft to be the whole chariot.

REFERENCES

Anālayo, B. (2020). Buddhist antecedents to the body scan meditation. *Mindfulness, 11*(1), 194–202.

Arjana, S. R. (2020). *Buying Buddha, selling Rumi: Orientalism and the mystical marketplace.* Simon and Schuster.

Baer, D. (2017, June 4). *The father of mindfulness on what mindfulness has become.* Medium. Retrieved from https://medium.com/thrive-global/the-father-of-mindfulness-on-what-mindfulness-has-become-ad649c8340cf

Boyce, B. (2011). Introduction: Anyone can do it, and it changes everything. In B. Boyce (Ed.), *The mindfulness revolution: Leading psychologists, scientists, artists, and meditation teachers on the power of mindfulness in daily* life (pp. xi–xviii). Shambhala.

Buehler, A. F. (2016). *Recognizing Sufism: Contemplation in the Islamic tradition.* Bloomsbury.

Cooper, J. (2013). The pathless path of prayer: Is there a meditation method in Meister Eckhart? In H. Eifring (Ed.), *Meditation in Judaism, Christianity and Islam: Cultural historie* (pp. 123–135). Bloomsbury.

Crane, R. S. (2017). Implementing mindfulness in the mainstream: Making the path by walking it. *Mindfulness, 8*(3), 585–594.

Davis, L. S. (2010). *Advaita Vedanta and Zen Buddhism: Deconstructive modes of spiritual inquiry*. Continuum International Publishing Group.

Eifring, H. (Ed.). (2013). *Meditation in Judaism, Christianity and Islam*. In H. Eifring (Ed.), *Meditation in Judaism, Christianity and Islam: Cultural histories* (pp. 3–13). Bloomsbury.

Feldman, C., & Kuyken, W. (2019). *Mindfulness: Ancient wisdom meets modern psychology*. Guilford.

Frohlich, M. (2013). Teresa of Avila's evolving practices of "representing" Christ in prayer. In H. Eifring (Ed.), *Meditation in Judaism, Christianity and Islam: Cultural histories* (pp. 137–151). Bloomsbury.

Fronsdal, G. (1995). *The treasures of the Theravada: Recovering the riches of our tradition*. Insight Meditation Center. Retrieved from www.insightmeditationcenter.org/books-articles/the-treasures-of-the-theravada/

Gethin, R. (2015). Buddhist conceptualizations of mindfulness. In K. W. Brown, J. D. Creswell, & R. M. Ryan (Eds.), *Handbook of mindfulness: Theory, research, and practice*, 9–41.: Guilford.

Gleig, A. (2019). *American dharma: Buddhism beyond modernity*. Yale University Press.

Husgafvel, V. (2018). The "universal dharma foundation" of mindfulness-based stress reduction: non-duality and mahāyāna Buddhist influences in the work of Jon Kabat-Zinn. *Contemporary Buddhism, 19*(2), 275–326.

Hwang, Y. S., & Kearney, P. (2015). *A mindfulness intervention for children with autism spectrum disorders: New directions in research and practice*. Springer.

Ishvarananda, S. (1959). *God-realization through reason*. Sri Ramakrishna Ashrama.

Johnsén, H. R. (2013). *The early Jesus prayer and meditation in Greco-Roman philosophy*. In H. Eifring (Ed.), *Meditation in Judaism, Christianity and Islam: Cultural histories* (pp. 93–106). Bloomsbury.

Kabat-Zinn, J. (1982). An outpatient program in behavioral medicine for chronic pain patients based on the practice of mindfulness meditation: Theoretical considerations and preliminary results. *General Hospital Psychiatry, 4*(1), 33–47.

Kabat-Zinn, J. (1994). Catalyzing movement towards a more contemplative/sacred-appreciating/non-dualistic society. In *Meeting of the working group*. Retrieved from https://www.contemplativemind.org/admin/wp-content/uploads/kabat-zinn.pdf

Kabat-Zinn, J. (2003). Mindfulness-based stress reduction (MBSR). Constructivism in the Human Sciences, 8(2), 73–107.

Kabat-Zinn, J. (2011). Some reflections on the origins of MBSR, skillful means, and the trouble with maps. *Contemporary Buddhism, 12*(1), 281–306.

Kabat-Zinn, J. (2021). *Mind and life podcast transcript Jon Kabat-Zinn – the heart of mindfulness*. Retrieved from https://podcast.mindandlife.org/wp-con tent/uploads/2021/09/JZK_transcript.pdf

Kabat-Zinn, J., Lipworth, L., & Burney, R. (1985). The clinical use of mindfulness meditation for the self-regulation of chronic pain. *Journal of Behavioral Medicine, 8*(2), 163–190.

Kucinskas, J. (2019). *The mindful elite: Mobilizing from the inside out*. Oxford University Press, USA.

Lucas, P. C. (2014). Non-traditional modern Advaita gurus in the West and their traditional modern Advaita critics. *Nova Religio: The Journal of Alternative and Emergent Religions, 17*(3), 6–37.

Nisargadatta, M. (1973). *I am that: Talks with Nisargadatta Maharaj*. Chetana

McCown, D., Reibel, D., & Micozzi, M. S. (2011). *Teaching mindfulness: A practical guide for clinicians and educators*. Springer.

Morris, S. (2022). The rise of medicalised mindfulness during the 1970s and 1980s: The attempted convergence of religion and science. *Brief Encounters, 6*(1), 81–92.

Prabhavananda, S., & Smith, H. (1979). *The spiritual heritage of India: A clear summary of Indian philosophy and religion* (2nd ed.). Vedanta Press & Bookshop.

Rosenbaum, R. M., & Magid, B. (2016). Introduction: Universal mindfulness – be careful what you wish for?. In R. M. Rosenbaum & B. Magi (Eds.), *What's wrong with mindfulness (and what isn't): Zen perspectives* (pp 1–12). Wisdom Publications.

Seppala, S. (2013) Meditation in the East Syrian tradition. In H. Eifring (Ed.), *Meditation in Judaism, Christianity and Islam: Cultural histories* (pp. 107–121). Bloomsbury.

Shaheen, J. (2016, November 7). *The wise heart*. Tricycle. Retrieved from https://tricycle.org/magazine/wise-heart/

Shaker, F. S. (2015). *Al-Ghazali on vigilance and self-examination – kitab Al-Muraqaba Wa'l-Muhasaba*. Islamic Texts Society

Sharf, R. H. (2016). Is mindfulness Buddhist?(and why it matters). In R. M. Rosenbaum & B. Magid, *What's wrong with mindfulness (and what isn't): Zen perspectives* (pp. 139–152) Wisdom Publications.

Shaw, S. (2020). *Mindfulness: Where it comes from and what it means*. Shambhala Publications.

Shonin, E. (2015). This is not McMindfulness by any stretch of the imagination: Edo Shonin talks to Jon Kabat-Zinn. The Psychologist. Retrieved from https://thepsychologist.bps.org.uk/not-mcmindfulness-any-stretch-imagination

Varma, V. P. (1973). *Early Buddhism and its origins*. Munshiram Manoharlal.

Waite, D. (2012). *Advaita made easy* (reprint ed.). Mantra Books.

Weiss, A. (2004). *Beginning mindfulness: Learning the way of awareness: a ten-week course*. New World Library.

Wilson, J. (2014). *Mindful America: Meditation and the mutual transformation of Buddhism and American culture*. Oxford University Press.

Woods, S. L., & Rockman, P. (2021). *Mindfulness-based stress reduction: Protocol, practice, and teaching skills*. New Harbinger Publications.

Wynne, A. (2007). *The origin of Buddhist meditation*. Routledge.

APPENDICES

Intake Process

1 INTAKE FORM (SAMPLE)

The completed form will only be seen by the mindfulness teacher. All information you provide will be kept strictly confidential, and will only be used to help support you in achieving the full benefit from your efforts in the mindfulness program. Apart from the mandatory questions (indicated with an ★), if there are any questions in this form that you do not wish to answer, please feel free to leave them blank.

Part I

- Full name★
- Residential address★
- Year of birth
- Relationship status
- Gender identity
- Mobile/cell phone no.★
- Email address★
- Religion/faith
- Occupation
- Name of contact person and phone number in case of emergency★
- You will receive a "certificate" for attending at least 80% of the Mindfulness-Based Wellbeing Enhancement course. How would you like your name to appear on this certificate?★
- How did you come to know about the mindfulness course?

Part II

- What are your primary motivations and expectations for joining this course?
- Do you have any prior experience in meditation or mindfulness? Please share your experience.
- Do you currently have a meditation practice? If so, share some details with us.
- If you subscribe to a particular faith tradition, please state if you perceive any possible conflict between your faith tradition and the practice of secular mindfulness meditation.
- If you live with someone else, will they be supportive of your efforts to complete the eight-week program?
- Are there any events that might affect your participation in this course? (e.g. recent relationship breakup, retrenchment etc.)
- On a scale of 1 to 10, how certain do you feel that you will be able commit to approximately 30 to 45 minutes of practice a day, while you are undertaking the program. Please indicate, "1" being the least certain, "10" being absolutely certain. Indicate what you feel will be your biggest hindrance.

Part III

- Are there any health concerns/conditions that we should know about or you would like to tell us about? Please describe.★
- Are you currently undergoing therapy for mental health support?★
- Are you currently under any medical treatment? If yes, please explain, including any relevant medications.★
- Please list any allergies (including food allergies).★
- Please list any mobility issues.★
- What kind of exercise do you undertake each week and how often?
- Do you use any non-prescription drugs? If yes, please state the types of non-prescription drugs.★
- How is your sleep quality and pattern like? Please describe.★
- Is there anything else that you would like us to know about you that could help us in making this journey more fruitful for you?★

If you have experienced or are currently suffering from any mental illness (chronic depression, severe anxiety, etc.), please note that this course may not be suitable for you at this time.

2 INFORMED CONSENT FORM (SAMPLE)

In applying to register for the Mindfulness-Based Wellbeing Enhancement (MBWE) course, I hereby absolve and indemnify [your name] and all its servants, agents, employees from all liability arising from injury or damage in connection with my participation in programs provided by or in connection with [your name].

The MBWE course includes skills training in relaxation and basic meditation methods as well as gentle stretching exercises. I understand that if for any reason I am unable to, or think it unwise to, engage in these techniques or exercises either during the weekly classes or at home, I am under no obligation to engage in these techniques nor will I hold [your name] liable for any injury incurred.

Furthermore, I understand the MBWE course requires attendance at each of the eight weekly sessions, the half-day session, and 30–45 minutes' practice of home assignments each day during the duration of the course. In the event that I need to miss a class I will advise [your name] in advance so that either a brief make-up phone session or email summary of class content can be arranged, if necessary.

I am aware that I am free to refuse to answer any question or to discuss any matters that cause me any discomfort or feel my privacy invaded.

I also give consent to [your name] to contact me via email or by phone during the course and to include me in group messaging services (e.g. WhatsApp) for the duration of the eight-week program.

Refund Policy

[Add your refund policy in here, if you prefer]

Scripts for Moving into Specific Postures

1 MOVING INTO THE SUPINE POSTURE

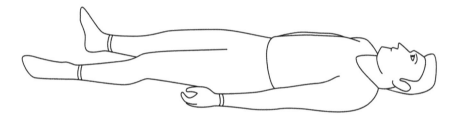

Figure A2.1 Supine posture

Sit on the mat with your knees bent, feet on the floor. And then use one hand to support your body as you lean on the forearm of the other arm. And then gently roll your back such that you are lying on your back with the front of your body facing upwards.

Close your eyes, and let your arms lie alongside your body with your palms facing upwards, and your feet falling away from each other. Allow your body to slowly sink into the mat and being relaxed.

[Strike chime/bell to signify the beginning of the mindfulness practice]

[After the end of the mindfulness practice]

Bring your awareness back to your body again, feeling the whole of it. You may want to wiggle your toes and fingers. Gently open your eyes. Roll your body either to the left or the right. Use the support of your hands and legs to support your body and slowly come to a seated position.

[Strike chime/bell to signify the end of the mindfulness practice]

2 MOVING INTO A SITTING POSTURE

Figure A2.2 Sitting posture

You are now invited to adopt an upright and comfortable seated posture on a cushion or a mat, that supports your intention to be awake. Keep your spine straight and shoulders relaxed. Rest your hands comfortably on your thighs with the fingers interlocked and at ease. Now close your eyes or adopt a soft gaze looking down on the floor a few feet in front of you.

> *[Strike chime/bell to signify the beginning of the mindfulness practice]*

> *[After the end of the mindfulness practice]*

Bring your awareness back to your body again, feeling the whole of it. Becoming aware of your posture, feel the weight of your body as you are seated here. And gently open your eyes at the sound of the chime.

> *[Strike chime/bell to signify the end of the mindfulness practice]*

Notes

Additional support (if required):

- **Back support:** if there are participants with spinal injuries or back challenges, they may consider sitting with their back against the wall, and using a rolled yoga mat, towel or cushion to support their lower back by placing it between their lower back and the wall.

- **Leg support:** if sitting crossed legged is challenging, the participant may consider sitting against a wall with their legs stretched out. To support their legs, it is recommended that they use a rolled yoga mat or towel or cushion placed beneath the knee.
- **Challenges sitting on the floor:**
  o Sitting on the floor might be challenging for some and they are encouraged to sit on a stable and firm chair without any castors. When seated, they could move their back slightly away from the backrest of the chair and place their palms gently on their thighs. Their feet should be placed firmly on the floor.
  o If the participants face difficulties or discomfort in placing the feet flat on the floor, they could use a rolled yoga mat or yoga block to place beneath their feet to support them.
  o If their back experiences discomfort while sitting on a chair, they may consider supporting their back with a rolled yoga mat, towel, or cushion placed between their lower back and the backrest of the chair.

3 MOVING INTO A STANDING POSTURE

Figure A2.3 Standing posture

Move into to a standing position with your back upright, feet parallel to each other, hips width apart, with your knees slightly flexed, allowing your arms to hang by your sides, and your shoulders relaxed. Direct your gaze softly straight ahead.

[Strike chime/bell to signify the beginning of the mindfulness practice and after the end of the mindfulness practice]

Standing here, feel the whole body in rest and in stillness.

Gently shift your attention to your breathing. Notice the inbreath and outbreath as the breath enters the body and as it moves out of the body. And when you feel ready, at the sound of the chime, gently open your eyes.

[Strike chime/bell to signify the beginning of the mindfulness practice]

Scripts for Formal Mindfulness Practices

Body Scan

Suggested length of practice: 30 mins

Sitting on the mat with your knees bent, feet on the floor. And then using one hand to support your body as you lean on the forearm of the other arm. And then gently rolling your back so that you are lying on your back with the front of your body facing upwards.

Closing your eyes, and letting your arms lie alongside your body with your palms facing upwards, and your feet falling away from each other. Allowing your body to slowly sink into the mat and be relaxed.

We shall now begin the practice with the sound of the chime.

[Strike chime/bell]

Gently bringing your attention to your breathing. Do not try to control your breath in any way but simply observing your inbreath and outbreath. Noticing the sensations as your belly expands with the inbreath. Then noticing the belly deflate with the outbreath.

And following the rhythmic movement of each breath . . . the expansion of the belly on the inbreath and on each outbreath just letting go, letting your body become heavy as it sinks a little bit deeper into relaxation. Just bringing full attention to each breath at each moment.

Now bring your attention to the right leg, and then to your right foot, becoming aware of whatever sensations are here.

Becoming aware of the shin and calf muscle and the sensations in the lower leg, not just on the surface but right down into the bones, experiencing and accepting what you feel here.

Then letting go of your lower leg as you relax into the mat. And now moving into the thigh and if there's any tension . . . just noticing it.

Then letting go of your thighs . . . bring attention to your left leg, and then to the left foot, becoming aware of whatever sensations are here.

Become aware of the shin and calf muscle and the sensations in the lower leg, not just on the surface but right down into the bones, experiencing and accepting what you feel here.

Then letting go of your lower leg as you relax into the mat. And moving now into the thigh and if there's any tension just noticing it.

Shifting your attention to the pelvis now, from one hip to the other.

Noticing the buttocks in contact with the mat and the sensations of contact and weight. Becoming aware of the genital region . . . whatever sensations or lack of sensations you are experiencing.

Totally present in each moment. Content to just be, and to just be right here as you are right now.

Direct your attention now to the lower back. And just experiencing your back as it is.

And then letting go of your lower back. And moving up into your upper back now. Just feeling the sensations in your upper back. You may even feel the ribcage, in the back as well as in the front expanding on the inbreath. Becoming aware of any tightness, fatigue, or discomfort in this part of your body.

And now turning your attention to your belly again and experiencing the rising and falling of the belly as you breathe. Feeling the movements of your diaphragm, that umbrella-like muscle that separates your belly from your chest.

And experiencing the chest as it expands on the inbreath and deflates on the outbreath. And if that works for you, tune into the rhythmic beating of your heart within your chest. Feeling it if you can.

As well as the lungs expanding on either side of your heart, just experiencing your chest, and your belly, as you lie here . . . the muscles on the chest wall, the breasts, the entirety of the front of your body.

Moving your attention now to your fingertips on the right hand and just becoming aware of the sensations now in the tips of your fingers and thumb where you may feel some pulsations from the blood flow, a dampness or a warmth or whatever you may be feeling. Just feeling them and letting them be.

And expand your awareness to include the palm of your hand and the back of the hand and the wrist. And here again perhaps picking up the pulsations of the arteries in your wrist as the blood flows to and from your hand. And becoming aware as well of the forearm. And the elbow. Any and all sensations regardless of what they are.

Now gently include the upper arm. Right up to your right shoulder. Just experiencing the whole arm.

Letting go of the right arm, directing your attention now to the fingertips on the left hand and just becoming aware of the sensations now in the tips of your fingers and thumb where you may feel some pulsations from the blood flow, a dampness or a warmth or whatever you feel. Just feeling them and letting it be.

And expand your awareness to include the palm of your hand and the back of your hand and the wrist. And here again perhaps picking up the pulsations of the arteries in the wrist as the blood flows to and from your hand. And becoming aware . . . as well of the forearm and the elbow. Noticing any and all sensations regardless of what they are.

Now gently include the upper arm, right up to your left shoulder. Just experiencing the whole arm.

Being present in each moment. Letting go of whatever thoughts that come up or whatever impulses to move and just experiencing yourself in this moment. Now focus your attention on the neck and throat and feel this part of your body, experiencing what it feels like perhaps when you swallow and with each inbreath and outbreath.

And then letting it go, becoming aware of your face now. Focusing on the jaw and the chin, just experiencing them as they are.

Bring your awareness to your lips and your mouth. And becoming aware of your cheeks now . . . and your nose, feeling the breath as it moves in and out at the nostrils.

And being aware of your eyes and the entire region around your eyes and eyelids. And just noticing if there's any tension.

And now the forehead. And the temples. And if you sense any emotion associated with the tension or feelings in your face, just acknowledging that emotion and be aware of that.

And now become aware of your ears . . . and the top of your head. For now, just letting it be as it is.

As this practice ends, bringing your awareness back to your body again, feeling the whole of it. You may want to wiggle your toes and fingers. Gently opening your eyes. Rolling your body either to the left or right. Using the support of your hands and legs to support your body and slowly coming to a seated position with legs crossed and spine upright and shoulders relaxed. Resting your hands comfortably on the thighs or the fingers interlocked and at ease.

[Strike chime/bell]

Sitting Meditation

SUGGESTED LENGTH OF PRACTICE: 30 MINS

We invite you now to adopt an upright and comfortable seated posture on a cushion or a mat, that supports your intention to be awake. Keeping your spine straight and shoulders relaxed. Resting your hands comfortably on the thighs with the fingers interlocked and at ease. Now closing the eyes or adopting a soft gaze looking down on the floor a few feet in front of you.

We shall now begin the practice with the sound of the chime.

[Strike chime/bell]

As you feel comfortable in your seat, bring your attention to your breathing. Being aware of the movement of your breath with each inbreath and outbreath. Not manipulating the breath in any way or trying to change it. Simply being aware.

And observing the breath deep down in your belly. Feeling the abdomen as it expands gently on the inbreath, and as it falls back toward your spine on the outbreath. Being totally here with each breath. Not trying to do anything or change anything but simply being with your breath.

You will find that from time to time that your mind will wander off into thoughts, about the future or the past, worrying, memories, whatever. When you notice that your attention is no longer here and no longer with your breathing, and without judging yourself, bring your attention back to the breathing.

Every time you find your mind wandering from the breath, gently bring it back to the present, back to the moment-to-moment observing of the flow of your breathing. Using your breath to help you tune into a state of relaxed awareness and stillness.

Now as you observe your breathing, you may find from time to time that you are becoming aware of sensations in your body. Just noticing them with curiosity.

As you maintain awareness of your breathing, expand the awareness so that it includes your whole body as a whole as you sit here. Feeling the body, from head to toe, and becoming aware of all the sensations in your body.

Being here with whatever feelings and sensations that come up in any moment without judging them, without reacting to them, just being fully here, fully aware of whatever you're experiencing. And again whenever you notice that your mind has wandered off, just bring it back to the breathing and the body as you sit here not going anywhere, not doing anything, just simply being, being whole, fully with yourself.

Now as you sit here, expanding your awareness to include thoughts as they move through the mind. Letting your breathing and sense of your body be in the background and allowing the thinking process itself to be the focus of your awareness. Rather than following individual thoughts and getting involved in the content and going from one thought to the next, simply seeing each thought as it comes up in your mind as a thought and letting the thoughts just come and go as you sit and dwell in stillness, witnessing them and observing them. Whatever they are . . . just observing them as events in the field of your awareness . . . as they linger and as they dissolve.

If you find yourself at any point getting involved in the content of your thoughts and you notice that you are no longer observing them, just return to observing them as events and use your breathing and the sense of your body to anchor you and stabilize you in the present.

Thoughts can take any form. They can have any content and they can be either neutral or very emotionally charged. This is the nature of thoughts and accepting them as they are. Regardless of the feeling that a thought might create for you, just observing it as simply a thought and letting it be here without pursuing it or without rejecting it. Noticing them from moment to moment, even when new thoughts come and go.

Bringing your awareness back to your body again, feeling the whole of it. Becoming aware of your posture. Feeling the weight of your body as you are seated here.

And gently opening your eyes at the sound of the chime.

[Strike chime/bell]

Mindful Movement

[This is a sample script for three postures.]

Coming to a standing position with your back upright, feet parallel to each other, hips width apart, with your knees slightly flexed, allowing your arms to hang by your sides, and shoulders relaxed. And directing your gaze softly straight ahead.

[Strike chime/bell]

The focus of this practice is to bring awareness to sensations in the body arising through movement and in different postures, letting go of thoughts about the sensations. We are not concerned about getting the poses right or getting into a perfect posture. Instead, we move our limbs with compassion and awareness of our limits.

Posture #1

As you are standing here, notice the sensations in both the feet.
Feeling the weight of the body on the feet.
Noticing how the body feels in stillness.

Posture #2

Bring the thumbs of both your hands together, and interlock them. With both arms outstretched, slowly raise them up, in front of you, all the way up, till both your hands are above your head. Noticing any, and all, sensations in the arms, as you gently bring them upwards.

Holding this position for a moment.

Releasing your thumbs from each other, gently lower your right hand, all the way to your side. And as you do so, become aware of the sensations in your right arm.

Now, gently lower the left hand, all the way to your side. And as you do so, becoming aware of the sensations in your left arm.

Just holding this position for a moment.

Posture #3

With both your arms outstretched by your sides, gently raise them up, to the shoulder level. Flexing only your wrists, lift up both your hands, such that your fingers point upwards.

Just holding this position for a moment. Becoming aware of any, and all, sensations in the arms, the wrists, and the hands.

Relaxing the right wrist, and then the right hand, lower the right arm to the side. Notice what is happening right there or perhaps nothing at all.

Now, relax the left wrist, and then the left hand. Lower the left arm to the side. Notice the sensations or nothing at all.

Just holding this position for a moment . . .

> *[Mindful movement practice continues until the planned posture sequence is complete]*

As this practice ends, bring your awareness back to your body again, feeling the whole body in rest and in stillness.

> *[Strike chime/bell]*

Complete List of Mindful Movement Postures

The recommended postures for mindful movement practice are listed below. There are two sets of sequences. You could use one set for any single practice session.

Set 1 – Sequence of Postures

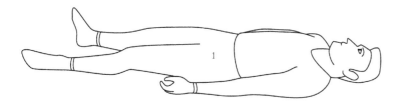

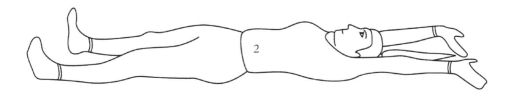

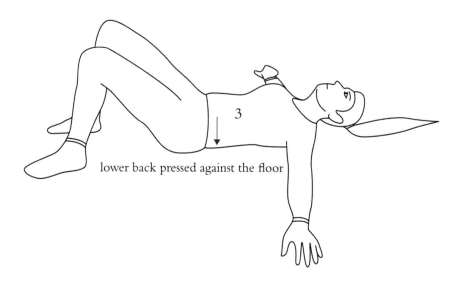

lower back pressed against the floor

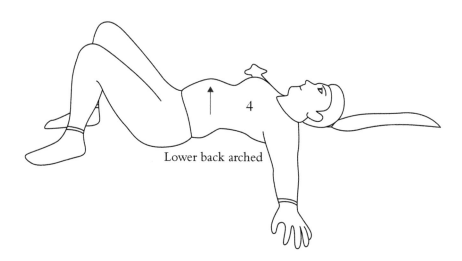

Lower back arched

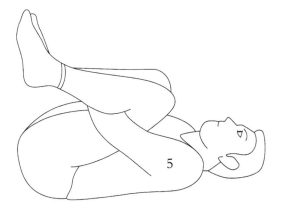

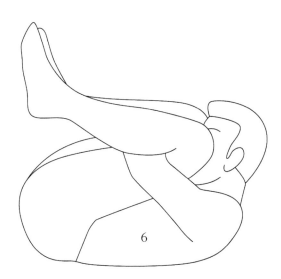

both sides

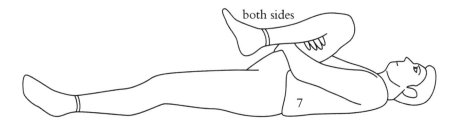

both sides

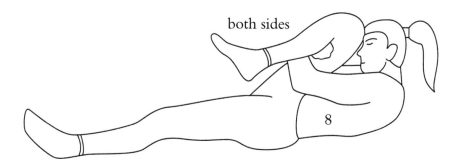

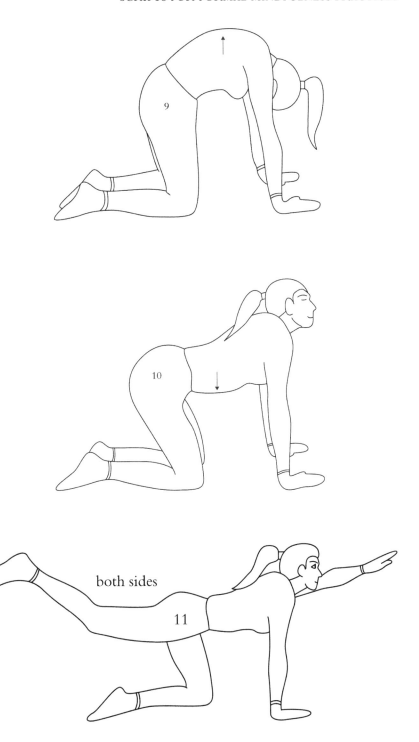

both sides

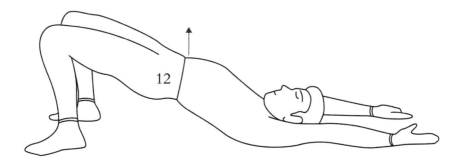

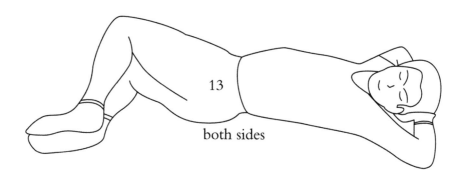

both sides

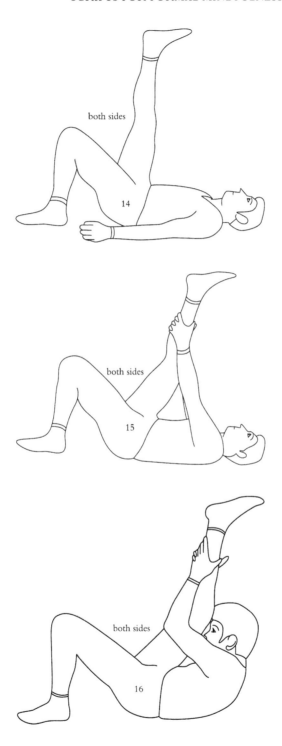

both sides

14

both sides

15

both sides

16

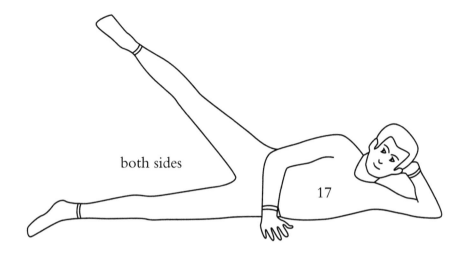

both sides

17

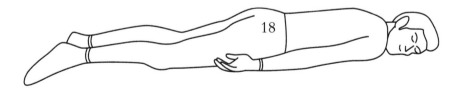

18

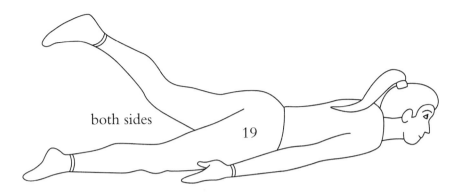

both sides

19

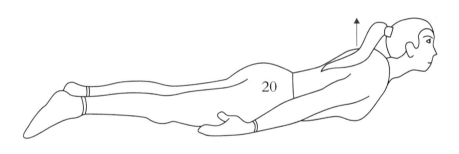

20

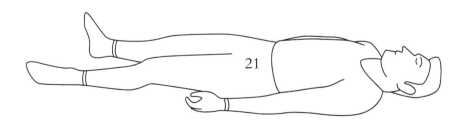

21

Set 2 – Sequence of Postures

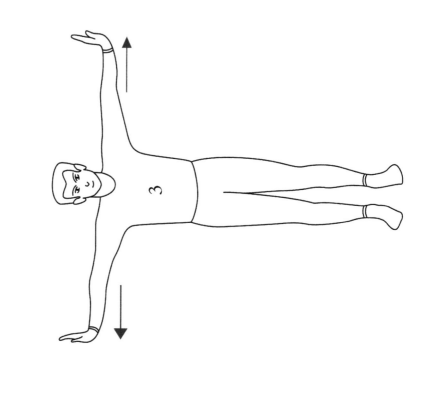

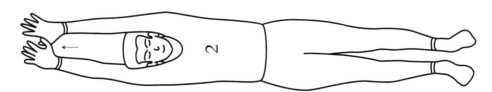

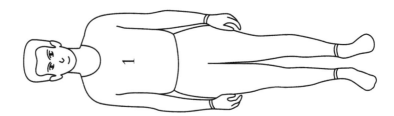

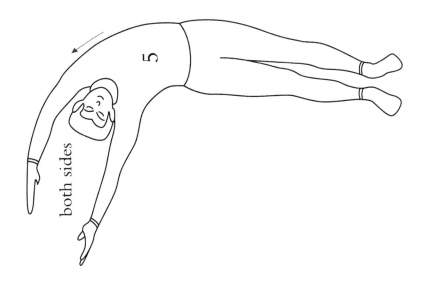

both sides

5

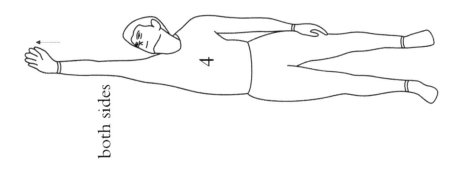

both sides

4

SHOULDER ROLLS

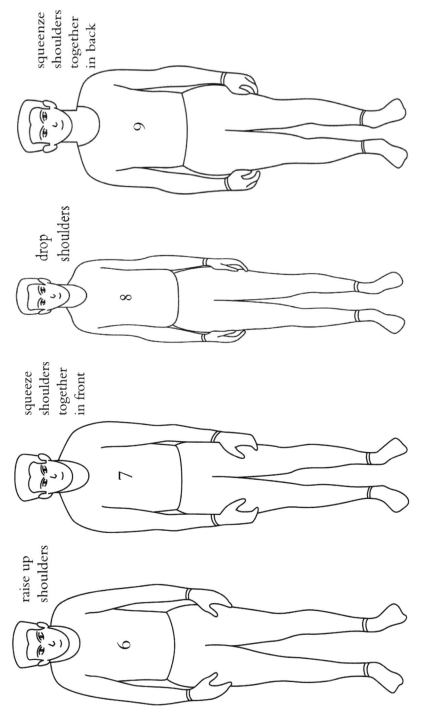

squeenze shoulders together in back

9

drop shoulders

8

squeeze shoulders together in front

7

raise up shoulders

6

NECK ROLLS

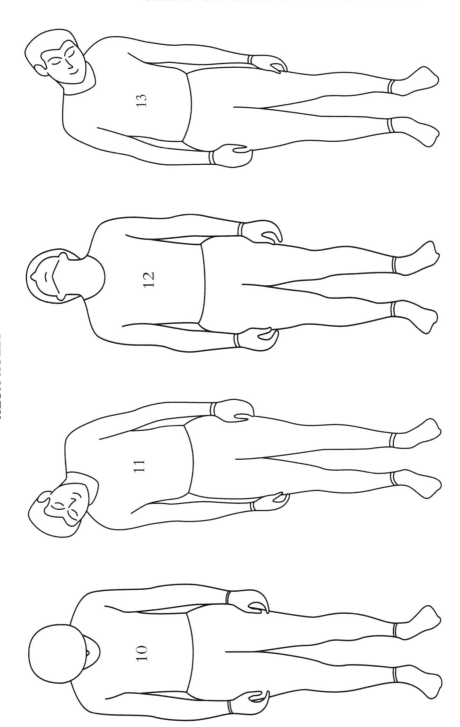

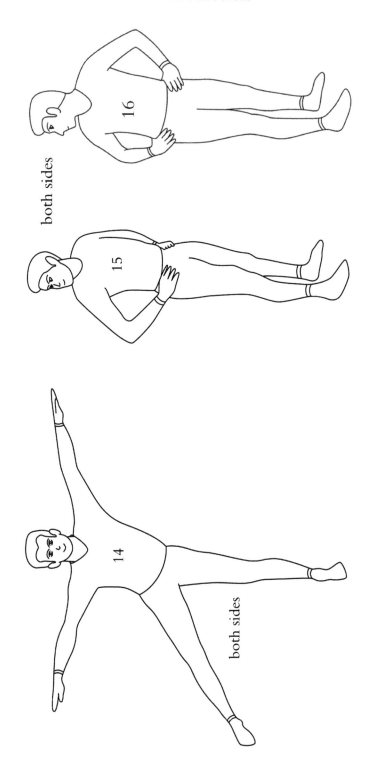

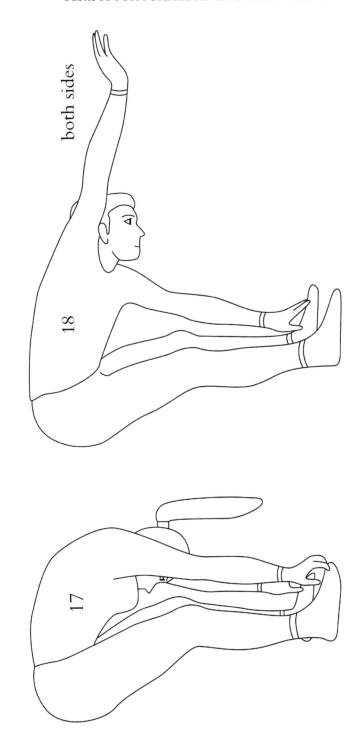

both sides

18

17

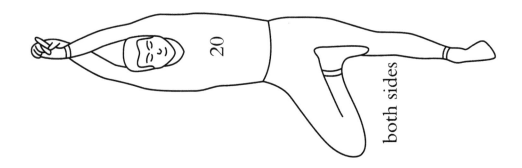

both sides

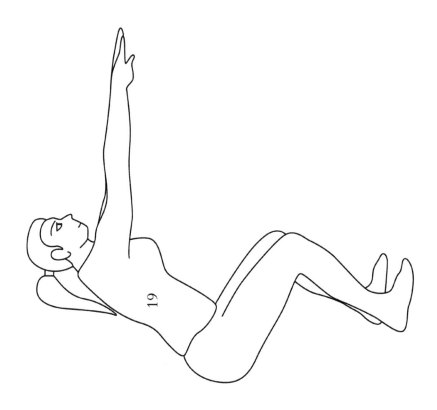

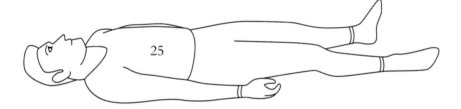

Scripts for Informal Mindfulness Practices

Centering

SUGGESTED LENGTH OF PRACTICE: 5 MINUTES

Coming into a standing position with your back upright, feet parallel to each other, hips width apart, with your knees slightly flexed, allowing your arms to hang by your sides, and shoulders relaxed. And directing your gaze softly straight ahead.

[Strike the chime/bell]

The purpose of this practice is to help you to know where you are in time and space. It grounds you in the present moment so that you are poised to begin anything.

As you are standing, bring your awareness to the weight of your body equally distributed on your feet. Noticing your body weight and your posture as you stand here.

Stabilize yourself and consider closing your eyes if that works for you.

Now, from the center, slowly shifting your body weight towards your toes. Staying in this position for a while and noticing the weight of your body on your toes. Noticing the changes in the body. Noticing the bodily reactions, the emotions, and thoughts as you stay in this position.

And now, slowly returning to the center and staying here in stillness.

And then slowly shifting your body weight towards your heels. Staying here and noticing the weight of the body on your heels. Noticing the changes in the body. Noticing the bodily reactions, the emotions and thoughts as you stay here.

And now, slowly returning to the center and staying here in stillness.

And then slowly shifting your body weight onto your right foot. Staying here and noticing the weight of your body on the right foot. Noticing the changes in the body and the feet.

And now, slowly returning to the center and staying here in stillness.

And then slowly shifting your body weight towards your left foot. Holding this posture and noticing the weight of your body on the left foot. Noticing the changes in the body and the feet.

And now, slowly returning to the center and staying here in stillness. Noticing all the changes in the body. Noticing your breathing as you naturally inhale and exhale without the need to change anything.

With the sound of the chime, gently open your eyes.

[Strike the chime/bell]

Mindful Perception

SUGGESTED LENGTH OF PRACTICE: 10 MINUTES

We now invite you to adopt an upright and comfortable seated posture on a cushion or a mat, that supports your intention to be awake. Keeping your spine straight and shoulders relaxed. Resting your hands comfortably on the thighs or with the fingers interlocked and at ease. Now closing the eyes or adopting a soft gaze looking down on the floor a few feet in front of you.

We shall now begin the practice with the sound of the chime.

[Strike the chime/bell]

Directing your attention to the eyes. Bringing awareness to seeing. Perhaps, noticing the darkness behind your eyelids.

Focusing, now, on the ears. Listening to the sounds around you. What are some sounds that are close to you? How about those that are further away? Noticing the different sounds around you. Now focusing your attention on only one sound. And now letting go of that sound, listen to another one.

Now, turning your attention to your mouth, bringing awareness to taste. What can you taste in your mouth right now or perhaps the lack of it? Or maybe an aftertaste. Is your mouth wet or dry?

Now, focusing on your nostrils. Bringing awareness to the sense of smell. What can you smell right now? Is there more than one scent around you? Noticing the smell of the air with every inbreath, or perhaps no smell at all.

Now, turning your attention to your skin. Bringing awareness to the sense of touch. How do the clothes feel on your body? What is the temperature in the space that you are in? Perhaps you can feel the wind or heat or coolness where you are seated.

[Optional segment begins]

Now opening your eyes and seeing what you have in front of you. Be curious about what your eyes are landing on. Noticing all the details. What are the colors and intensity of the colors in your surroundings? What shapes and sizes are they? What objects are closer to you and what are further away? What do you notice that you had never noticed before?

When you are ready, closing your eyes and focusing on your breath, noticing every inbreath and outbreath.

[Optional segment ends]

Bringing your awareness back to the body, feeling its wholeness. Becoming aware of your posture. Feeling the weight of your body as you are seated here.

And gently opening your eyes at the sound of the chime.

[Strike the chime/bell]

Raisin Practice

SUGGESTED LENGTH OF PRACTICE: 15 MINUTES

[There are eight stages in the raisin practice]

1. **Holding**: hold it in the palm of your hand or between your index finger and your thumb.
2. **Seeing**: take the time to notice it; gaze at the raisin with full attention as if you are seeing it for the first time: the darker hollows, the folds, and ridges . . . being curious . . .
3. **Touching**: feel the raisin by rolling it between your fingers, exploring its texture.
4. **Smelling:** hold the raisin beneath your nose. With each inbreath, take in any smell. Does it smell like anything else you know? Are there any emotions that come up with the smell?
5. **Hearing:** bring it to your ears. Notice the sound . . . Are you hearing anything?
6. **Placing**: place the raisin on your tongue, noticing how it gets into your mouth. Leting it be on your tongue, noticing its contact with the surface

of the tongue and its weight. Perhaps noticing the urge to take a bite. Now, tossing the raisin to one side of your mouth, and noticing how its contact with the inside of the cheek feels. Noticing the urges that may rise.

7. **Tasting:** take just one bite into it and notice what happens. Noticing the juice, sensations. And then the next bite, noticing the sensations and taste. And then continue chewing it without swallowing it.

8. **Swallowing**: now swallow it while noticing the sensations of this experience.

Awareness of Breath Meditation

SUGGESTED LENGTH OF PRACTICE: 20 MINUTES

We now invite you to adopt an upright and comfortable seated posture on a cushion or a mat, that supports your intention to be awake. Keeping your spine straight and shoulders relaxed. Resting your hands comfortably on the thighs or with the fingers interlocked and at ease. Now closing the eyes or adopting a soft gaze looking down on the floor a few feet in front of you.

   [Strike the chime/bell]

Being aware of the movement of your breath with each inbreath and out-breath. Not manipulating the breath in any way or trying to change it. Simply being aware, by observing the nostrils or the rise of the chest or the belly.

Observing the breath deep down in your belly. Feeling the belly expand gently on the inbreath, and as it falls back toward your spine on the out-breath. Be totally here with each breath. Not trying to do anything or change anything but simply be with your breath.

Bringing curiosity to the practice. Is the breath fast or slow? Is it deep or shallow?

From time to time the mind will wander off into thoughts, about the future or the past, worrying, memories, whatever. When you notice that your attention is no longer here and no longer with your breathing, and without judging yourself, bring your attention back to the breathing.

Whenever you notice that your attention has drifted off and is becoming caught up in thoughts or feelings, simply acknowledge that the attention has drifted, and then gently bring it back to the breathing.

It is acceptable and natural for thoughts to enter into your awareness, and for your attention to follow them. No matter how many times this happens, just keep bringing your attention back to the breathing with compassion and kindness.

Bring your awareness back to the body again, feeling its wholeness. Becoming aware of your posture. Feeling the weight of your body as you are seated here.

And gently opening your eyes at the sound of the chime.

[Strike the chime/bell]

Coping Breathing Space

LENGTH OF PRACTICE: 3 MINUTES

Coming into a standing position with your back upright, feet parallel to each other, hips width apart, with your knees slightly flexed, allowing your arms to hang by your sides, and shoulders relaxed. And directing your gaze softly straight ahead.

Awareness of Body – 1 min

Becoming aware of your body and the surface upon which you are standing (or sitting). Noticing your posture. Mentally scanning your body and noticing all of the sensations from the toes to the head.

Breathing Awareness – 1 min

Then, gently redirecting full attention to breathing, to each inbreath and to each outbreath as they follow, one after the other. Your breath can function as an anchor to bring you into the present and help you tune into a state of awareness and stillness.

Expanding Awareness – 1 min

Expanding the field of your awareness around your breathing, including the sense of the body as a whole.

Lovingkindness Meditation

We now invite you to adopt an upright and comfortable seated posture on a cushion or a mat, that supports your intention to be awake. Keeping your spine straight and shoulders relaxed. Resting your hands comfortably on the thighs or with the fingers interlocked and at ease. Now closing your eyes or adopting a soft gaze looking down on the floor a few feet in front of you.

> *[Strike the chime/bell]*

Becoming aware of the movement of your breath, each inbreath and each outbreath.

And now bringing to mind someone for whom you have deep feelings of love. Seeing or sensing this person and noticing the feelings for them arising in your body. It may simply be a smile that spreads across your face, or your chest becomes warm. Whatever the effects, allow them to be felt. And offer loving-kindness to this person, by letting these words become your words mentally . . .

> May you be well
> May you be happy
> May you be healthy
> May you be free from distress

Now letting go of this person in your mind, and seeing if you can offer loving-kindness to yourself, by letting these words become your words mentally . . .

> May I be well
> May I be happy
> May I be healthy
> May I be free from distress

And noticing the feelings that arise and letting them be.

Now offering lovingkindness to someone who supports you, who has always "been on your side." Bringing this person to mind, imagining them perhaps across from you, and letting these words become your words mentally . . .

> May you be well
> May you be happy
> May you be healthy
> May you be free from distress

(Optional) Once your feelings flow easily to a loved one, turn your attention now to someone with whom you have difficulty – it is best not to start with the most difficult person, but perhaps someone who provokes feelings of irritation or annoyance. And seeing if you can let these words become your words mentally as you keep this person in awareness . . .

> May you be well
> May you be happy
> May you be healthy
> May you be free from distress

Noticing the sensations and feelings that arise within you. And seeing if you can just allow them and let them be.

And now bringing to mind the broader community of which you are a part of. You may imagine your family, your workmates, your neighbors, or fan out your attention until you include all persons and creatures on the planet. And including yourself in this offering of lovingkindness, as you let these words become your words mentally . . .

> May all be well
> May all be happy
> May all be healthy
> May all be free from distress

And now turning your attention to the breathing. Noticing each inbreath and each outbreath.

Bringing your awareness back to your body again, feeling the wholeness of it. Becoming aware of the posture. Feeling the weight of your body as you are seated here.

And gently opening your eyes at the sound of the chime.

[Strike the chime/bell]

Mindful Walking
(Walking Meditation)

SUGGESTED LENGTH OF PRACTICE: 10 MINUTES

Coming into a standing position with your back upright, feet parallel to each other, hips width apart, with your knees slightly flexed, allowing your arms to hang by your sides, and shoulders relaxed. And directing your gaze softly straight ahead.

[Strike the chime/bell]

When you are ready, bringing your focus to the bottom of your feet. Being aware of the direct sensations in the feet in contact with the ground, and the sensation of your muscles supporting and stabilizing your body all the way to your feet on the ground. In this stillness, remain relaxed and alert.

As you begin walking, starting at a slower pace than usual, paying particular attention to the sensations in your feet and legs – the heaviness, lightness, pressure, tingling, energy, even pain if it's present. Noticing this play of sensations.

Be mindful of the sensations of lifting your feet and of placing them back down on the floor or earth. Sensing each step fully as you walk in a relaxed and natural way to the end of your chosen path. When you arrive, stop and pause for a moment. Feeling your whole body standing, allowing all your senses to be awake, then slowly and mindfully – with intention – turn to face in the other direction. Before you begin walking, pause again to collect and center yourself. If it helps, you can even close your eyes during these standing pauses.

Continuing to walk slowly in this way walking from one end of the walking lane to the other. Choosing a pace that allows you to focus most clearly on the lifting, moving, placing and landing in each turn. Each time when your foot is landing, notice the sensations of the heel touching the ground, then the ball of the foot, then the toes.

When you come to the end of your path, pausing, turning slowly around, noticing the complex pattern of movements through which the body changes direction. And when you have turned perhaps pausing again for a moment to notice the stillness of your body. Notice the weight of the body carried through your feet to the ground.

And then continuing to walk on your path noticing the sensations on the heel, ball, and the toes.

As you are walking, it is quite natural for your mind to wander. Whenever it does, you might mentally pause, perhaps noting inwardly the fact of thinking, or even where your mind went: planning, worrying, fantasizing, judging. Then, gently return your attention to the sensations of the next step. No matter how long you have spent lost in thought, you can always arrive right here, bringing presence and care to the moment-to-moment sensations of walking.

If your mind is very agitated or keeps wandering away from your intended focus, it is perfectly fine to pause for a moment and stand here, feet hips width apart, in touch with the breath and the body as a whole. Noticing the body in stillness. And gathering the attention that has been scattered and resuming the mindful walking when you are ready.

At a certain point, if you would like to, you could expand the focus of your awareness to the whole of the body as it moves in this way. Noticing what other sensations there are in your body as you walk. Always remember that you can return to the sensations in the heel, ball, and toes if the mind begins to wander.

At a certain point, feel free to expand the awareness around the body to notice the air on the skin as you move, the sounds around you, the sense of the body moving through space. Always remember that if your mind keeps wandering you can pause anytime or simply return to the sensations on the heel, ball and the toes of your feet as you walk.

Now slowing down to stillness and coming to a stop. Feeling the whole body in rest and in stillness. Gently shifting your attention to the breathing. Noticing the inbreath and outbreath as the breath comes into the body and as it moves out of the body.

[Strike the chime/bell]

Five-Finger Gratitude Practice

SUGGESTED LENGTH OF PRACTICE: 5 MINUTES

[Strike the chime/bell]

This is a practice that reminds us of what we can be grateful for every day. Bring to mind five things for which you are grateful, counting them on your fingers. Noticing the sensations of gratitude in the body emerging at the present moment.

Remind yourself daily of what you are grateful for no matter how small or big with a sense of appreciation.

And gently open your eyes at the sound of the chime.

[Strike the chime/bell]

Five-Finger Pro-Social Gratitude Practice

SUGGESTED LENGTH OF PRACTICE: 5 MINUTES

[Strike the chime/bell]

This is a practice that reminds us of the people whom we consider as others or who are not part of our immediate family for whom we can be grateful for every day. Bring to mind five people whom you are grateful to, counting them on your fingers. Noticing the sensations of gratitude in the body emerging at the present moment.

Remind yourself daily of the people in your community, locality, or country you are grateful to.

And gently open your eyes at the sound of the chime.

[Strike the chime/bell]

Mindful Eating

SUGGESTED LENGTH OF PRACTICE: 15 MINUTES

[This practice requires the participants to prepare a food item that can be consumed within 15 minutes. This could be a very small meal in a container or sealed package. Drinking water should be available as well.]

We shall now begin the practice with the sound of the chime.

[Strike the chime/bell]

During this practice, we will be focusing on the present moment by engaging our five senses. Being open and curious in this practice as we pay attention to the experience of the body and the mind.

Place the food item in front of you without removing the packaging. Closing your eyes and connecting to your breath and body as you sit here. Noticing any thoughts, bodily sensations, or emotions that you might be experiencing. Tuning in to the awareness of feeling thirsty, hungry, full, or perhaps neutral.

Now opening your eyes and bringing your attention to the food packaging, seeing it as if you are seeing it for the first time. Observing it with curiosity. Paying attention and noticing the packaging. Perhaps there are words on the packaging, or the colors and the details.

Now opening the packaging or container and noticing the sounds as you do that. Now examining the food closely as if you are seeing it for the first time. Noticing the color, shape, size, regularities, and irregularities if any.

And now bring the food closer to your nose. With each inbreath, take in the smell from the food. Noticing if you have any bodily reactions or sensations to the smell.

Now noticing the sensations and movements as you take a mouthful and letting it stay in the mouth. Take a pause here, without chewing, and noticing the sensation of the food in your mouth.

Continuing to focus on the sensations of the food and exploring it with your tongue by rolling it around the different parts of your mouth. How does it feel as you move the food from one side to the other side of the mouth?

Without swallowing yet, take one bite and notice the juice, flavor, and sensations. Taking another bite and noticing any new flavors and how the texture is changing.

Now as you continue chewing without swallowing it, notice the sound of the chewing process.

Now as you swallow, notice the sensations of swallowing your food from your throat and down to your stomach as it transits. Notice the aftertaste that may linger in your mouth.

Now, at your own pace, eat the rest of the food, chewing it as slowly as you can and paying attention moment to moment as you eat.

[Allow the remaining time for the participants to finish their meal]

Bring this experience of mindful eating into your daily life as you eat your meals to nourish your mind and your body.

[Strike the chime/bell]

Mountain Meditation

SUGGESTED LENGTH OF PRACTICE: 15 MINUTES

We now invite you now to adopt an upright and comfortable seated posture on a cushion or a mat, that supports your intention to be awake. Keeping your spine straight and shoulders relaxed. Resting your hands comfortably on the thighs or with the fingers interlocked and at ease. Now closing your eyes or adopting a soft gaze looking down on the floor a few feet in front of you.

[Strike the chime/bell]

Bring your attention to the flow of your breathing. Feeling each inbreath and each outbreath. Just observing your breathing without trying to change it or regulate it in any way, allowing the body to be still and sitting with a sense of dignity, a sense of resolve, a sense of being complete, whole, in this very moment, with your posture reflecting this sense of wholeness.

And as you sit here, picturing in your mind's eye, as best you can, the most beautiful mountain you know or have seen, or can imagine, just holding the image and feeling of this mountain in your mind's eye, letting it gradually come into greater focus.

Observing its overall shape, lofty peak high in the sky, the large base rooted in the rock of the earth's crust, its steep or gently sloping sides.

Noticing how massive it is, how solid, how unmoving, how beautiful, both from afar and up close.

Perhaps your mountain has snow at the top and trees on the lower slopes. Perhaps it has one prominent peak, perhaps a series of peaks, or a high plateau.

Observing it, noting its qualities and when you feel ready, seeing if you can bring the mountain into your own body so that your body sitting here and the mountain in your mind's eye become one so that as you sit here, you share in the massiveness and the stillness and majesty of the mountain. You become the mountain.

Rooted in the sitting posture, your head becomes the lofty peak, supported by the rest of the body and affording a panoramic vista. Your shoulders and arms are the sides of the mountain. Your buttocks and legs are the solid base, rooted to your cushion or your chair, experiencing in your body a sense of uplift from deep within your pelvis and spine.

With each breath, as you continue sitting, becoming a little more a breathing mountain, unwavering in your stillness, completely what you are, beyond words and thought, a centered, unmoving, rooted presence.

As you sit here, becoming aware of the fact that as the sun travels across the sky, the light and shadows and colors are changing virtually moment by moment in the mountain's stillness.

Night follows day and day follows night – the canopy of stars, the moon, then the sun. Through it all, the mountain just sits, experiencing change in each moment, constantly changing, yet always just being itself. It remains still as the seasons flow into one another and as the weather changes moment by moment and day by day, calmness abiding all change.

In any season, it may find itself at times enshrouded in cloud or fog or pelted by freezing rain. People may come to see the mountain and comment on how beautiful it is or how it's not a good day to see the mountain, that it's too cloudy or rainy or foggy or dark.

None of these matter to the mountain, which remains at all times its essential self. Clouds may come and clouds may go; tourists may like it or not. The mountain's magnificence and beauty are not changed one bit by whether people see it or not, seen or unseen, in sun or clouds, broiling or frigid, day or night. It just sits, being itself. Through it all, the mountain sits.

In the same way, as we sit in meditation, we can learn to experience the mountain, we can embody the same unwavering stillness and rootedness in the face of everything that changes in our own lives, over seconds, over hours, over years.

So, in the time that remains, continuing to sustain the mountain meditation on your own, in silence, moment by moment.

Bringing your awareness back to your body again, feeling the whole of it. Becoming aware of your posture. Feeling the weight of your body as you are seated here.

And gently opening your eyes at the sound of the chime.

[Strike the chime/bell]

Mindful Stretching

SUGGESTED LENGTH OF PRACTICE: 10 MINUTES

[This is a sample script for mindful stretching which can be done informally during the self-retreat. This practice can also be done unguided by the participants who are familiar with the practice of mindfulness.]

Coming to a standing position with your back upright, feet parallel to each other, hips width apart, with your knees slightly flexed, allowing your arms to hang by your sides, and shoulders relaxed. And directing your gaze softly straight ahead.

The focus of this practice is to bring awareness to gentle stretching exercises.

Posture 1

Turning your head to the right and gently looking over your right shoulder and noticing the *stretch* in your left shoulder. Continue to breathe normally. Returning to the center and noticing the difference between your right and left shoulders.

Turning your head to the left and gently looking over your left shoulder and noticing the *stretch* in your right shoulder. Continue to breathe normally. Returning to the center and noticing the changes in the shoulders.

Posture 2

Now gently look down bringing your chin toward your chest and noticing the muscle *stretch* at the back of your neck. Continue to breathe normally. And now raising your chin and looking straight ahead.

Now, gently, raising your chin as you look toward the sky and noticing the *stretches* in the front of your neck. Continue to breathe normally.
And now gently releasing the hold and returning to the center and looking straight ahead.

Posture 3

Now slowly roll your shoulders three times in forward circles noticing the *stretches* in the shoulder muscles.
And now releasing the shoulders and come to the center.
Now slowly roll your shoulders three times in backward circles noticing the *stretches* in the shoulder muscles.
And now releasing the shoulders and come to the center.

> *[Mindful stretching practice continues till the planned exercise sequence is complete]*

Bringing Mindfulness to Routine Activities

Choose one routine activity that you do daily without fail and bring attention to the moment-to-moment experience with this activity. You could explore this with any of the following activities but not be limited to them:

- Brushing teeth
- Washing face
- Showering
- Drying of hair or body
- Combing hair
- Applying face and body lotion or aftershave lotion
- Getting dressed
- Having a drink/meal/snack

Explore each experience with an attitude of curiosity no matter how mundane or repetitive it might be. Engage your senses with purpose and notice your bodily sensations, movements, thoughts, and emotions as they rise, linger, and fall. Welcome all of the experiences regardless of whether they are positive, neutral, or negative.

Metaphors, Visual Illusions, and Stories

Session 1: Being Curious

1 COMPONENT 2 – THE AUTOPILOT

The teacher can choose either one of these metaphors as the opening metaphor in this session.

Option 1: The Pilot

[Script]

You are on a flight to your holiday destination. The pilot has welcomed everyone onboard, introduced his co-pilot and crew, and announced the estimated arrival time.
You sit back and relax.
Little do you realize, apart from the pilot and co-pilot, there is another pilot in the cockpit with them – a non-human one, the "autopilot."
This pilot has no heart, and neither does he have a brain like yours.
And yet he knows your destination like the back of his hand and needs no control from the human pilots.
Are we on autopilot, like this plane?

Option 2: Cow's Milk

This is an interactive activity to present how autopilot works. This may work better with a younger audience as it induces a fun experience.

Get the participants to say aloud the word "milk" ten times. And then ask them immediately "What does a cow drink?" It is likely that you will hear "milk" as the response.

2 COMPONENT 4 – YOUNG WOMAN OR OLD WOMAN

Figure A5.1 Young woman or old woman. Visual illusion by William Ely Hill

The optical illusion popularly known as the "The Young Girl – Old Woman" could be used as way for participants to gain insight into how our minds interpret what it sees with memories, knowledge, and more importantly what we pay attention to. Interestingly only one woman can be seen at any present moment. Many participants would not be able to see "both" the women at the same time.

Session 2: Holistic Wellbeing

1 COMPONENT 1 – A CAR WITHOUT A STEERING WHEEL

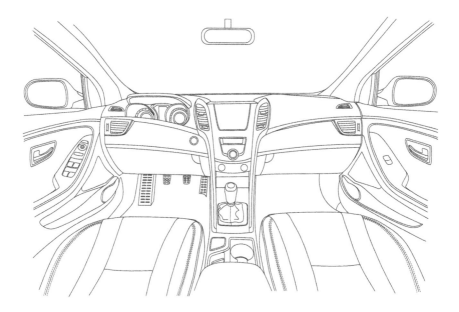

Figure A5.2 An image of a car dashboard without a steering wheel

2 COMPONENT 7 – LIKE A TORCHLIGHT

[Script]

Our attention is like torchlight. Its light falls on whatever object the torch is directed at. You can also brighten the light if it is dim. Our attention too can be enhanced with curiosity if we wanted to. Imagine a small torch tied to the neck of a cat. And the light gets scattered whenever the cat runs. Or you can get hold of that torch and shine it on one place brightening that spot. The light of awareness is always available, and we can choose to direct it with our attention.

Session 3: Response-Ability

1 COMPONENT 1 – SHOOT AND LOOK OR LOOK AND SHOOT

[Script]

I am a soldier called to war to protect my country, my family, and myself against invading aggressors. Here am I in the trenches in the cold and wet weather. I now hear footsteps right in front of me charging towards me. Shall I shoot and then look, OR shall I look and then shoot?

Session 4: Focusing on What Works

1 COMPONENT 1 – CAMERA AND ITS LENSES

[Script]

I am a photographer. I am now in the highlands looking down at a valley. To my right I see a tiger attacking a deer. Right in the middle I see a beautiful river flowing down to the lowlands. To my left I see a herd of elephant calves playing in the sand, cooling themselves in the sweltering heat. Here am I with a camera and a zoom lens. Shall I shoot the tiger, the river, or the elephant calves? [*silence for a few moments*] Attention is like the camera. The choice about what I want to shoot is the flexibility of attention. The zoom lens is my curiosity and concentration.

Session 5: Meaningful Engagement

1 COMPONENT 1 – ARE YOU A PASSENGER?

[Script]

Imagine you at a bus stop, and you are waiting for a bus to arrive. As you are waiting, there are other buses that stop at the bus stop and depart. And when your bus arrives, you board it. You are an observer when you are waiting at the bus stop. You can choose to become a passenger when you want to, willfully.

[silence for a few moments] Similarly, we can witness our thoughts as they arrive and depart and choose to identify with thoughts that help enhance our wellbeing. At times we are observers and at other times passengers of our thoughts.

2 COMPONENT 8 – ANIMALS WITHIN RHINO

Figure A5.3 Image of animals within rhino

Session 6: Generating Perspectives

1 COMPONENT 1 – CLOUDS IN THE SKY

[Script]

Like clouds that appear in the sky, thoughts appear in our awareness. The clouds could be dark, white, threatening, or pleasant, but the sky does not get affected by it. Regardless of how the clouds are, the sky lets them be. In fact, it is because of the sky that we can see the clouds. *[silence for a few moments]* The clouds come and go, but the sky remains unaffected by it. Thoughts come and go, but awareness remains unaffected by it.

Session 7: Mindful Living

1 COMPONENT 1 – ROPE AND SNAKE

[Script]

I was walking in a dark alley, and there I saw a snake coiled up.
I was startled, jumped, and ran straight back to the main road.
My heart was racing, breathing became shallow, muscles tightened
My friends who met me there immediately brought a torch and a stick to kill
that snake, after I had shared what I saw.
We ran into the dark alley again and shone the light at that snake to strike it.
And there we saw a coiled rope. [*silence for a few moments*]
But my heart was still racing, breathing was still shallow, muscles were still
tightened.

Session 8: The Future in the Present Moment

1 COMPONENT 1 – RIVERS AND OCEAN

[Script]

Like an ocean that does not resist the rivers, awareness does not resist thoughts.
Like waves that rise and fall in the waters of the ocean, thoughts rise and fall
in awareness.
This awareness does not reject, nor does it pursue thoughts.

Poems

1 THE GUEST HOUSE BY JALALUDDIN RUMI (TRANSLATED BY COLEMAN BARKS)

This being human is a guest house.
Every morning a new arrival.

A joy, a depression, a meanness,
some momentary awareness comes
as an unexpected visitor.

Welcome and entertain them all!
Even if they are a crowd of sorrows,
who violently sweep your house
empty of its furniture,
still, treat each guest honorably.
He may be clearing you out
for some new delight.

The dark thought, the shame, the malice.
Meet them at the door laughing,
and invite them in.

Be grateful for whatever comes.
Because each has been sent
as a guide from beyond.

2 TWO WOLVES – A CHEROKEE PARABLE

An old Cherokee chief was teaching his grandson about life . . .

"A fight is going on inside me," he said to the boy.

"It is a terrible fight and it is between two wolves.

"One is evil – he is anger, envy, sorrow, regret, greed, arrogance, self-pity, guilt, resentment, inferiority, lies, false pride, superiority, self-doubt, and ego.

"The other is good – he is joy, peace, love, hope, serenity, humility, kindness, benevolence, empathy, generosity, truth, compassion, and faith.

"This same fight is going on inside you – and inside every other person, too."

The grandson thought about it for a minute and then asked his grandfather, "Which wolf will win?"

The old chief simply replied,
"The one you feed."

3 *THOUGHTS BY* WALT WHITMAN (AN EXCERPT)

Of the visages of things—And of piercing through
to the accepted hells beneath;

Of ugliness—To me there is just as much in it as
there is in beauty—And now the ugliness of
human beings is acceptable to me;

Of detected persons—To me, detected persons are
not, in any respect, worse than undetected persons—and are not in any respect worse than I
am myself;

Of criminals—To me, any judge, or any juror, is
equally criminal—and any reputable person is
also—and the President is also.

4 *THREE GIFTS BY* CONFUCIUS (TRANSLATED BY L. CRANMER-BYNG)

A royal gourd was given me,
And in exchange an emerald I gave,
No mere return for courtesy,
But that our friendship might outlast the grave.

A princely peach was given me,
And in exchange a ruby gem I gave,
No mere exchange for courtesy,
But that our friendship might outlast the grave.

A yellow plum was given me,
And in exchange a sardonyx I gave,
No mere return for courtesy,
But that our friendship might outlast the grave.

5 *LOTUS* BY RABINDRANATH TAGORE

On the day when the lotus bloomed, alas, my mind was straying,
and I knew it not. My basket was empty and the flower remained unheeded.

Only now and again a sadness fell upon me, and I started up from my
dream and felt a sweet trace of a strange fragrance in the south wind.

That vague sweetness made my heart ache with longing and it seemed to
me that is was the eager breath of the summer seeking for its completion.

I knew not then that it was so near, that it was mine, and that this
perfect sweetness had blossomed in the depth of my own heart.

6 *THE BLIND MEN AND THE ELEPHANT* BY JOHN GODFREY SAXE

It was six men of Indostan
To learning much inclined,
Who went to see the Elephant
Though all of them were blind,
That each by observation
Might satisfy his mind.

The *First* approached the Elephant,
And happening to fall
Against his broad and sturdy side,
At once began to bawl:
"God bless me! – but the Elephant
Is very like a wall!"

The *Second*, feeling of the tusk,
Cried: "Ho! – what have we here
So very round and smooth and sharp?
To me 't is mighty clear
This wonder of an Elephant
Is very like a spear!"

The *Third* approached the animal,
And happening to take
The squirming trunk within his hands,
Thus boldly up and spake:
"I see," quoth he, "the Elephant
Is very like a snake!"

The *Fourth* reached out his eager hand,
And felt about the knee.
"What most this wondrous beast is like
Is mighty plain," quoth he;
"'T is clear enough the Elephant
Is very like a tree!"

The *Fifth*, who chanced to touch the ear,
Said: "E'en the blindest man
Can tell what this resembles most;
Deny the fact who can,
This marvel of an Elephant
Is very like a fan!"

The *Sixth* no sooner had begun
About the beast to grope,
Than, seizing on the swinging tail
That fell within his scope,
"I see," quoth he, "the Elephant
Is very like a rope!"

And so these men of Indostan
Disputed loud and long,

Each in his own opinion
Exceeding stiff and strong,
Though each was partly in the right,
And all were in the wrong!

Exercises

Session 2: Holistic Wellbeing

1 COMPONENT 4 – MY WELLBEING INTENTIONS

Materials needed: laptop and projector or a large drawing of the image below (see Figure A7.1).

Facilitation Instructions

- Briefly present the five selves of wellbeing of the Integrated Wellbeing Model (IWM) either through projected slide or on a writing board (refer to Table A7.1):

Table A7.1 Elements of the IWM

	Aspect	Elements
1	Spatial self	• Space and environment we are in • Interaction of the body with the environment
2	Physical self	• Engagement with physical activity • Physiological health
3	Emotional self	• Emotional experiences • Emotional resilience • Emotional intelligence • Emotional regulation
4	Intellectual self	• Wisdom and knowledge • Values • Attitude and strengths • Locus of control • Decision making • Religiosity and spirituality • Relationships • Personality
5	Eudaimonic self	• Purpose • Meaning in life

- Divide the space in the room into fifths based on the five selves (see Figure A7.1). You can allow participants to imagine the boundaries or set some markings as indicators. Ideally the participants should be able to understand this by looking at the projected image or the drawing.

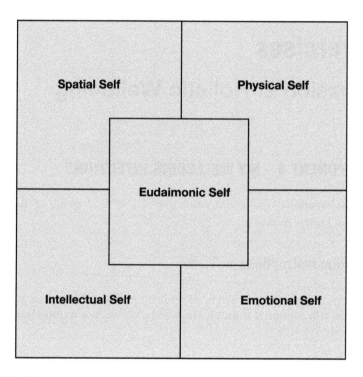

Figure A7.1 Floor layout corresponding to the five selves

- Part I (10 mins)
    - o Invite the participants to move into one of the boxes by saying,
        - "Which area of your wellbeing do you feel that you are most satisfied with? Move to that area within the room."
    - o After they have moved into a box, instruct them to,
        - Find another person in the same box (or if they are unable to find someone in the same box, to find someone close) to have a conversation about what is going well and how they feel about it going well.

- Teacher facilitates a short debrief asking about emotions or thoughts that they are experiencing in this present moment as they reflect on this aspect of their life.

- Part II (10 mins)

  o   Invite the participants to move into another box by saying,

    ▪   "Now, move to the box where you feel your wellbeing can be better or an area that you would like to focus more."

  o   After they have moved into a box, instruct them to,

    ▪   Find another person in the same box (or if they unable to find someone in the same box, to find someone close) to have a conversation about how they feel about this area of their life.
    ▪   Teacher facilitates a short debrief asking about emotions or thoughts that they are experiencing at this present moment as they reflected on this aspect of their life.

[Alternative] One possible alternative in this component is for teachers to use other wellbeing models if they so desire.

2 COMPONENT 7: THE NEGATIVITY BIASED BRAIN

Materials needed: the exercise sheet (see Table A7.2) and writing tools. This sheet could be included in the handout distributed in the first session or be distributed on the day of the session.

Facilitation Instructions

- Instruct the participants to complete the pleasant experience journal (see Table A7.2) daily for a week.
- Invite participants to bring a sense of awareness to pleasant experiences in their daily living. While they need not actively seek it, the intention is to be aware of it and the resulting bodily sensations, emotions, thoughts, and behaviors that arise.
- The teacher can give an example of an event.
- The teacher should note that the same facilitation process is used for the unpleasant experience journaling exercise.

Table A7.2 Pleasant experience journal

Day/ Date	EVENT What was the pleasant experience/ event?	SENSATIONS How did your body feel (physical sensations)?	EMOTIONS What emotions were present for you?	THOUGHTS What thoughts went through your mind?	BEHAVIOR What were some immediate actions/ urges that you noticed?
Day 1					
Day 2					
Day 3					
Day 4					
Day 5					
Day 6					
Day 7					

Session 3: Response-Ability

1 COMPONENT 5 – THE BRAIN AND MINDFULNESS

Materials needed: none

Facilitation Instructions

- Option 1: 3–6–9 Clap (suitable for a group of about 15 or fewer participants)
  - o   Instruct the participants to form a large circle where everyone can see everyone in the circle (see Figure A7.2)

o   Explain the instructions of the game:

▪   Each participant is to shout the numbers from 1 to number 60 (or 100 depending on the group size) as they move down the circle. However there is a condition. When the numbers 3, 6, or 9 appear in the number that is being shouted out, they should just clap instead. For example, this is how it would sound like – 1 2 clap 4 5 clap 7 8 clap 10 11 12 clap 14 15 clap 17 18 clap 20 21 22 clap 24 25 clap 27 28 clap clap clap clap . . . 40 41. . .

▪   Give them a practice round with the numbers up to 10 as a warm up. The game begins with the first participant saying "One," the one on his right (or left) saying "Two," and the next person on the right *claps* and so forth. If a person makes an error, you are to restart the counting from number 1 with the person who made that error.

▪   The counting gets repeated until number 60 is reached or if five minutes is up.

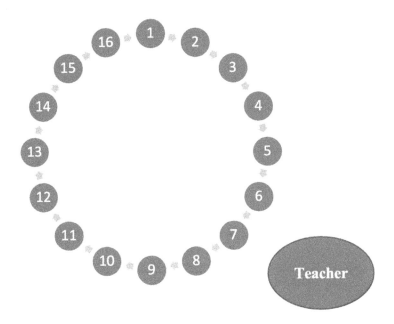

Figure A7.2 3–6–9 Clap-game formation

• Option 2: Stroop effect activity (suitable for any group size)

o   Materials needed: PowerPoint slides.

o   Create a PowerPoint slide with the following:

- First slide:

  - Create boxes or circles with colors. See the example below in figure A7.3.
  - Animate for each colored box to appear on transition from the earlier one every 1 second.
  - Tell the participants to shout out the color as it appears.
  - After the game has ended, ask them if it was easy or difficult. The majority, if not all, will find it easy.
  - Inform that they are going to do it again with words instead.

Figure A7.3 Stroop effect slide 1 sample

- Second slide:

  - Create words with colors that do not match the words. For example, type the word "blue" but choose the color to be red. See the example below in figure A7.4.
  - Animate for each colored word to appear in transition from the earlier one every 1 second.
  - Tell the participants to shout out the color as it appears, not the words. So for example, if you see the word "blue" in red color, you have to say red (the color).
  - After the game has ended, ask them how the experience was for them and what was the difficulty they faced.

- Do a debrief and link the insights to the purpose of this segment.

Say Aloud the Colour of each Word

BLUE **YELLOW** RED GREEN BLACK

YELLOW GREEN **RED** BLACK BLUE

GREEN **RED** YELLOW BLACK BLUE

Figure A7.4 Stroop effect slide 2 sample

Session 4: Focusing on What Works

1 COMPONENT 4 – SHIFTING PARADIGMS I ACTIVITY

skrow tahw no gnisucof

The teacher shows the statement above to the participants for five seconds and then shields it for ten seconds. And then she shows the above sentence again, but this time asking the participants to read it from right to left.

Participants will learn that when they changed their paradigms of how sentences should be read, they could derive meaning from the "meaningless."

2 COMPONENT 4 – PAPER FOLDING ACTIVITY

Materials needed: one A4 or letter-sized paper per participant

Facilitation Instructions

• Distribute a sheet of A4 or letter-sized paper to each participant.
• Demonstrate to them by folding the paper five times to the size of the shaded portion (see Figure A7.5).
• To begin, instruct all of them to hold the sheet of paper in their hands and then to close their eyes.
• Instruct them to fold the paper into the size of the shaded portion with their eyes closed. Invite them to raise their hands when they have completed it and keep them raised until they are told to lower them.

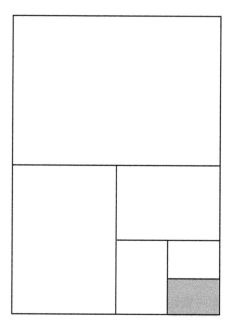

Figure A7.5 Paper folding activity

- Once all of them have completed the task, tell them to lower their hands and invite them to unfold the paper back to its original size.
- Now for one more time, invite them to close their eyes and get them to fold that paper into the size of the shaded portion and raise their hands when they have completed it. Once all of them have completed the task, invite them to lower their hands and open their eyes.
- Now ask the participants why the second time was easier. And the reasons would revolve around the fold in the paper already created during the first round. You can connect these folds to the new neuropathways that mindfulness creates in our brains. With each practice we create new pathways of thinking, feeling, responding, etc.

Session 5: Meaningful Engagement

1 COMPONENT 8 – MEANINGFUL ENGAGEMENT EXERCISE

Materials needed: exercise sheets and writing tools. This sheet could be included in the handout distributed at the first session or be distributed on the day of the session.

Facilitation Instructions

- Explain to the participants that they will be looking through their daily activities during a typical week and evaluating them on the criteria of whether it is uplifting for them or depleting them.
- Instruct them as follows
  - o   Part A: Daily activities exploration (Table A7.3):
    - Step 1: the first step is to write down at least ten activities in the "Daily activities" column, e.g. showering, jogging or working. Give them 5 minutes to complete this.
    - Step 2: next, look through each of the activities and tick either the uplifting or depleting column. If the activity makes them feel refreshed, energized, good, or is enjoyable, then they can tick in the uplifting column. If they find the activity to be energy

Table A7.3 Daily activities exploration

(A) Daily activities			
No	Daily activities	Uplifting (Energizing, enjoyable, make you feel good)	Depleting (Energy draining, tiring, makes you feel low)
	[Examples] a. Shower b. Housework/working long hours	☐	☐
1			
2			
3			
4			
5			
6			
7			
8			
9			
10			

draining or exhausting, they can then tick the depleting column. Give them 3 minutes to complete this task.

- Step 3: once they have completed this task, ask the large group for any insights.

o   Part B: Pleasurable and mastery-type activities (Table A7.4):

- Now get them to bring the insights they got from the last exercise to now write up to ten activities that they are good at, enjoy, or find meaningful to do. For example, I might be good at playing the guitar or enjoy playing with my children. Activities that were uplifting from the previous exercise could also be included in this list. Give them 5 minutes to complete this.

- Instruct them to look at their list and find at least one or two of these activities which they are willing to commit to daily and write them in the "My commitment" box. They may even consider modifying the depleting activities so to make them pleasurable or more like mastery-type activities. For example, if doing housework is depleting and listening to music gives me joy, I could consider combining this two into my daily plan. Give them 2 minutes to complete this.

- Invite three or four participants to share their commitments.

Table A7.4 Pleasurable and mastery-type activities

(B) Pleasurable and mastery-type of activities	
No	Daily activities
	e.g. listening to music, reading a book, playing a game of chess, playing a musical instrument
1	
2	
3	
4	
5	
6	
7	
8	

(B) Pleasurable and mastery-type of activities	
No	Daily activities
9	
10	
My Commitments:	

Session 6: Generating Perspectives

1 COMPONENT 4 – PERSPECTIVE TAKING

Materials needed: writing board, markers, exercise sheet. The exercise sheet (refer to Table A7.5) could be included in the handout distributed on first session or be distributed on the day of the session.

Preparation

- Draw a table with five columns on a writing board. Each column should have one of these five headings in this order: Event, Sensations, Emotions, Thoughts, and Alternative perspectives.

Facilitation Instructions

- Ask someone from the room to share an incident that was positive or pleasant during the last week. And then ask what sensations, emotions and thoughts about the incident they had. Invite others to contribute by imagining or recollecting a similar incident. Ask deeper questions as to how this impacted the rest of the day or the week.
- Now ask them for another incident but this time it should be something negative or unpleasant such as:
  - o Caused by Self – at work where you felt judged, disrespected, or criticized
  - o Caused by Others – where you felt that the other person was not competent in doing something that you wanted to be done

Table A7.5 Perspective taking

EVENT What was the experience or event?	SENSATIONS How did your body feel (physical sensations)?	EMOTIONS What emotions were present for you?	THOUGHTS What thoughts went through your mind?	ALTERNATIVE PERSPECTIVES: What alternative viewpoints could you have?				
Susan walked past me and didn't even say hi. This is the 2nd time this week.	increased heart rate, warmth around my face and chest area, clenching of jaw	Rejected, angry, disappointed, sad.	How could she ignore me? Did I do something wrong? What's her problem? I shall ignore her in future too.	• Maybe Susan didn't see me. • Maybe Susan is in deep thought. • Maybe Susan is going through a tough time this week.				

- As the participants share, just note one or two incidents on the events column of the table drawn on the board. Inquire into what their sensations, emotions, and thoughts were at the time of the incident and note them down in the appropriate columns of the table. Ask deeper questions on how this impacted the rest of the day or the week, and whether the thoughts were helpful or not.
- Teach how our experiences are interpreted as realities and thus impact our thoughts, emotions, sensations, and actions. To be happy, we can accept a negative experience and re-interpret it with new perspectives.
- Revisit the unpleasant incidents and ask the participants to think of possible alternative perspectives about it.
- Distribute or refer to the perspective taking exercise sheet (see Table A7.5) and invite the participants to journal the events, their bodily sensations, emotions, thoughts, and alternative perspectives for any negative or unpleasant event in the next seven days.

Session 7: Mindful Living

2 COMPONENT 6 – JOHN THE JANITOR ACTIVITY

This short paragraph, below, is spoken by the facilitator one statement at a time with an eight-second gap between statements. This short exercise would allow participants to see how our minds interpret statements and that thoughts are not facts.

> John was on his way to school;
> He was worried about the math lesson;
> He was not sure he could control the class again today;
> It was not part of a janitor's duty.

3 COMPONENT 7 – MY FIRST MONTH OF WELLBEING

Materials needed: exercise sheet (the exercise sheet (refer to Table A7.6) could be included in the handout distributed in the first session or distributed on the day of the session).

Facilitation Instructions

- Tell participants to write the month and year in Table A7.6 e.g. October 2025.

- Based on the chosen month, participants are to write in all dates for that month in the calendar.
- Once the above is complete, they are to plan their daily mindfulness practices and meaningful engagements and note it in the calendar as part of their homework for the week. Some examples are shown in Table A7.7.

Table A7.6 My monthly wellbeing calendar

Month and year: _____						
Mon	Tues	Wed	Thurs	Fri	Sat	Sun

Table A7.7 My monthly wellbeing calendar (sample)

Month and year: October 2025						
Mon	Tues	Wed	Thurs	Fri	Sat	Sun
					1 • Reading a novel • Mindful eating • Body Scan	2 • Gardening • Mindful walking
3 • Listening to music on the way to office • Mindful walking @ lunchtime	4	5	6	7	8	9
10	11	12	13	14	15	16

Month and year: <u>October 2025</u>						
Mon	*Tues*	*Wed*	*Thurs*	*Fri*	*Sat*	*Sun*
17	18	19	20	21	22	23
24	25	26	27	28	29	30
31						

4 COMPONENT 9 – SHIFTING PARADIGMS II ACTIVITY

stcaf ton era sthguoht

The teacher shows the above statement to the participants and asks what it means.

Participants are likely to read it from the right to left, and even if they don't, that is fine. It is a demonstration of how paradigms can take time to shift or it could be immediate for some.

Session 8: The Future in the Present Moment

1 COMPONENT 9 – MINDFUL LETTER TO SELF

Materials needed: one sheet of writing paper and a sealable envelope per participant.

Facilitation Instructions

- Brief participants that they are going to write a mindful letter to themselves to encourage themselves to continue this journey. This letter will be posted by the teacher to them after three months.
- Instruct them to:
  - o write their home or office address on the envelope.

o   take 15 minutes to write their mindful letter to themselves. Assure them no one else will be reading this letter except them so encourage them to be frank, positive, and motivating toward themselves. They can include something they wish to remind themselves of or nuggets of wisdom from their experience that can guide them in their journey. They are to address the letter to themselves and to sign off the letter and date it before placing it in an envelope and sealing it.

- Collect all the envelopes and assure them that you will be mailing them in three months.

Index

Note: Locators in *italic* indicate figures, in **bold** tables.